Can I Be Earnest?

Ernest K. Aning

Dedication

To my daughter, grandmother and introverts worldwide.

Acknowledgments

This portion of the book has always been my favorite. Considering how small my circle is, the list should be short and sweet. So, let's do it!

First and foremost, none of this is possible without the acknowledgment of God and His presence in my life. He kept this vision alive in all aspects of writing, whether through minuscule *journal entries, current event reports, letters to the op-ed sections of major newspapers, or songwriting* – until it evolved into a book release! My pen stayed active and I watched how the whole process played out. I'm not taking *any* credit for that.

I must thank my former teasers, ex-friends, friends-turned-associates, exes and anyone who has given me their ass to kiss over the years. I sincerely mean that. You all were the fuel to my fire and I have enough material to write for a lifetime. Without you, I am truly nothing.

A *big* thank you to the hundreds of employers who denied me opportunities when I was only looking for a way to survive (I've saved many of these job applications in an email folder titled, 'wishful thinking'). I guess this was a blessing in disguise.

To my former employer, for remaining mum for nine months as I completed this book on company time. I know deep down it pissed many of you off, but I was simply multitasking. Just one of my many skills.

To the skewed child support court system for their arrogance and blatant targeting of men. I know too many good fathers affected by this for it to even be a debate. But I was driven to speak up on the undeniable unjust. The system may *never* change, but at least I can become a voice for those mistreated fathers through literature.

Amy Lane, Amanda Rich, Erica Young, thank you so much for assisting me on delivering my book to the world.

Lee Weston, big bro, you've been the battery in my back since day one. I don't think there's a topic we haven't discussed. You are a major part of this book. We've both crawled, kicked and punched our way through many obstacles, hoping to one day knock down that ii Can I Be Earnest?

door. This is a start. Thank you for your presence, persistent inspiring pep talks and supporting my dream. I can't begin to tell you how much it means to me.

Tamara Smith, the sister I never had. I knew you'd be a key component in my life from the onset. On the first day we met (working at Radio Shack), I recall sharing a full-fledged conversation with you about 80s music. I don't remember how the topic arose, but I was blown away – you *really* knew your stuff (I nearly lost it when you mentioned being a Madonna fan). I can be quite eccentric... thank you for accepting that. Thank you for sharing stories, listening to my gripes and more importantly, forcing me to watch *Dirty Dancing* (although, I still think the movie sucks).

Mom – Thank you for your unconditional love and support. It amazes me how you continue to possess that same *proud parent* glow when we connect. While I'm at it, I should probably thank you for those *three-minute long* voicemails (ugh!) when you'd announce, "Hi, Son, I *only* wanted to say *hi!*" followed by stories about your day, the week ahead and everything else going on in your life! (I learned my long-windedness from you). You're a loving Mom and I don't take you for granted. Thank you for your tasty *home-cooked* meals and having my back through all the ups and downs.

To my namesake – You have done your devoir quite well, Sir. I am extremely proud to have you as a father. I credit you most for this book as you've passed the torch, I will stake my claim and carry on. It almost took an eternity, but I found my lane and I hope I've made you proud.

To my other half – Thank you for restoring hope that there are still good women in existence and thank you for bringing life to a once lifeless one. You are an overall incredible human being, I am truly fortunate.

Stink – You are the light of my life and one of my biggest inspirations. I love you with all of my heart. Always remember: quality over quantity – P.S. I know you enjoy reading, but you're not allowed to read this book until you're 18!

Finally, a HUGE thank you to my grandmother – Words cannot possibly explain what you've meant to me (that sentence alone gets me choked up, so I will keep this short). Thank you for providing confidence and being a listener when it felt like I had nobody else.

Thank you for the life lessons, the laughs and teaching me how to navigate through the dark (using my five senses) while preserving the electric bill! Through you, I've learned of the importance of rest, waking up early and keeping my faith in God to a maximum... and for *humanity* to a bare minimum. Thank you for bringing home the newspaper each day. Thank you for watching the news *three times* a day (sometimes four). Thank you for allowing me to watch *$100,000 Pyramid, Press Your Luck, General Hospital, Supermarket Sweep, Shop 'til You Drop, Jeopardy* and *Wheel of Fortune* with you. Finally, thank you for *always* being there. You didn't have to take on that role, but you were there every step of the way. Thank you for being my best friend... from day one!

Anyone I haven't mentioned by name – If you've been a part of this ride and we're still on speaking terms, just know that I appreciate and value what you've brought to my life. If we are no longer cordial, but you recognize my name on the book cover and decided to pick it up, thank you! I am certainly not here to win back your friendship, but hopefully you'll enjoy the reading and get a chance to understand me better.

A Note to the Reader

The PC climate has severely stripped the population of healthy banter… until now! Through my disorderly adventure (a.k.a., *Can I Be ~~E~~arnest?*), we will *temporarily* return to the glory days; a time where men and women stood behind their words…without the mere thought of ~~damage control, deleted tweets~~ *an apology.*

No more!

In addition, you'll notice a theme where *strike-throughs* are placed on letters (as seen by the book cover), words, or terms which I originally intended to use (until I thought of something better). Do not be alarmed! The strike-throughs are deliberate and were left alone by my editor (at my request). Why? Because I wanted you to witness my *original* thought in its rawest form.

Transparency isn't only a noun, it's a way of life. I just wanted to be earnest!

CONTENTS

Prologue

Finally, the moment arrived. I took a deep breath, gathered my belongings and put on my winter coat. There was a sudden urge to make a quick run to the men's room, but I convinced myself to wait – further increasing the chances of an enlarged prostate. It was 5 p.m. and I needed to get the hell out of the office. I gave a half-hearted wave to a few co-workers. *We'll do this again tomorrow!*

Deep down, I was praying it was the last time I'd see their miserable faces… but it was only Monday. Another day, another ~~pointless eight hours in the bag~~ *dollar*. I scurried through the office in sight of the elevators, hoping to get a head start on the evening rush. My body language conflicted with the thoughts in my head… I was thrilled to be heading home, yet, saddened at what I'd become.

I was in what I considered to be the *third quarter* of life and it was getting critical:

- First Quarter: Ages 18-25
- Second Quarter: Ages 25-35
- Third Quarter: Ages 35-45
- Fourth Quarter: If you haven't figured out what to do with your life by now, bury your head in the sand!

If life was predicated upon change, I needed to dig deep and figure my next move instead of presuming a new job would fix this. I'd done that before… it was like applying a band-aid to a bullet wound.

I'll be okay once I get away from the city. I'll head over to the gym, decompress… everything will be fine. But it wasn't. Now standing at the elevator, expecting to beat the other five o'clock departures, I mashed on the down arrow vigorously. Nothing irritated me more than boarding a packed elevator – especially in this building. That awkward feeling of passengers staring unceremoniously while I attempted to squeeze inside, was enough to make me consider taking the twelve flights of stairs down. Much to my surprise, an empty elevator arrived at the floor, while a familiar face from the office entered my periphery.

"Hold the door!" he yelled.

Rather than oblige, I fired away at the *close door* button in typical asshole fashion. To my delight, the doors promptly closed within a few feet of his face.

The nerve of that prick giving ME orders! I thought.

I don't know when it developed, but I've always had asshole ways – usually kept under wraps, unless someone prompted me to reveal that ugly side. But the elevator episode signaled a major problem: My office mannerisms had clearly abandoned me.

Office Etiquette 101 says:

- Hold the elevator doors for your colleagues
- Laugh at your boss's unfunny jokes
- Always give a tight lip smile when in passing
- Exchange "Happy Friday" pleasantries

I purposefully neglected all four rules. My arrival at the office was typically met with a vibe of dejection, but I'd *shake it off* like a Taylor Swift song as the day progressed. Not today. Today, I was overtaken by the feeling of entrapment. As a substitute for the gym (where I didn't want to subject myself to the annoying grunts of a bench-presser), I made the executive decision to go home.

Maybe I'll have time to drink a beer and unwind. I imagined eating an early dinner while catching up on recorded episodes of *Ancient Aliens* which had been sitting idle on my DVR for months. But my evenings tended to run away from me… even on those straight-to-home days.

Instead of *by the minute*, time appeared to move *by the hour*. Before long, the neighborhood birds were outside my window callously chirping – which meant one thing: *It was time to make the donuts…*

Where was the time going and why didn't it go at this pace during work hours?!

Public transportation was abounding in downtown Philadelphia and there was an existing shuttle bus taking employees from the building directly to the train station, something my boss often recommended.

"Great way to beat the cold", he'd say.

Great way to beat the cold, I mimicked in my head. But I was fixed on taking the 25-minute walk. After all, I sat on my keister for a good stretch of the day, the last thing I wanted was to subject my glutes to the numbness of more sitting. In addition, I had no interest intermixing with evening commuters – who openly coughed and sneezed in such tight quarters.

Walking was therapeutic, adding some much-needed cardio to my work out schedule on those non-gym days. Aside from that, it gave me an opportunity to take in the scenery of the city, while listening to one of my favorite sports radio personalities through an app on my cell phone. The only thing standing in the way of walking home altogether, was the Delaware River… but swimming wasn't one of my strong suits.

Mike Francesa's array of sports knowledge accompanied me upon my arrival to the train station and again on the car ride home. I was more than a listener of 25 years, I was a cult follower. His sports talk show was usually the highlight of my day, as he enlightened the audience on *the amount of people he knew, how right he was and how wrong you were!* Despite his bevy of critics, it made for great radio and I couldn't get enough.

Unfortunately, on this dreary winter afternoon, a hiccup with the app was the source of disarray to my usual flow. Standing in the middle of the lobby floor – blindsided by the turn of events, the issue was of paramount importance. It needed to be resolved before making my way outside. After a few attempts to uninstall/reinstall the app, I tried restarting my phone. Nothing.

What was going on?

Light traffic formed in the lobby and I felt my attitude shift from bad to worse. Having spent most of the day listening to a playlist featuring some of my favorite *80s artists*, I was in desperate need of a sports fix – but there I stood… helpless without a Plan B, like a woman who unreservedly forgot about that drunken one-night stand after Happy Hour. In a matter of minutes, old man winter's untimely presence would extend his hand and here I was without a form of entertainment.

Fuck!

The blustering winds howled through the cracks of the lobby door, but the sound of my teeth sucking overshadowed the noise. Were there more things to be upset about? Sure. But nothing of

greater significance than the New York Jets not going for it on
4th & 1. I needed to hear Francesa's take on it. But, nothing…

Maybe I could reminisce about the good ol' days as a way
around the kerfuffle. I'll close my eyes and transport myself to a
time where drama didn't exist in my world. A point where child
support payments weren't depleting my pockets, unruly bill
collectors weren't calling my phone and my only agonizing thought
was whether Hulk Hogan would retain the WWF championship.
Over the next few minutes, I ran across some insane ideas, leaning
towards something more subdued.

I'll give Wesley a buzz.

Wesley could have a full-blown conversation with himself,
that's how much he talked. At times, the only way to escape (or get
a word in) was to make up a cockamamie excuse to hang up:

Dude! I've gotta go! The house is on fire!

But I was in desperate need of entertainment and he would have
to do. Unfortunately, one look outside of the lobby window changed
that thought. A man was running down the street chasing after his
hat – meaning one thing: the wind gusts would greatly impact our
listening abilities.

I'll pass.

One of my biggest pet peeves, is having to constantly repeat
myself. I just wasn't in the mood. Adding insult to injury, I left my
gloves in my cubicle and was unable to muster enough energy to
head back upstairs to retrieve them. The decision not to go back was
much ado about nothing, I just wanted to avoid the ensuing
conversation:

"Hey Ernest! I see you're *early* for tomorrow!"

Seriously?! Office folks are so damn predictable.

It was time to get a move on. The evening was near, I'd be right
back in this gloomy place in only a few short hours. Left without a
choice, I placed my ear buds in and proceeded outdoors. I'll *pretend*
to listen to something. No one will know a thing.

Whooooosh!

My shoulders hunched to the tips of my earlobes, as old man
winter struck with a flash of cold – traveling through my body at the
speed of light.

What was that?!

The wind attack felt personal. Old man winter has been depicted as a white male for centuries and I seriously considered pressing charges. *What? It felt like a hate crime!* Thankfully, I came to my senses. Filing a police report over a "wind assault" would've caused a lifetime of embarrassment. I popped the collar to my pea coat in preppy fashion, pulled the zipper up to the point of suffocation and went on my way.

I couldn't believe how angry I'd gotten. Had it really come to this?

Maybe the "attack" was the bolt of energy I needed – a wake-up call of sorts. In a considerable amount of time, I grew mildly inspired by the people and images abroad, taking a moment to reflect on life. I aimlessly wondered how well it treated others, as I came across disheveled faces and others filled with glee. What precipitated the appearances of these total complete strangers?

Are people truly living the lives they've envisioned?

Was this couple walking in front of me as happy as they appeared?

What does he do for a living?

Isn't that child too big for a stroller?

How did this young man become homeless?

Is her ass really that big?

Is she wearing any underwear?

Questions we've all had in mind, at one time, or another.

WALK WITH ME

Over the years, I found myself taking copious notes, hoping to spark a new interest in writing. Since 2007, the year of my original book plans, I've experienced additional life, having grown a prodigious amount of confidence in my abilities to express thoughts through words. To be straightforward, 2007 wasn't the right time.

Today, *reality* was staring me down, as if I was eye candy – attracted to my *failures and missed opportunities*. I'd explore various *jobs* over the years and considered starting a few businesses but didn't have a *career* in sight. Time was running out.

With my daughter on the brink of her teenage years, it was imperative to disclose my true passion, as a form of inspiration to follow her own dreams. In addition, I needed to prove to myself that I wasn't a failure.

"How cool would it be to see a book written by your dad?" I asked.

"That would be awesome! Can I help?"

You already did Princess... you already did.

No longer could I sit idle, watching others with the vocabulary of a four-year old receive lucrative book deals. Visit your local bookstore and you'll see exactly what I mean. The market is disturbingly flooded with useless material and it was starting to get under my skin. If publishers were going to continue handing out deals like Halloween candy, I wanted my share of the cavities!

My mind was entranced, consumed by a world of thought and that's when I had a revelation: I needed to make an *immediate* life change. Former U.S. President, Barack Obama – *change*. Baseball great, Jackie Robinson – *change.* Heck, Caitlyn (Bruce) Jenner – *change!* Something impactful, something rewarding, something to get people talking, something that would cement my place in history! Just moments ago, my entire world was about to crash over an app. Now, I had new life. Nothing could steer me away from what was becoming the crowning moment of my week.

As a child, I'd write articles to various newspaper and magazine op-ed sections, until an editor felt they were worthy enough to publish. It was a trait I picked up from my father, who commonly shared his written pieces on politics. With a growing passion for sports, I'd grab Sunday's paper (or the latest edition of *Pro Wrestling Illustrated*), eagerly turning to the fan forum section anticipating my presumed published article – only to hang my head in disappointment. The rejection created an uncanny work ethic to improve linguistics and sentence structure. No longer would they reject me. In hindsight, maybe I shouldn't have cared so much about this type of stuff. Besides, I had other fish to fry... like trying to figure out how Ric Flair and Bobby Heenan carried the WCW big gold belt on WWF Television! But the feeling was indescribable once I came across my personal work of art printed in the *New York Daily News* for all to see.

"They printed my letter!" I'd yell.

Sooner or later, I caught the eye of *Ms. Glynn,* my 5th grade teacher, who'd give the class weekly current event assignments. If your topic of choice piqued her interest, she'd ask that you present it to the class – usually the part I dreaded most. *It was supposed to be a simple homework assignment, not the Gettysburg Address!* All I wanted to do was write, but Ms. Glynn recognized my abilities, appointing me class valedictorian, beating out the overall favorite, *Sasha Dawes*.

With a commitment to making a *life* change in full effect, I was cognizant of the opinions shared by others, fully aware of the struggles involved when trying to cut your teeth in the writing industry. My decision would likely come under some scrutiny, but I couldn't allow it to demoralize me.

Taking a leap of faith – without the security blanket of a college degree (or a Reparations check from the 6.4 trillion dollars owed to black America – stemming from the 40 acre & mule agreement) is daring... but working a dead-end job 40 hours a week was unfulfilling!

As my daughter elegantly puts it: 'What's the point of living, if you don't take chances?' *Writing* has long been a part of my genetic makeup – what was I waiting for? It was time to turn the page on this ugly chapter in life, resign from my unavailing job and embark on a new journey!

In the land of public perception, conveying to others about an outlandish career choice (without a body of work) creates preconceived notions.

"Either this dude is unemployed, broke, or hanging onto a dream."

I'll take, 'unemployed, broke, or hanging onto a dream for $1000', Alex! Telling the world that I'm an author before releasing a book, would be equivalent to a "movie extra" telling friends that he/she is an actor, but my livelihood was at stake – their opinions didn't matter. Rather than stick around a corporate environment where I was heading nowhere fast, I wanted to follow my passion and remove myself from:

- Ho hum team meetings
- Overused buzzwords like, *perspective*
- Useless performance assessment reviews

And worst of all: OFFICE PRETZELS. Good fuckin' riddance! I knew it was time to part ways from the nine-to-five grind as my habits grew uglier by the day:

- **Daily Pep** – When you remind yourself each morning, that no matter what anyone says (or does) at work, you won't allow it to affect you… until that *very first* encounter pisses you off!
- **Weekend Blues** – When you've spent *all day* Sunday complaining about Monday!
- **Sayonara** – When you've used 95 percent of your vacation time by March!

If this describes you, get out now and reassess everything! I was unquestionably non-committal to the corporate world – where my only excitement was derived from dressing up for the part and reading the Yahoo! comment section on company time!

* * * * *

Author's Note: *If you ever wanted to know where all of America's racists hide, try reading the Yahoo! comment section after a black person commits a crime. You'll be in for a treat.*

* * * * *

The question remained: How long should I commit to a profession that offers annual ten cent raises? Was that my worth, after all the time and effort I'd put forth? Aside from that, I couldn't overcome the disconcerting feeling of being the lone black male in the department. It was a never-ending story… *like racism in America… like black on black crime… like one of my favorite 80s films.*

* * * * *

Author's Note: *I'm sure I was hired to placate the Department of Labor's diversity standards, but being the "token black guy" in department photos was exasperating! We'll save some of my thoughts on this topic for a later chapter.*

* * * * *

Q: Okay, Ernest, so what about a switch to a blue-collar field?
A: *My intestinal fortitude for a blue-collar job is imaginary at best.*

- *Construction* involved too much manual labor; climbing tall buildings, braving the outside elements. Returning home in filth wasn't conducive to my well-being.

- *Law enforcement* starts with being patronized in boot camp, followed by having my life endlessly on the line. Plus, I wasn't comfortable with the thought of one day staring inside the barrel of a gun... simply for pulling someone over for a broken tail light!
- *Fire Department*... Not enough people of color to even give it a thought.
- *Sanitation*... No thanks. I'm not picking up another person's trash.

Before anybody out there blows a gasket, this isn't a knock at those making an honest living in each of the listed professions. For the record, I've met quite a few people in these fields, who have enticed me with *salaries, stock options, 401K plans, health benefits, vacation time* and the opportunity for an *early retirement.*

It all looked wonderful on the surface, but were the rewards greater than the ONE reward I've been seeking?

Q: What reward is that?

A: *HAPPINESS...*

And the answer is an emphatic, *no!* Outside of sports, there hasn't been another hobby or profession that produces the same adrenaline rush as *writing...* and at this stage in life, I'm too old to try and hit a curveball.

"ERNEST, I SEE HERE YOU'RE AN ANALYST... AN ANALYST OF WHAT EXACTLY?"

I've been asked this question on job interviews. My reply? Life! Why did I choose *Analyst?* Because an analyst can serve many purposes, as I finagled my way through an imaginary career.

Hell, I tinkered with the title, *Special Executive Office Analyst Administrator Account Manager to the CEO* (hoping to appease potential employers), until that windy winter afternoon, when I relinquished all corporate ties, threw up my arms and officially designated myself: *Author!* At that moment, ideas materialized and the excitement to get started on a book grew. I was undeterred by the *senseless honks and obscenities blaring from vehicles stuck in traffic...* I kept my composure when *police sirens wailed, as jackhammers walloped against the concrete.* Usually, I would have sunken into a deep abyss from the flurry of activity (where I'd somberly question my existence), but today, I used it as motivation.

BEFORE I GO

I wouldn't allow the bitter cold or the earlier discouraging thoughts, detract me from my new goals:

- Waking up each morning to freshly brewed coffee
- Creating new writing content in my personal office… with my own choice of breakfast!

I wanted to open my laptop and review the new & improved itinerary:

- Writer's conference on Monday
- Book signing on Wednesday
- Podcast interview on Friday

I wanted to intensify my gym schedule between days and possibly join an adult basketball or softball league on the weekend. I could include more travel and find time to learn new recipes. Heck, just to exercise the mind, I'd consider taking up a new language, learn to play the guitar, *even* take a few online college courses!

I was through with setting an alarm clock to attend a job I detested, while someone in the world made a handsome living as a *Taste Testing Expert.* No more! With a few minutes remaining before I headed underground to my arriving train, I wondered: *Am I prepared to reveal some of my innermost, deepest thoughts on life, people and everything between? Would readers find interest in my hobbies and quirks? Does anyone care to know about my collection of house plants?*

In the current age of A.D.D. (Attention Deficit Disorder), capturing the undivided attention of a reader is more challenging than finding someone *without* a social media account! Couple that with the constant distractions of electronic devices and what do you have?

A generation of walking zombies probably disinterested in a book penned by a no-name? If that was your first guess – nice job! We have some wonderful parting gifts for you in the back!

All joking aside, I'm sure many would prefer to scroll through a complete stranger's timeline, than to read how I once cried watching the movie *Pretty in Pink.*

Have I grabbed your attention yet?

Were readers willing to spend time perusing a book, to find out what goes on in this twisted brain of mine? Somehow, I managed to convince myself – it was time to invite you to my nonconformist views, obsessions, passions and devotions. The world needed to know of my adoration for *pornography, Archie comics and Jesse Frederick TV show themes* (take advantage of Google if you're unfamiliar). My hankering for *women, fitness, 80s culture* and why the smell of *gasoline* and the crackling sounds of *vinyl records* captivate me.

Could I potentially alienate readers with unmentionable topics?

How would the consensus handle my antagonistic views on?

- Single mothers who seek child support through court, WITH the father complying to the child's needs, while actively involved?
- Women with the names of exes tatted across their private areas?
- Bad hygiene?
- Black women wearing *blonde* wigs?

And for the women who feel I'm only looking to badger them?

- Men choosing the name 'Dick' over Richard
- Prolonged handshakes
- The lack of courtesy flushes in the restroom
- Senseless stare downs
- White men and entitlement
- Black men and bravado
- Morgan Freeman and Harrison Ford wearing earrings
- Men who get their eyebrows done

My take on:

- Disliking the term *African-American*
- The grammatical goof – 'stay woke'
- UFO's
- Valentine's Day

Could my thoughts and opinions have great implications down the road?

My mind was at a standstill as I walked past a couple of vagrants in front of a 7-Eleven convenience store. The Powerball jackpot skyrocketed to a robust *$400 million* with a sea of hopefuls entering to purchase a ticket. The thought of living life as a *one percenter* was intriguing, so I gave it a quick thought:

Maybe this book thing is wishful thinking. I can hit the jackpot and have all my problems immediately solved. Besides, the current generation is too fixated on selfies and telling the world 'what they ate for dinner'. Who am I fooling? Perhaps those with similar personalities have perished like the dinosaurs, or what if they've all fallen into the traps of the new age? Maybe my story doesn't resonate with the current group of narcissistic ass-clowns. What if they find reading laborious? What if I've lost a good percentage of readers using words like 'LABORIOUS'?

The overanalyzing sent me into a state of frenzy. After giving the Powerball some thought, I realized my chances of hitting the jackpot were pure fantasy, as I backpedaled away from the 7-Eleven faster than Tonya Harding at the '94 Winter Olympics!

With roughly seven billion people roaming the earth, I liked the odds of someone relating to my story a lot better. In a world where bills pop up as frequently as 'hey stranger' text messages, I understand the importance of earning an income. Bills must get paid if you hope to get a good night's rest, and I'll have to keep *some* form of a job until further notice. But maybe my dream will lead to a guest spot on a college radio station, a 'meet and greet' session at a local library, or eventually a top seller on somebody's list!

That was the type of excitement I desired and it would supersede anything I've ever accomplished in the work place. *Of course, there is always the possibility of my book becoming another piece of literature, buried in the annals of literature history (or, used as a table coaster). But there's only one way to find out!*

PAY ATTENTION, MILLENNIALS... and OTHERS!

One of the goals I wish to accomplish with this book, is to inspire those who have fallen victim to becoming attention whores. You don't have to do that anymore.

Let's stop wasting valuable years doing unnecessary things for views, like *twerking in the middle of a highway, punching random people in the face, or taking thousands of selfies in every imaginable position known to man.* Are we really doing this for the irresistible impulse of likes and views? For goodness sake, just be normal!

If you're one of those people who find *normal* "boring", understand that life has great rewards for simplicity. Try and figure out how to maximize "boredom". Make it work to your advantage, that way you're not constantly in search of the *next* high.

Don't lose your sense of self for the allure of emulating friends and entertainers who *appear* to be living "exciting lives" on social media. It's an illusion and a clear recipe for disaster! You'll soon develop a complex, finding yourself faced with a series of *sentences:*

- **Jail:** 3-5 years (literally or relationally)
- **Kids:** 18-21 years (self-explanatory)
- **STD's:** LIFE

Now, how important was it to "stay lit"? Let's face it, most of us weren't put on earth to "entertain". For those who were, I am sure the road to success didn't require the level of atrocities happening today. I can't stress the importance for *owning your idiosyncrasies* in lieu of feeding your ego. Please don't mistake my disquisition as "not having fun and enjoying life". Have as much fun as you wish. I get it, "YOLO" (You Only Live Once). But I encourage you to pay attention to your activities.

Remember – you're only in control of your actions, not the consequences that come with them. If you desire to "stand out" from the crowd, try "fitting in" less! I promise you, it works. I've used this as my prime motivator through life. It was one of the many inspirations used to write this book;

Sure, there are plenty of authors and writers in the world, but how many "non-celebrity writers" have the courage to put it all on the line? I wanted to create a lane for people with similar personality traits and life experiences. Why should we be made to feel like outcasts?

- If you don't have a social media account?
  So, what!
- If you don't own a pair of *Yeezy* sneakers?
  Who cares!

- If you've never enjoyed the club scene?
  Join the club!
- If you'd rather be a hermit crab on New Year's Eve?
  High five!
- If you're unwilling to engage in the foolishness of today?
  It's okay!

Many people will conceal their normalcy, in fear of being labeled by the "cool people". I personally got tired of living a façade. It wasn't until my latter twenties (a little too late, if you ask me), when I wanted to *finally* treasure my true self. That is when I started receiving tons of *unwanted* attention – primarily from women.

Unwanted attention: *When you draw the attention of others without seeking it.* Outside of achieving personal goals, most men are driven by vagina. It doesn't mean we don't aspire for long-term commitments, but a horde of our antics are caused by a compulsive desire to sleep with as many women as we can. We will do just about anything for the *kitty*… until realizing how often it is handed on a silver platter… *if* you've allowed *patience* to be your friend.

You should also subscribe to the following: Acting normal! Stop forcing the issue – with everything! Guys be yourself, just make sure to sprinkle a little of the below ingredients to your character. Before long, you'll stick out like a hard-on after a good night's sleep!

- Confidence
- Wit
- Sense of humor
- Style
- Proper hygiene practices
- Good etiquette
- A contagious smile

This isn't a P.S.A., nor am I looking to pontificate upon a certain group of society. If you're able to look at this objectively, you'll see that my only aim is to help those struggling with their own identity. Who better to coach you on the road to recovery than a *Generation X'er* (the generation *before* millennials), who is helping raise a *Generation Z'er* (the generation *after* millennials)? Meaning… I'm not *that* old!

Don't take life for granted, or it will pass you by like a Pharcyde song, leaving you with nothing but fond memories… and a whole lot of *should've, could've, would've*. Soon, a third of your life will be down the shitter, with only *death* to look forward to!

THE END… OF THE BEGINNING

So, maybe this book won't connect with all. There is widespread apathy for owning your idiosyncrasies, getting on the right track and I am privy to this. For some, social media relevancy is the *only* way. Maybe you cherish forming duck lips and posting selfies before washing your ass. My words alone won't move an entire generation, but here's hoping that my book reaches you… before your next *follower!*

For the rest? I advise you to buckle your seatbelts, as I proudly give you a peregrination of my life. Prepare yourselves for a wild rollercoaster ride through *Weirdoville*, as I bring you *adventure, mayhem, befuddlement and boredom* with enough self-deprecating jokes to make you feel better about yourselves! Stop second guessing the individual God intended you to be and don't give a second thought about what others think. Find your passion and leave your own footprints in the sand!

We all have a journey to travel. I am just thankful to have found mine before my ashes were sprinkled along the Atlantic Ocean!

* * * * *

Disclaimer: Certain names in this book have been changed for obvious reasons and if you happen to find a few topics cringe worthy, keep in mind – I am unapologetically me!

Put down your electronic devices and let's read again (unless you've purchased the e-book, of course)!

Bon Appetit!
* * * * * * * * *

The **present** of my *past*

is the **gift** of *future* jubilation…

* * * * * * * * * *

Chapter One: Ernest Goes to Jail!

If you play with fire, you'll get burned...

* * * * *

The stench of urine and unwashed clothes rose from the filthy white floors as I strategically positioned myself on the corner of the twin sized bed. Seated in a slouched position, resting my face between both palms, no longer could I fight the tears. Overpowered by thoughts of despair, I'd become muddled as to what happened.

Only a few years ago, I was adding *blocks of time* to my credit card, listening to the voices of hopeless women searching for love. Now, I was examining four walls, a dirty toilet and a hollow steel door. As a last attempt to wake from this nightmare, I gave a lengthy pinch to my left forearm, anticipating a sudden jolt from my pillow – in a cold sweat. Instead, the pinch left a deep bruise. This wasn't a dream, it was reality staring me in the face. I was a product of the system.

As a kid, I used to laugh at the 80s cult film, *Ernest Goes to Jail,* starring the late Jim Varney. But never in a million years did I expect my life to imitate art. The movie was fiction, but my ordeal wasn't. The only comedy involved was my poor choice in women.

My yearning for acceptance finally caught up. All the years of desperately wanting a relationship… and here I was, stuck behind bars because of a toxic one. Four years of walking through quicksand, now buried down to the last set of fingers – trying to hold on for dear life.

The *writing was on the wall* years ago, right around the three-month relationship mark, to be exact. That's when I should've sprinted for the hills. Instead, I was staring at a different type of *wall writing*: *Mark V. was here '03.* Inscribed on the yellow block wall – filled with the names of prior jailbirds.

With nothing but time on my hands, I used it wisely to reflect on the poor decisions that ushered me to this point. My mind raced aimlessly, thinking of all the missed opportunities to break away unscathed, yet I stuck around – like an annoying housefly that stubbornly avoids the open window.

All the good people I'd let slip away. The lost friendships, the missed opportunities to travel, the potential to achieve greatness… all of it down the drain. Why God? Why did I waste my time on her? Why did I brush off the people who said she wasn't any good? What was I thinking? I wasn't, which is why I was stuck inside of a cell, pondering whether life was even worth living.

To the officers, I was just another *nigger*. Little did they know, I had solid foundation and a strong moral compass to speak of. Raised by my parents and a loving grandmother, I was all the rave of teachers, family and friends, having traveled to *three* different countries by the age of 18. To top it off, I was offered a scholarship to play basketball at a Division II school – only to decline and enroll in an *academically acclaimed* university instead.

How did I reduce myself to this? The closest I'd ever been to a cell was from the comfort of my living room… watching TV! Surely, they had the wrong guy. My track record was sound – if anything, I was the victim!

During my treacherous young adult years, I was seemingly willing to sell my soul and endanger my livelihood for the sake of a relationship. The amount of bending I'd do, would've made a street hooker jealous. Except I wasn't looking for a *good time* – I only wanted to love… and be loved.

I lacked the patience to wait my turn, convinced my past experiences were a precursor of things to come. The last thing I wanted, was to grow into being a miserable old man, sitting in a rocking chair, surrounded by house cats… screaming at children to *get off my lawn!*

I grew tired of meeting *shallow, superficial* women, but it appeared to be the only type I'd attract. Rejecting them would only send me into a deep despondency – soon faced with the threat of the *Three Deadly D's*:

- Desolation
- Depression
- Desperation

My frivolous chase for love backfired, plenty – but I was going to find it one way or another. Tapping into my inner Al Green, I was simply "tired of being alone".

I was confounded by my involvement with *Hershey* from the start. She lacked the qualities, principles, attractiveness and wisdom that would entice a person of my caliber. I'd been around better suited women, usually shying away (from exploring relationships) if there were noticeable character flaws. Perhaps they weren't as "classy" as I'd prefer... *a couple of chronic smokers, one or two who were missing a few appointments with the dentist, or those with a lurking ex-boyfriend constantly interfering in our affairs.* I'd also lose interest at the drop of a dime, if someone was too demanding or had an inability to communicate on broader subjects.

As expected, during my time with Hershey, my connection to women (who fit the mold, yet had significant others), substantially grew. Ultimately, I'd find myself stuck in the dreaded "friend zone", which is where I'd act as a *listener* – relying on a pending breakup, hoping to make a swift move and leave my own sorrowful situation.

"I'm so over my boyfriend... when are *we* hanging out?" a question many asked.

Hang out, eh?

I knew what 'hang out' meant – we *all* do. It's usually music to a man's ears and I took full advantage when the opportunity came about. But I had a thirst for more. On this quest for love I remained persistent, because *playing friends* got old.

HOW DID I GET HERE?

All I needed was a chance. I knew what I could bring to the table and it was time that I stopped being so damn picky. I wasn't perfect by any means, so why was I searching for the perfect type? Who was I to judge? So, I made the unwise decision to lower the bar.

It's okay to have high expectations, but never under any circumstances should you lower the bar when hopeless!

My interest during our cluster-fuck of a relationship lasted about the lifespan of a mayfly. But that didn't stop me from overextending my stay. It was the first *real* relationship I'd been involved in and I didn't quite know how to break up. She experienced many emotional issues, stemming from a troublesome upbringing. I genuinely felt sorry for her. Although I lacked a physical attraction to Hershey, her character flaws were imperceptible... or maybe I foolishly ignored them due to my infatuation with being somebody's boyfriend.

I had a disturbing quirk for trying to play Mighty Mouse, hoping to "save the day" by lending Hershey a hand. The calculated move was ego driven and ill-advised, as I hoped to distinguish myself from the guys in her past. The clouded judgment steered me onto a hazardous road – a road full of *potholes, warning signs and a death-defying cliff ahead*. Instead of making a clear escape (when the opportunity presented itself), I sat back and agonized over the *what if's:*

What if my phone stops ringing after I dump her?
What if I don't find a replacement?

I'd been a "hot commodity" for a few years and was unwilling to revisit my teenage agony. Despite our complications and indifferences, she looked to me for guidance. I tried to provide as many pointers as I could. She had an older male deficiency and I knew she couldn't afford to refute the wisdom of the *one* older guy in her life with vision... even if I was on the verge of making one of the biggest mistakes of my life.

They say humans utilize 10 percent of their brains, but that's being generous. Hershey and I shared absolutely nothing in common, proving that I was clearly out of my mind! It may be that my father was onto something when he suggested I eat more fish as a child. Deemed as brain food, it would have served a great purpose, preventing the calamities of my teen years leading to this point. My neglect of the aquatic animal put me in jail, confirming two things:

I didn't know my worth...

I was clearly brain dead!

LET'S MAKE A DEAL

During livelier times, when Friday night bowling was a staple and I was only home to grab shut-eye, my mother commonly brought home affordable housing applications. It wasn't that she was looking for me to move-out at once, after all, I had a full-time job and occasionally helped with the smaller household bills. But she felt it would be wise including my name to the list of *thousands* looking for inexpensive housing – in an exceedingly expensive city.

It wasn't a secret how much I anticipated bachelorhood. I had a couple of friends who were thoroughly enjoying life on their own. I couldn't wait for the day. But sadly, the thought was a fool's paradise. My *first home* became Hershey's *first home* and bachelorhood was out the door... like a thief in the night.

After a transient living experiment which saw inadequate house cleaning and constant bickering, we finally called it quits. It was a momentous feeling, albeit bittersweet, but I could finally revel in the bachelor years that I bitterly missed out on.

I immediately found a spacious one-bedroom apartment, ~~hurdling, jumping,~~ *leaping* at the chance of starting over! The feeling of coming to a clean home, lined with pictures of serenity, houseplants and the opportunity to entertain company was imposing but unfortunately short-lived. We'd been apart less than a year when her misfortune reared its ugly head, hitting an immediate soft spot.

In a world governed by hard luck, Hershey couldn't sustain a life on her own. She expressed great concern over a pending eviction and with family hours away, the onus was on me to provide immediate assistance. Besides, I didn't know how much longer I could be of any financial support – while simultaneously paying *my own* expenses. It wasn't that I was flexing my wealth – I was working a dead-end job (where I got paid to watch X-rated videos), accompanied by a part-time weekend gig for spending money. But I was a proud holder of an American Express card, the owner of *Grade A* credit and my saving habits were superb. Simply put, I was in a better financial position.

She was unwilling to move back with family and I wanted to shield us from the potential embarrassment. The nay-sayers would have had a field day had she returned:

"I told you not to move in with him in the first place!"

Perception meant everything.

My back was against the wall and it was Mighty Mouse to the rescue once more! We had several conversations and that's when I agreed to offer shelter.

My ambivalence was well noted, but she constructed a plan to resign from her job as a cashier and become a full-time medical student. There's nothing like a good plan. For the sake of solidarity,

I *tried* putting on my best face, but couldn't imagine relinquishing the freedom I worked so hard to obtain. I constantly reminded myself to relax.

The move is *only* temporary.

The medical school offered swift job placement, often boasting on their ability to find employment faster than its competitors. Suffice it to say, once the nine-month program was completed, paychecks would soon roll-in and she'd be off to resume her previous life. A verbal agreement was in place:

Rent-free stay for the duration of the school term, followed by an imminent move-out.

Maybe this wouldn't be so bad after all. The task ahead was challenging to say the least, but I wanted to prove to those on the outside that I wasn't a bad guy. She'd often accentuate my selfish ways, but that assertion no longer held any weight. What I was about to attempt was extraordinary and couldn't be ignored. We weren't married, so I had no obligation to share the same roof.

THE OTHER WOMAN

Once I met *Dana,* the connection was unlike anything I'd ever been a part of. We were at different points in our lives, with neither of us looking for a relationship. But somehow, we managed to turn an innocent conversation into a phone number exchange.

As we conversed by the vending machine at work, I was instantly attracted by the way she conducted herself. Dana articulated words in an unfamiliar fashion and I was reinvigorated by her drive and ambition – after being around the complete opposite with Hershey. She expressed a strong desire to become a career woman, where she hoped to run multiple businesses and travel the world – all of which were right up my alley. We appeared to be the perfect match, but the timing couldn't have been any worse.

While on *cloud 9,* the excitement grew as talks of starting a life together intensified. I couldn't wait to spend the remaining hours of the evening with her following work. Our situation was refreshingly unique, it was important that I surround myself with her positive energy. She was witty and had a sense of humor to die for.

Dana often asked, "Ernest, where did you come from? Are you Godsent?"

But I couldn't take any credit. I was just over the moon about our association. It also marked the first time I dated anyone who was *God fearing, culturally in tune, with a face that could grace the cover of a magazine.* Typically, those women were snatched up quicker than a hot meal at a homeless shelter on Thanksgiving morning! My past dealings included women who were missing a key component... the "it-factor". But Dana was seemingly unmatched, it was the happiest I'd been in quite some time.

Her living situation was almost as dicey as mine, sharing a home with a girlfriend – who wasn't all too fond of me. I suspected a bit of jealousy (with a hint of conviction, she had an eye for Dana), but I wasn't going anywhere. We were madly in love and I certainly wasn't sharing, so her friend had no choice but to get used to my glowing face.

Our prior relationships left us in a vulnerable state, leading to a rapid fellowship once we hit it off. Having an attraction is one thing, but when you've made a mental connection – the feeling can be outright intoxicating. Nevertheless, there was a slight hiccup in our situation which I'd been through in a prior affair, but managed to elude:

Dana was an *expectant mother* – already six months into a pregnancy.

* * * * *

Unlike most men, once the *mental* stimulation for my partner dies, the *physical* aspect vanishes like a fart in the wind. Depending on the severity of the breakup, I'm a firm believer of *when it's over – it's over!* The relationship with Hershey expired long ago and most importantly, we slept in different rooms. But the living arrangement was new grounds for Dana. I couldn't jeopardize losing her trust.

I kept her abreast of the activities at home, from the moment I walked through the door, until I hit the bed – and once more after waking up. She wasn't the jealous type, but I wanted to reduce any preexisting insecurities since we'd only been dating for a couple of months. It was the least that I could do. What amazed me about her? She was all too encouraging, offering a world of support, convincingly mentioning how my situation at home would soon pass. Maybe it was my look of disgust whenever I discussed my home life that provided Dana with enough comfort to trust me, but she exuded the necessary patience required for a lifestyle comparable to a soap opera.

It is unquestionably difficult convincing a new partner about an ingenuous living arrangement with an ex. Had the shoe been on the other foot, I would have fallen on the job... like a one-legged ice skater! But I knew once the smoke cleared, we'd have our moment in the sun and less uncompromising intimacy in her Ford Escort.

Those in the know, were completely blown away:

"You're dating a pregnant chick, while shacking up with an ex?! Are you fuckin' insane?"

Yes.

But their opinions didn't matter. Dana didn't beg me to date her and I certainly didn't ask for the other bullshit... *or, maybe I did.* My issue was solely with Hershey. I had no idea what I walked into, ditching my once *drama-free* life for future years of anguish. I'd mistakenly given her access to a once heavily guarded heart and my life would never be the same.

YOUNG & THE RESTLESS

We'd reached the dog days of summer and the apartment search narrowed down. After nine long months, the feeling of happier days ballooned; Hershey received her long-anticipated certificate! Though, a job wasn't in place, a couple of developments were brewing behind the scenes. To stay ahead of the game, we set a move-out date. After all, the school promised to deliver, so we anticipated scores of incoming phone calls from potential employers.

Thrilled by the news, Hershey's family offered to assist with a rental deposit for the future apartment, eliminating the possibility that I'd be asked for *another* favor. I wasn't in the position to do anything more – my good deed had already been recorded.

Although the job progression was moving at a snail's pace, we'd drive around the area during some down time to get a feel of what was on the apartment market. She had a pretty good idea of what she wanted, but her financial track record and money management was porous at best.

Hershey needed something feasible, conveniently located near public transportation, but we wanted confirmation that help was on the way. The clock was ticking and as someone who tends to overthink, my mind amassed doubts... with more *what if's*:

What if she's faced with another scenario where she's unable to pay rent?

What if her family doesn't have the funds to accommodate the move?

What if no one hires her?

I thought back to a time where I narrowly escaped cosigning a car she was looking to purchase. It was likely the first time I'd ever listened to my brain, instead of my heart (concerning Hershey) and my declination to tie myself into potential debt caused a major rift.

"You would've helped me, if you cared!" she declared.

But I didn't. Not enough to jeopardize my credit. Attaching your name to hers was the equivalent of signing your life over to the devil. The threat of encountering lifelong debt and tarnished credit scared me out of my wits! I was already filled with indignation, convinced she was the individual *most* responsible for shifting me away from my dreams. All that was left were my balls, my word and an *impeccable* credit score... I'd be damned if I allowed her to take that too.

She compared our situation to that of a co-worker whose boyfriend cosigned a car without breaking a sweat. But we weren't them. They were happily engaged, I was a disconsolate boyfriend regretting the day I injudiciously answered that *private call* on New Year's Eve.

I couldn't afford to be inconvenienced anymore and if she faced another moment of financial unrest, she'd have to look elsewhere for help. As the pressure to find employment mounted, so did the tension around the house. The job updates went from *pending* to dead and I was splitting time between houses, spending additional time with Dana after she gave birth. I simply wanted to provide her with the same level of support that she provided to me.

I watched my Mom go through trials and tribulations with my father and *Terrance*, so I was fully aware of the sensitivity levels after a break-up. If one happens to recover from the break up before the other? Run! *The slow recoveree carries an attitude of, 'How dare you get over me so soon?' That's when things tend to get sticky.*

The idea of living under the same roof – a second time – was strictly business. I stressed on the importance of maintaining a healthy living environment from the onset. All personal matters would be kept at bay and neither of us would come home to find strangers sitting on my sofa. *Respect the household by any means necessary!*

I knew her feelings hadn't completely dissolved, I was holding on by a thread (since I'd been pulling for her during the moments she had no one to turn to). I figured we'd pull off the *unthinkable* and gracefully go our separate ways. But, as with everything else, I thought wrong.

Hershey's suspicions of my personal dealings with Dana grew, causing her to ask unusual questions. She needed closure, but I was an unwilling participant in supplying answers. So, she sought them out herself. That was her M.O. and she admittedly played Inspector Gadget many times, snooping through my belongings while I was out. She'd come across a few items – namely a photo of Dana (which I secured in such an unlikely hiding spot that even I forgot about it!), in addition to picking the lock to a safe where I kept personal documents. But the straw that broke the camel's back, was when she courageously threw away my *Black Bubble Butts Vol. 3 DVD,* featuring the one and only, Cherokee D'Ass! That did it!

It was abundantly clear we'd reached our peak as roommates and it wasn't a secret that I was dating someone new. But I wasn't going to throw it in her face. Yes, my moods were light-hearted as I was regularly seen floating through the air – showing no inclination of wanting anything to do with Hershey. In fact, that light turned off quicker than an *unpaid* electric bill through the four-year relationship. But I tried diligently to remain cordial during our arrangement.

As with most uninformed women, if a man isn't making a pass at them, they're promptly regarded as a homosexual or there must be somebody else – because heaven help us all if a straight male is simply uninterested in a female! (some of you need to get over yourselves.) There was somebody else and I'd given Hershey the signs long ago that I was uninterested, so why would she even care about what I was doing and who I was with? We weren't together!

I grew weary of being a prisoner in my own home. But what set me off was having to constantly place my newfound relationship on the back burner. Dana and I had no control of our feelings or the timing we met, but how long was this charade at home supposed to continue? I was the one in need of answers! The intro to *60 Minutes,* became the soundtrack of our incommodious summer;

Tick, tick, tick, tick, tick, tick, tick…

More calls were placed to family members, but the responses were absent… as were the job offers.

Please, Lord, don't let this happen…

I imagined mustering up a thousand dollars for a rental deposit was harder than anticipated, but I couldn't understand why they'd make a promise they couldn't keep. Her family bailed on her with past monetary requests, but considering the circumstances, no way would that same act be repeated. Something had to give – even if it meant robbing a fuckin' bank!

With less than two weeks remaining before the proposed move-out date and no clue how this would play out, Hershey had her eyes set on an apartment only *minutes* from the house – without a pot to piss in. It was less than a year ago when we concocted this grand plan to get her on the right track and there we stood… facing another failing effort. The momentum shifted from *hopeful* to *hopeless,* but I was positive my prayers would be answered… until the unthinkable happened.

"Can you extend my stay until the end of the year?"

No. Fuckin'. Way!

We were already a month removed from her graduation without an inkling of a job and now she wanted four more months? How would I put up with her shenanigans for an extended period? Was I supposed to make another sacrifice? I'd been sacrificing since the day we met! I couldn't fathom telling Dana to wait another four months before receiving an invite to my house. So, I responded with the *one* word that could have saved me so long ago:

No!

Tempers flared, it was about to go down… like a fat kid on a see-saw. The threat of a war loomed as a thunderous conversation sparked inside of the apartment. She was feistier than usual, showing a pugnacious side that I was familiar with from past quarrels, yet I kept my cool, reminding her of the verbal agreement in place. My benevolence wasn't good enough… she wanted more.

The exchange of words continued until she'd had enough. Grabbing a swan figurine off the wall unit, she struck it against the marble surface of the dining room table shattering it into pieces.

Hershey stormed off into the bedroom, retrieved the cordless phone from the night stand and hurled it in my direction with the speed of a Nolan Ryan fastball – missing my face by a few inches. No way was this happening… again. I pleaded for her to calm down as she hurried off into the bathroom.

"Fuck you!" she yelled, slamming the door with prodigious force. Stunned, I followed her, like an animal hunting its prey. After several unsuccessful attempts at turning the doorknob, I looked around the bedroom door for the skeleton key.

Hershey had moments in the past of being unable to control her temper, but her aura that afternoon was unusual. I am fully convinced that her next course of action was carefully planned and crafted.

"Calm down!" I exclaimed.

"Leave me the fuck alone, you only care about yourself!" Two F-bombs in a span of minutes, from an individual who rarely used profanity. It was at that moment reality hit me square in the face… like her *right hand* a couple of years prior:

She never appreciated what I'd done. The sacrifices made in our once turbulent relationship; the mental torment, emotional angst, health scares, lost friendships, family divisiveness, all of which she brought to the table! And this is how I was being repaid?

Fuck that!

I barged through the bathroom door, like a swat team executing a drug raid – toppling her over. As we fell to the floor, I made a last effort to calm matters.

"Get off me! Get off me!" she screamed.

"Calm the fuck down!" I yelled back.

Incensed, she reached for my face while I attempted to hold both of her hands down onto the bathroom mat. Somehow, she managed to evade my grip, sliding her fingers towards my bottom row of teeth, as if she was feeling for a loose tooth, but she wasn't a dentist. Regrettably, that's when my instincts got the best of me.

"Aaaaaaaah! You bit me? You fuckin' bit me?!" As she threatened to call police, I got up and grabbed my cell phone, hoping to locate Dana. If there was anytime I needed her, it was now. Dana was privy to everything going on up until that point and I knew she would have blood in her eyes upon arrival. Never in a million years did I anticipate my skirmish with Hershey as the reason for Dana's first visit to my home, but I didn't have anyone nearby to turn to.

"Call that bitch, I don't give a fuck, call her… she won't do shit!" Hershey yelled.

Dana, who was on the other end of the line, jawed back with belligerence, ready to take matters into her own hands. I knew she'd be there in mere minutes, so I stepped outside to distance myself from the chaos.

While awaiting the arrival of the police, Hershey was on the phone with a friend – explaining the bite, attempting to further antagonize me with unruly comments about my act. Within minutes, multiple police cars pulled up to the scene. It was as if we lived on *Bundy Drive*.

A couple of officers entered the home to attend to the *victim*, while I managed to express myself to those remaining outside.

My guard had been up from our previous battles – signaling a *preemptive strike* from my brain once her fingers entered my mouth. It was a traumatic experience, but I was left with no other choice than to protect myself. Of course, there was a better chance of *pigs flying,* than Hershey causing any real physical harm, but she carried a Napoléon complex – and hell hath no fury like a woman scorned.

After being fueled with anger for so long – feeling as if my life was in shambles, I was thankful the outcome wasn't worse. Quite frankly, she was lucky to be alive. *The results can be disastrous once testosterone is mixed with a spurned female – which is why men are oftentimes told to walk away.*

I took pride in containing my emotions, refusing to fall victim to the deadly traps set during domestic disputes. Had I acted on my true emotions, my freedom would've been stripped away quicker than a burning victim's clothes. I'd never been exposed to physical violence before this inessential relationship – all it took was a couple of silly arguments to transpire and I'd detach myself from an individual for good. There were plenty of other fish in the sea and I didn't have the energy to engage in any back and forth jibber jabber.

But our situation went deeper. Hershey's paltry attempts at humor in the presence of police mystified us all, having the audacity to question my manhood for *biting.*

I towered over her by a foot and could've easily turned her into a personal punching bag. Yet, there she was. Trying to be funny, instead of being thankful I showed restraint.

The officers were equally astounded by the venom spewing from her mouth, requesting that she stop at once and return to the apartment. *Did she sound like a victim or an antagonist?*

I continued chatting with *Officer O'Hare,* as a Ford Escort entered our sight. Inquiring if I could place a quick call to my father (who was all too familiar with our struggles, yet unaware of the madness that occurred), I stepped aside once receiving his blessings – as Dana began to exchange profanity-laced *pleasantries* with Hershey. Minutes into the conversation, I directed my attention to *Officer Carrillo,* who approached with some discouraging news.

"Sir, the victim is pressing charges and will be requesting a restraining order against you."

What?! My mind was racing in a thousand directions. What was happening?

"Dad, I'll call you back."

When I was on the receiving end of her aggression, I didn't bat an eye. But the *one* time I act out of character, this was her response?

"Officer, I could've put a restraining order on this girl three months after we met. She would've been out of my life for good!" My retort fell on deaf ears.

Here I was, faced with a charge for a scratch about the size of a mosquito bite – when they should've thrown the book at her for years of distress!

That's when it occurred to me. The restraining order gave her full access to my home. The coveted extension she longed for was happening… courtesy of my teeth!

According to state law, an individual can claim a residence as their own upon receiving mail at the address – *even* if their name doesn't appear on the lease. I was the lone lessee, but she had *squatter rights.* This was her home too!

Son of a bitch! It explained why she rejected the idea of renting a P.O. Box when she moved in.

"Well, if I live here, I should get mail here too."

It all started to make sense. I'd allowed her to outsmart me… again.

With a restraining order in place, I was to inform an officer and await their arrival at a neutral location – to be escorted to the apartment, if I needed to return for any reason. The "victim" was given full autonomy over *my* personal belongings. What a turn of events!

Dana was running late for work and fully exhausted after using every cuss word in the book. Before departing, we embraced as she assured me that I'd have a place to stay once the dust settled. Officer Carrillo slowly approached, wearing a grimace on his face, as he placed handcuffs on my wrists.

A few of the resident neighbors gathered around to observe the scene as I was led to the back seat of the police car. I made sure to avoid eye contact, ashamed of my actions and my entire involvement with this individual. Taking one last look at the apartment, an image of my face stood in the living room window … except, *younger.* Figuring it was just my imagination, I blinked several times, yet the image remained.

Why wouldn't it go away?

The car pulled off as a hard lump emerged in my throat. I put my head down and wept, until we arrived at the police station.

* * * * *

Author's Note: *Domestic disputes are about as recurrent as the common cold, but this was new territory for me. Prior to this relationship, I'd managed to escape the unfair conventional stereotypes placed on black men. However, due to my inexperience, I was baited. Like an amateur, I ate the cheese.*

Chapter Two: New York, N.Y.: Big City of Dreams, Rats and Attitudes!

Very little scares me as an adult. What is there to fear, when you've been exposed to kidnappings, robberies, murders, open drug deals and equally alarming – rats?! I never needed a big brother when I had the city take me by the hand – leading me to the fire to walk alone. That is how I became a man.

* * * * *

It's quite easy to figure out why *New Yawkers* are detested; we're arrogant, brash and say dumb shit like *fuhgeddaboudit!* (we *really* don't). The world seemingly revolves around us and *New Yawkers* aren't afraid to thumb their nose at the tourists. I get it – our city is overcrowded, fast paced, overpriced and we're named after each other *twice*. Pretty lame, if I must say.

We have rats the size of women's shoeboxes, the quality of life absolutely sucks and living here will shed your life expectancy about *ten years!* But that doesn't stop you from adding us to your bucket list. We're a big deal to most – the buck stops here… literally. Home to Wall Street and the Stock Exchange, New York City is the *money* capital of the world, the *fashion* capital of the western world and the home to many landmarks you've seen on your television:

- The Empire State Building
- Statue of Liberty
- Central Park
- Times Square
- Radio City
- Rockefeller Center
- Lincoln Center
- Apollo Theater
- Madison Square Garden
- Yankee Stadium

Our sports fans have a false sense of entitlement. Due to the enormous pressure, athletes err on the side of caution (before signing contracts) to play for one of our many teams.

Ol' Blue Eyes said it best: *If you can make it here, you can make it anywhere.* He wasn't lying.

It's the birthplace of hip-hop and some of the biggest actors in Hollywood got their start here.

We have Broadway shows, an abundance of museums and restaurants and our city is divided into five-boroughs; *Brooklyn* being the largest. I'm sure you've heard of it before. That borough alone has a population larger than some U.S. cities!

Our skyline is legendary, and the street names are world-renowned:

- Broadway
- Park Avenue
- 5th Avenue
- Madison Avenue
- 34th Street
- 42nd Street, Times Square
- Grand Central
- 125th Street

This is the Big Apple! Yes, there is a lot to be proud of, but the narrative about *New Yawkers* is true: We are a *different* bunch. Spend a little time here and watch how quickly we rub off on you. You'll turn from an *optimistic soul,* to an *acrimonious prick* in no time!

In a city of eight to ten million people, where we trip over one another like lab mice, it's hard to circumvent our personality traits. We *want* to be perceived as *Good Samaritans*, but honestly, we don't care what you think. Why should we, when the rest of the world is too busy trying to emulate us? It's the land of the 'frowner', where we walk with a noticeable scowl (except for those living in the "nicer" parts of the city). If you find a *New Yawker* smiling, you've *probably* bumped into someone on the other side of crazy!

We drive like lunatics – find a driver who uses their signals and I can assure you they were taught their driving skills elsewhere. We jaywalk at will and if you *even* think about honking your horn – as we *illegally* cross the street – you'll get flipped the bird… maybe even a swift kick to your car if we're close enough.

"What's your problem?" you ask.

No, no, Sir, what's *your* problem?! We don't follow rules, we defy them! Our style of dress is distinct, we have a contrasting swagger and our accents – yes, let's talk about those "silly" accents…

"Why do you pronounce words that way?"

Because we fuckin' can! Is that alright with you? You mock us, but you secretly like our broken English and women from other cities are oftentimes intrigued. Don't try to deny it now. I'm living proof. I've watched women's *eyes enlarge, lashes bat and thoughts wander* – during colloquy. If that was your girl… she may not be for long.

For those looking to relocate, or simply pay us a visit? Don't fret! We will kindly roll out the red carpet – just try to remain on our good side:

- **Do not stare at others while riding public transportation** – Look at the floor, scroll through your phone, or read the same poster advertisement – until your eyes permanently hate you!
- **Do not stop the flow of pedestrians by *casually* walking through our busy streets** – If you notice everyone walking at *100 MPH*, try your best to keep up! We're unafraid to give you a shoulder bump (without an apology) if you're standing in the way.
- **Do not stall at a green light (if you're behind the wheel)** – Green means *'go!'* Either move the fuckin' car or get off the road!

Finally, let's talk about the trademarks of our wonderful city: ~~Yellow cabs, skyscrapers, bodegas, graffiti,~~ *Rats & Pigeons!* Has anyone noticed how unbothered they are by our presence? We fear them more than they fear us. Doze off on the subway and you might find a *four-legged critter* running up your leg. That's a *New Yawker* greeting you – bold and in your face! Show some respect or may you never ride the subway again.

Pigeons are equally brave and in the good ol' days, a simple flinch into the direction of these *rats with wings* would have them scurrying quicker than Usain Bolt at a track meet. But the grittiness of the city has rubbed off on the latest generation of birds. Try flinching now – I dare you! Watch as they brush off your weak attempts at striking fear, *walking* audaciously to their destination. That's right, *walk!* They aren't *flying* anywhere. They're not frightened by you.

I am a proud product of this cesspool called New York City and couldn't imagine being born anywhere else… *well… yes, I can.* But the question is: How did I get here?

I LOVE N.Y… SOMETIMES

Phyllis Norflis, my grandmother (known as Gran), made the move to New York City during the early 1960s, after brief stints on the West Coast and Midwest. Originally from the rural town of Monroe, Louisiana, she lived on a farm with her parents and three siblings. She found farmland life to be a drag, seeking a little excitement as she neared her latter teenage years. To combat the boredom, Gran asked her parents for permission to move to the Bay Area with additional family and friends. With enough tugging and pulling, her father obliged. She was obviously a *daddy's girl.*

Some years passed, Gran found herself miles away in Detroit, Michigan where she settled down – eventually giving birth to two girls. With a new lease on life and mouths to feed, she had an impulse to start a career in the medical field, but Detroit's job market was meager at best. Through word of mouth, she found out about the immense job opportunities available in New York City and pondered relocation once more.

Not one to shy away from adventure, Gran informed her mother (Ms. Viola Manning, my great grandmother) who still resided in Louisiana (after her husband's passing) of the desire to make the gutsy trip to the "Empire State" as a trial run. Ms. Viola welcomed the idea, packed up her belongings and migrated to Detroit to look after the girls while Gran attempted to establish herself in the big city. Once the family reunited, there were several apartment visits around the boroughs, before fixing in on a *one-bedroom* unit on the Upper West Side of Manhattan; my second home.

The apartment was the originator of loud furniture colors, fond memories and where Ms. Viola, Gran, my aunt (eventually joined by her two kids) and Mom resided... *simultaneously.* Perhaps occupancy laws were lax during the 60s.

New York City was a different animal than the one we've grown accustomed to. When nostalgia comes over me (which is often), one of my favorite pastimes is watching movies filmed in the city. Movie favorites include films from the 70s, 80s and early 90s, showcasing the *old* New York:

- The Warriors
- The Godfather
- Ghostbusters
- Fatal Attraction
- Wall Street
- Kids

I will admittedly watch any movie filmed in Manhattan, just to pinpoint familiar neighborhoods captured on camera. It's one of those bizarre things I do – and if anyone is wondering, yes, I've watched "Sex and the City" and plenty of romantic comedies... and yes, I still consider myself a man – thank you!

The *old* New York is the city I identify most with and I'll proceed to explain why. With all its glitz & glamour, the city experienced its share of dark moments, noticeably in the 70s and 80s, when New York City and crime went hand in hand... like Jergens lotion and a strong Wi-Fi connection.

A period where street signs were an ugly mustard yellow, police cars looked like they were taken off the set of *Dragnet* and checkered cabs roamed. Graffiti permeated the outside of buildings, subway cars and the insides of tunnels. Drugs and homelessness were rampant, the playgrounds were a haven for junkies. If *little Bobby* wanted to play on the slides, he'd better watch out for the hypodermic needles and *red tops* on the way down. There was the *old* Times Square – considered a wasteland, with scores of *naked women, pimps, prostitutes and drug dealers* within arm's reach.

Fast forward to today? Tourists and Disney characters. *Thanks, Rudy!* (Former Mayor, Rudolph Giuliani, credited for cleaning up the filth).

I miss the aroma from the *old* diners; the smell of *French fry grease and gluten products.* I miss the *Twin Towers;* the buildings that once defined our skyline, until that horrific September day in

2001 – when they were eradicated. *The replacement tower doesn't do it for me.*

New York City is where Jason Voorhees washed away in the sewers in, *Friday the 13th Part VIII: Jason Takes Manhattan.* The very same sewers the *Teenage Mutant Ninja Turtles* called home. Nino Brown became a New York drug kingpin in, *New Jack City,* while Macaulay Caulkin and Fivel Mousekewitz got lost here in *Home Alone 2* and *American Tail,* respectively. (*The latter being the first movie to put a tear in my eye.*)

I miss the mystique of the *old* New York – a time when you didn't know whether you'd make it home alive...

We had gangs like the *Decepticons* and the *Lo-Life Crew* and didn't look to copy the gang culture of Los Angeles. The only group parading the streets in *all red,* were Curtis Sliwa and the Guardian Angels (responsible for targeting criminals and protecting lives, while the NYPD was consumed with corruption).

Through the heroic efforts of the Angels, I still miss the infamous drug kingpins and mob bosses, who wreaked havoc through the five-boroughs. Not for their senseless acts of crimes, but for their backstories, which are at the crux of our city's history. *They just don't make gangsters like they used to.*

I miss subway tokens and *redbird* subway cars. Telephone booths and video arcades. I miss when the city had character, a time when car radios were stolen in abundance and tourists thought twice about holding up sidewalk traffic for pictures. I miss Woolworth, Tower Records and the infamous Skate Key.

The current New York City is a farce, dominated by *Hipsters, Yuppies* and a *Cowboy who makes a living strumming a guitar in his tighty-whities.* Sadly, a slew of out of towners call New York home – without a clue of our past.

You're all very welcome.

MEET THE PARENTS

My father (also my namesake), a native of Ghana, West Africa, made the lone journey to the states in the early 1970s – in pursuit of opportunity and the "American Dream". With his fate in the western world unknown, it was while attending a local college that he met *Charlotte.*

I don't know the exact verbiage *Ernest Sr.* used to sweep my mother off her feet, but it must have been something for the ages. Before long, the two were a hot item and to the chagrin of Ms. Viola and Gran, Mom ditched her educational obligations for the allure of love & marriage. *Because we all know how important it is for women to get married in their 20s!* (eye-roll).

Nothing could stand in the way of their undefined love... not even birth control. As legend has it, once moved into a studio apartment (in the Hamilton Heights section of Manhattan), the lovebirds consummated the marriage... and somewhere along the way... Mom's diaphragm slipped. *Whoops!*

Before long, your author arrived with a head full of hair, face full of cheeks, on a mission to take the world by storm... *or maybe not.*

My father went on to graduate with a bachelor's degree in economics, thriving in banking and finance – pissing off a couple of in-laws in the process as they accused him of sending my mother off track, while Mom moved around a few big named companies, only to stunt her professional growth – entangled in *unrelenting* love quests. *Unfortunately, a trait I would pick up in the coming years* (we will revisit in a later chapter).

To my parents' credit, they were the prime example to emulate: *marriage first, children second.* Such an easy template to follow, yet it remains a deficiency in many communities – particularly, the black community.

HOME BITTER HOME

My childhood neighborhood was truly one of the hidden gems of the city. Located in the Hamilton Heights section of Manhattan, I lived on a tree-lined block with some of the prettiest tenements and brownstones around. The ones you'd commonly see on *The Cosby Show.* Hamilton Heights was once the home of thousands of European immigrants during the 1950s and 60s until *prominent* people of color migrated to the area. A cue for the immigrants – who wanted nothing to do with comingling – to transition out.

With Harlem only a few miles away, I was thrilled to witness a smidgen of black renaissance happening in my part of town. They weren't the customary blacks we've all grown to witness through deficient media images; they were of the upper echelon. *Yes, America, we exist*. The euphoria of spotting brown faces (young and old), mixed in with a few ethnic groups who hadn't scurried out of town yet, was unparalleled!

To understand New York City, one must have comprehension of "white privilege". Luxurious living is offered to all, but when the going rate for a one/two-bedroom apartment (in a good neighborhood) averages between 2500–3000 dollars/month and the top salaried jobs are generally offered to Caucasians... who do you expect the occupants to be? I'll wait...

For every rule there is an exception, but do you think it's coincidental that the primary residents in the better parts of town are non-black? Certain minority groups are not making the incomes to support luxurious living in major cities. Sometimes it's through faults of our own, other times through blatant racial profiling. Unlike 'The Jeffersons', my family 'moved on up' ... to the WEST side... of Manhattan.

We moved from the mouse infested studio, into a two-bedroom unit (inside of a tenement building), around the time I could crawl. This is where I spent most of my early childhood, thinking back on many fond memories.

I had a good variety of activities to keep me engaged; *children's books, encyclopedias, comics, science kits, a TV, Sega Master video game system, toy chest and a collection of vinyl records* (kept in my room for extra storage). However, I remained fixated on the images outside of my window, where I had a bird's-eye view of minorities getting a taste of prosperity. The feeling was empowering.

My analytical abilities started young and though I was enamored by what was on display outdoors, I was confounded by the intensity existing outside of my room. Like most kids, I wasn't privy to the everyday struggles of adulthood – circumstances that can alter a relationship and affect the mood of the house. I noticed how exceedingly different my parents were and it showed in their body language. Their open display of affection was limited, and the conversations were succinct.

On many accounts, my father sat quietly on the sofa, fully immersed in the latest edition of *Time* magazine (the first "book" I attempted to read as an infant – how many of you can say that?), listening to the Jazzy sounds of CD 101.9 FM, while Mom usually chatted away on the phone with her best friend. There was the occasional moment we'd eat at the kitchen table or watch our favorite TV shows in the living room – *MacGyver* and *The Cosby Show*, but for the most part, we kept to ourselves. My father wasn't concerned with *indoor* activities if it didn't include books, usually scoffing at the idea of playing with toys or the mere thought of watching television.

"Why don't you turn off the TV and read a book?"

The programs I watched were harmless, as I only had access to local stations; CBS, NBC, FOX, ABC, WWOR-TV, WPIX, PBS. Not many opportunities to catch a titty... unless, there was grave concern over Bugs Bunny tonguing down Elmer Fudd every Saturday morning (which was admittedly disturbing).

I often joked, if it were up to my father, I'd still be a virgin – enrolled at a University in another continent! I didn't understand his issue with television, until I was old enough to realize how injurious it is to the mind. 'Tel-LIE-vision' – it can be destructive.

My mother was what they call a "fun mom", regularly tapping into her inner child. We played cards, board games, danced to Bobby Brown songs, recited Keith Sweat lyrics, sharing a ton of laughs.

As a family, *outdoors* was contrastingly different. We spent a lot of time attending free summer concerts in Central Park and there were plenty of cultural events and African gatherings to drop in on around the city. That's when my parents would dress up in African garbs, mingling with other couples, while I attempted to break out of my shy spell busting a few moves on the dance floor with the other children in attendance. But the icing on the cake was our trip to the U.K. when I was five years-old – specifically London. What a blast! We took enough pictures to last a lifetime.

I traveled to England again, alone... at the age of seven! There aren't many children who can say they've been across the pond multiple times before the age of ten, but I was very fortunate to have such exposure (I would also travel to Ghana as a teenager). Despite my parents' vast differences, they were loving and heavily invested in a future that looked promising to say the least.

"GO TO YOUR PLAYGROUND... I MEAN, ROOM!"

My room was used as a source of punishment, but also served as my personal playground. To those who grew up with nice sized backyards... well, the bedroom (*courtyard, or rooftop* – depending on where you grew up in the city) was *our* backyard. This is where I played indoor hoops, mimicking the deafening dunks of Dominique Wilkins, or the heroic efforts of Michael Jordan and Larry Bird, courtesy of my *Nerf* basketball set. It was also where I'd practice my driving skills, with the *Tomy Turnin' Turbo Dashboard Steering Wheel.* In those rare moments when I'd get into some serious trouble and my parents made the command of "no TV or toys", my imagination *really* went to work!

I'd stare at the sky in search of a Goodyear blimp or attempt to identify the shapes of the clouds. I'd trace the album covers of my father's vinyl records or grab an encyclopedia and read up on the dinosaurs and solar system. Is that boring enough for you? The adage of turning *lemons into lemonade* was discovered young and if sending me to my room was considered a form of "punishment", they'd have to try much harder. Ladies and Gentlemen: This is where spankings were added to the mix. *Be careful what you wish for!*

My mother tries to have collective amnesia on this topic, but I never understood how a woman *so sweet and playful, delicate and kind,* could dish out the lashings rivaling an overzealous slave owner! She was the lone enforcer responsible for 99.9 percent of my whooping's... and my ass remembers each one vividly.

Wapeeesh!

That was the sound of the belt striking across my thigh. Man! She was a wizard with that thing, homing in on a meaty part of my body with her eyes closed. Mom would have me hopping around the room, like someone standing on a bed of hot coals!

On the other hand, my father was *quiet and short-tempered,* using the simple (but effective) tactic of *putting the fear of God in me* with one stare. If looks could kill, he'd put you six-feet under! I'd never seen anything like it.

Collectively, my parents had the patience of a cat in heat, but I gravitated towards my father's demeanor, and used that stare tactic on my daughter plenty of times. Let me tell you – it works like a charm!

* * * * *

I started off overly-sensitive, persistently allowing my emotions to get the best of me. Any sign of trouble (or being told 'no') was generally met with a hard lump in the throat and a sea of tears. Boys are oftentimes told not to cry:

- Big boys don't cry!
- You *must* be strong!

Roarrrrrrrrr!
Mannnn, puh-lease!

The world needed to know if my feelings were hurt. I'd deal with the consequences later. But my problem? I'd allow *everything* to touch a nerve! It was difficult not to give the go-ahead for that single tear to form, as I constantly blinked my eyes to avoid the tear from gaining enough traction. Cause if that son of a bitch left my eye socket (and Mom got a sense of it), I was as good as done!

"And I better not see any tears in your eyes!"

* * * * *

Author's Note: *Why must parents discern whether their child is vexed? Message to parents: Continue to look forward and allow your child those few seconds to shed silent tears. Making further threats of, "I'll give you something to cry about!" won't defuse the situation. Only when your child becomes publicly disruptive should you pull them aside and scare the bejesus out of them!*

* * * * *

There were days I'd go to school with welts on my legs, struggling just to sit down. Mom's form of discipline was merely a part of the era I grew up in. An era where there was no such thing as "timeouts".

What the fuck is a time out? If the situation called for an ass beating, that's exactly what you got. Any problems – go pout about it with someone who cared! Namely, your *favorite pillow* – as was the case with me.

Mom's approach had its pluses and minuses. Yes, it was a template for establishing a healthy fear of authority. But ultimately, beating my ass like I stole something, turned me into a complete sucker! Before the wrath of her belt, I'd wince at the moment she uttered these familiar words:

Take off your clothes!

Gulp! Followed by that stupid, lone tear.

"Why are you crying? I haven't even hit you yet!" she'd shout.

Genius... I knew what was coming! *Mom, relax... I'm grown now...*

And when she asked that I remove my clothing, she *meant* every single layer... until I was left standing in my *Thundercats* underwear and striped white tube socks. If there was a sudden draft in the room and I thought for one second that I'd keep my socks on? Guess again.

"Take off your socks!"

Great. Thanks for allowing me to keep on my underwear!

I was quiet and obedient; my only *real* trouble came from imitating the misbehavior of classmates. As a parent, I understand the idea of beating your child's ass (hoping they will renounce their insubordinate behavior), but some of my spankings were unmistakably unjustifiable.

It seemed like she'd tear my legs up – no matter the cause and I never knew what justified a spanking.

Would she spank me if I incorrectly tied my shoe laces? No. But rest assure my father wouldn't be all too pleased. At times, I didn't know what was worse: a spanking from Mom or a death-stare (followed by a hard-grunting sound) by my father. Talk about a Double-Whammy!

My parents claimed to have wanted more children, but I was the lone sperm cell to persevere – taking the brunt of ass beatings – on behalf of my phantom *brothers and sisters* who couldn't make it. You're all very welcome!

I wouldn't classify my folks as abusive; like most parents, they simply wanted to flex their muscle... in case you'd forgotten who was in charge. But I knew not to test them. It was only at the start of adulthood when I felt comfortable enough to express myself!

* * * * *

Gran is the culprit for contributing to my wussy behavior, since I spent a lot of my earlier years running around her apartment. I was the youngest of three grandchildren, so rightfully, she spoiled and coddled me. She could whoop some tail in her heyday. I've heard some great stories over the years, but I was fortunate to catch her at a different time. I was raised under the *sweeter, kinder* Phyllis – the causing of gratuitous pettiness with family members lasting to this day.

Gran's pampering was a concern, but it wouldn't compare to the parenting style of my folks – which Gran greatly disapproved. She felt their demands were irrational and detrimental to my well-being – and she couldn't have been any more correct. I was constantly walking on eggshells, too shy to socialize with visitors to our home – terrified of the consequences if I didn't.

At Gran's house, I was given liberties that my parents (particularly, my father) wouldn't entertain... like opening the refrigerator without permission. Not a big deal, right? Wrong. Dead wrong! My father once scolded me for neglecting to *ask* if I could make a bologna and cheese sandwich! The infringement prompted hard time in the ~~slammer~~ *room*... door closed, TV off and a few more tears... silent ones. Shhh! Without a sibling around to toughen me and the threat of not making any friends emerging, who would save me from this mess?

THREE KNOCKS TO THE DOOR

My Saturday mornings started off with a bowl of *Ghostbusters cereal* and my favorite Saturday morning programs; *Alvin & The Chipmunks, Pee Wee's Playhouse, The Real Ghostbusters, Bugs Bunny and Tweety show,* ending with *WWF Superstars.* If we didn't have any plans for the day, I'd get started on a few chores, before turning my room into fantasy land. At that point, you wouldn't see my face around the house again until lunch, which is when I'd prepare my customary bologna and cheese sandwich – *with permission*, of course.

* * * * *

Author's Note: *In case you're wondering, I do not eat bologna these days and I have no idea why I was allowed to as a child!*

* * * * *

Play time usually ended around five o'clock, as I geared up for an hour of the *A-Team,* followed by *Knight Rider* (or some random

Charles Bronson/Chuck Norris movie). I was quite regimented with my weekend schedule, but three unexpected knocks to the front door changed everything that afternoon. I raced to see who was gracing us with their presence.

"Peek through the peephole first, boy!" Mom declared. Either the knocks belonged to a stranger who managed to slip through the lobby door, or to a group of Jehovah's Witnesses. *Sometimes, you'd prefer the knocks of a stranger because Jehovah's Witnesses can be relentless!*

It was the latter part of the 80s and our neighborhood had started to change for the worse. Moreover, there was an abrupt increase in Latin and low-scale blacks to the area, leading to a growth in drug related crimes.

An expected visitor needed to be buzzed in through the lobby door before gaining access to the other floors. So random knocks were usually nerve-wracking. But I had an inkling of who it was. I looked through the peephole, as Mom ordered, catching a glimpse of the one soul responsible for saving me from obscurity.

"What's up, Fran?!"

We stood in the middle of the doorway glowing like two kids in a candy shop – *probably a little too much glow when I think of it.*

"Nothing much, can you come over?"

I asked Fran to wait by the door as I petitioned Mom for approval. Now racing around the house, after she acquiesced, I grabbed a few items and took one last look at the "Million Dollar Man" Ted DiBiase – stuffing money down his opponent's throat. The next few hours called for Fran's vast collection of Nintendo games, strategy guides and *the one* item we couldn't live without. A gleam of happiness crossed my face, thinking about all the fun that was in store.

I felt compelled to protect Mom whenever my father was out of the house, but he was only up the street with his best friend (and fellow countryman), *Kodwo* – who resided in our old studio apartment. That was a regular thing for the guys on a light-scheduled weekend and it allowed Mom an opportunity to unwind. This is when she'd emulate her favorite dance moves on *Soul Train*. I said goodbye and met Fran in the hallway, where he was busy shooting away at imaginary aliens.

Pew! Pew! Pew!

The Tomlinson's were amazing. The grandparents of *Francis (Fran) Tomlinson,* resided in our five-story building and were members of Riverside Church, where my parents and I regularly attended.

We were leaving service one Easter Sunday, when the Tomlinson's spotted us on the way out of the door. A light conversation ensued, where Mrs. Tomlinson complimented my clip-on bowtie and fedora, further stating how her youngest grandson made frequent visits to their home – and needed a friend.

"His name is Francis and he can sure use a play buddy… that way he can leave us alone!" The comment was followed by laughter, but considering my emotional rollercoaster, the news couldn't have come at a better time.

Francis was a year older, but the youngest of two siblings who lived with their mom in a Northern New Jersey suburb. His older siblings often stayed in trouble, doing very little to shield him from their imprudent behavior, while their father remained in and out of jail.

The Tomlinson's top priority was keeping their youngest grandchild out of harm's way. He was quite the scholar, enrolled in a top-flight academy, but Fran's mother was unwilling to disrupt his academic achievements by forcing a school transfer. Fran was their prized possession – the crown jewel. *Always* protect the jewel.

* * * * *

Mrs. Tomlinson was loving, kind and often found concocting a snack when informed of my arrival, while Mr. Tomlinson commonly greeted me with a warm pat on the back, before disappearing into the kitchen where he'd nod off amid our noise. I remember the scent of their home – an inviting cinnamon aroma emanating from their plush wine-colored carpet, blended with the smell of something tasty in the oven. My parents routinely reminded me to be back by dinner, but I had a difficult time leaving the Tomlinson's on my own. I didn't know what "overstaying my welcome" meant, nor did I care. We were having too much fun.

Fran and I played uninterrupted for hours; bathroom breaks weren't allowed. *Find a kid concerned about his prostate and there's a good chance you have a child prodigy on your hands!* We configured some crafty ideas, using Fran's *Panasonic tape recorder*

– what a life saver! When our creative juices flowed…there was no stopping us.

We had the remarkable ability to make magic with one press of the *record/play* button, acting out our own Variety Show. Whether it was performing as game (or talk) show hosts, stand-up comedians, or simply *tickling the ivories* of the Casio player – we achieved it.

There once lived:

- Abbott & Costello
- Laurel & Hardy
- Sonny & Cher

And now? *Fran & Ernie.*

Our names didn't have quite the same ring, but it worked for us. Adrift in thoughts, with limitless imaginations, I was fascinated by our relatability and my aptitude for making him laugh. I discovered a scintillating wit that lived inside, usually losing track of time through our escapades. The experience made for a swift recovery in my confidence and his grandparents' home became my sanctuary.

"Can Ernest have dinner here?"

Fran often posed the question once playtime winded down. I'd stand in the hallway – puppy-eyed, awaiting the Tomlinson's reply… attempting to keep my emotions in check.

"He'll have to ask his parents."

When the Tomlinson's were completely over our noise, in search of a little peace and quiet, they'd ask:

"Haven't you guys played long enough today?"

"No!" we'd yell collectively.

I was a huge admirer of Fran, and so were my parents, who treated him like one of their own and I tried my very best to mirror him and his organizational skills. He had the mannerisms of someone who served in the military and was quite the joy to be around. He always kept the latest gadgets and I nearly blew my top when Fran drank from a cup with his name engraved! You know what followed... I wanted a cup with my name engraved too. That was a BIG deal!

Naturally we had our differences, but there weren't many. The common denominator behind an incredible chemistry was our nerdy behavior – likely derived from being two kids who spent a lot of time alone. Despite his conditions at home, Fran always kept a positive attitude and we had an indissoluble friendship. Without him, who knows where I'd be in the years to follow.

CITY OF PITY

Gunfire erupted one evening on the same block I once marveled at. The neighborhood of inviting smiles and working families became the section of the city many began to flee.

The courtyard where we once hung our clothes to dry (using a clothesline extending from our kitchen window to the next building) was now a hiding spot for drug dealers. The lights were dimly lit – sometimes not lit at all. The area was secluded; the perfect location for dealers to sell their poisons and for users to get high. That very same bedroom window where I stared out at the clouds, is where I observed the spark from a handgun – and residents scattering like roaches. It was total chaos and my neighborhood wouldn't be the same again.

* * * * *

Sometimes I'd get home around dusk, after my parents picked me up from Gran's. I stayed with her periodically after school, awaiting their arrival, as they alternated pick-up days. I remember one evening walking with my father, feeling his ire, as we approached the apartment. *Kenny* and his crew assumed their regular position posted up against the parked cars, blasting music from a boom box. Once upon a time, my father and Kenny exchanged hellos… but not anymore.

Kenny lived on the first floor of the building with his grandmother, who could no longer restrain him. Now a teenager, he was heavily influenced by his crew of lowlifes; they disturbed the peace whenever they chose. With their eyes commonly glazed over and the stench of marijuana encompassing the night air, a boisterous conversation was usually underway.

"Ou-oooooooo!"

That was the chant made by someone in the group if they sought the attention of a familiar face closing in on the block. And *just* when the noise simmered down? *HOCCCCKKK – PFFT!* Phlegm – which usually littered the ground.

I kept my head down, counting the crevices in the concrete as we approached our building. It was *that* – or get caught in an ugly stare down with a bunch of guys who would've gladly knocked my teeth out – spreading them along Broadway.

During my rare moments of bravery, I'd notice a menacing glare made by the group towards my father, I'm sure they sensed his disgust a mile away (fully prepared to do the same with his teeth). The tension in the air was unbearable and I never felt safer than when we made it inside. Many in the neighborhood were left feeling hopeless and afraid.

I can probably count on one hand the number of times I played outside (in front of our home). There was a better chance of spotting Waldo... in the middle of Manhattan... while standing atop the Empire State Building – than to find me frolicking around. The city had gone up in flames and I grew a sudden awareness for current events – watching *ABC's Eyewitness News* with Bill Beutel most evenings. I'm unsure how other children spent their time, but with Kenny and his crew directly impacting the neighborhood and crime reaching all-time highs, I was left without a choice. I wanted to learn about the events surrounding me.

* * * * *

Author's Note: *I read about the doom and gloom of the late 70s and early 80s, but I was living through the crack epidemic, drug crimes, the "Central Park Five", John Gotti and the rest of the upheaval. My parents feared for our safety and little did we know the elements would soon affect someone close to home.*

* * * * *

"¿ARROZ CON POLLO?"

Gran was my primary babysitter after the completion of her day job (splitting time with a few peculiar choices), but she couldn't commit to a full-time schedule once Ms. Viola passed. Finances were tighter than usual, she needed to supplement her income with a part-time job. This is where *Carmella Perez* and her family came into play.

Carmella was a relative of a coworker at Gran's job, who offered to assist with babysitting duties once word got around. Originally from Puerto Rico, Carmella lived up the road from my apartment in Hamilton Heights, a short distance from my school's drop-off point for students living in the area. Hoping to get the families acquainted, she invited my parents to her home for dinner over a nice Spanish dish. Joining us were Carmella's husband, *Jorge*, her mother (superbly named, "Ma-ma") and their two teenaged daughters, *Jeanette* and *Yancy*.

I found their brightly colored three-bedroom home entirely cozy as I sat quietly counting the number of *White Jesus* portraits on the wall. Ma-ma attempted to play nice, molding her face with her hands, while Yancy sought eye contact, only to bashfully turn away. Mom joined Carmella and Jeanette in the kitchen as they prepared our meal, while my father struggled to make conversation with Jorge who didn't speak much English.

Carmella was short in stature, with a robust figure, while her daughters stood tall and slender. Both girls were soft and eloquent in their tone, with a strong command of the English language – quite the opposite from their boisterous mother, who was a proponent of using *Spanglish* (the fusion of Spanish and English) to translate words back to her husband.

We sat at the dining room table, digging in on some mouth-watering *arroz con pollo* – boy, what a treat! I appreciated the dish so much, I'd regurgitate the food after a few bites, just to enjoy the taste again. Yeah, I was *that* guy. Gross.

After dinner, Carmella shared pictures from the family photo albums, in addition to pointing out Jeanette's artwork exhibited around the house. It was clear she was the overall favorite. Carmella was jovial most of the evening but used this moment to get serious as she discussed her background in childcare. I was captivated by the chirping parakeets, yet caught a part of the conversation where she explained the importance of staying on top of her daughters.

The girls were honor-roll students at a nearby Catholic high school and it showed through their character. A stickler for etiquette, my parents raved about Jeanette and Yancy for their level of academic success and were completely sold on their maturity and mannerisms.

We were informed of Jorge's long hours as a carpenter, while Carmella worked periodically off the books as a receptionist for her brother's sheet roofing business. On non-working days, she'd run early errands with Ma-ma (in the family's tan colored Astro van), assuring us it wouldn't interfere with afterschool pick-up. If, by chance, something unexpected occurred, her daughters were more than capable of picking up the slack. And *that* they did!

My folks were thoroughly impressed by the family's hospitality and more than thrilled about the location of their home. Before long, an offer was made, which they cheerfully accepted. My weekday afternoons were set and any concerns regarding safety were put to rest – thanks to Carmella (not to mention, my hormones were *awakened* – thanks to her daughters).

* * * * *

Chapter Tidbits:

Riverside church featured a basketball program, home to many former college and NBA stars from the New York area: Kenny Anderson, Malik Sealy, Lamar Odom, Ron Artest, Elton Brand and others. What saddens me? I'm in the same age bracket as a few of these men, having followed them intently throughout their collegiate and professional careers. All this time, while I was singing hymns and serving the Lord, these gentlemen were under my nose playing inside of a cramped basement gym at the church. Just goes to show you, the NBA wasn't my calling.

Chapter Three: Ugly as Ever!

The bathroom is my sanctuary. It is the one place in the house where privacy isn't a concern. I can stare deeply into my soul and with good lighting, observe my imperfections. I'll spend as much time in there as needed and if you have a bad bladder? Too bad!

Someone once told me: "You stay in the bathroom about as long as a woman does..."

My reply? Really? Well, that's one smart gal! I'm unsure if that comment was meant to hurt my feelings, but you'll have to try harder than that. I spend a minimum of thirty minutes in the bathroom each morning and if that's a bit "too feminine" for readers – brace yourself! I've got a few more tricks up my sleeve!

I'm an admitted procrastinator and I don't mind sitting on the throne for umpteen minutes at a time catching up on last night's scores, watching YouTube, or analyzing my fantasy sports lineups. It's a celebrated act by most guys and more importantly, there's really no time limit for waste removal, followed by a long, hot shower. It is safe to say – personal hygiene means the world to me. Some of my antics may come across as silly, but it didn't always start out that way...

* * * * *

My parents elected to separate when I was in the 3rd grade; a move to Gran's house was imminent. After catching up on a few bills, she was in a better position to keep me full-time while my folks worked out their convoluted living arrangement.

I was already acquainted with P.S. 199 and excelled there. It made sense to continue my studies at the Upper West Side school, considering Gran only lived minutes away. Thank goodness for that, I met some very good people! During that academic year, Gran did her best to shield me from my parents' messy situation. Surprisingly, their divorce didn't affect me or my grades. In hindsight, it was probably the best thing to happen to them.

I've never been a fan of parents staying together for the 'sake of the child.' What is that? By all means, if the matter is fixable, and both parents are eager to work it out, go for it! But if there is irreconcilable damage – though it may sting (concerning the child's limited access to the non-custodial parent), life must go on. Just *try* to be cooperative when it comes to co-parenting. *Unfortunately, bitterness breeds pettiness and it doesn't always work out that way.*

* * * * *

I was a second-generation student, known as "Charlotte's handsome kid" to those who remained on the staff from the time Mom attended. The teachers were putty in my hands. I even had my share of "girlfriends". *I found it quite amusing, through all the tears and emotions, I never had a problem getting the attention of girls.*

It was around the 2nd or 3rd grade where I was often spotted under the desks of the school library kissing *Gina Anderson* and *Savannah Gill* at the same time (one kiss for *you* and a kiss for *you*) – and again, during recess behind the shed in the playground. The girls were ahead of their time and I was "pimpin" before I could grow a strand of hair on my balls. As one can imagine, my young hormones were raging!

I must admit… I was popular – like the high school jock wearing a stupid varsity letterman jacket, popular. But through the admiration, all it took was one disparaging remark about my complexion and I usually went home feeling hopelessly defeated.

MIRROR, MIRROR, ON THE WALL

I stared intently into Gran's bathroom mirror examining every aspect of my face; a bottle of rubbing alcohol in one hand, cotton balls in the other. Standing there motionless and confused, I thought to myself: *why hadn't they accepted me?* I gave the mirror one last look before an audacious feeling took over. Pouring a considerable amount of alcohol onto the cotton ball, I shifted my right hand in the direction of my forehead, attempting to wipe my skin away – *clockwise, counterclockwise* – down to my cheeks and jawline. I then dampened a wash cloth with warm water, rubbed enough Ivory soap to form a lather and proceeded to scrub my flesh away. The idiocy ended once my skin was abraded and the pain was too much to bear. However, I performed the act every day until enough *dirt* from my face was removed.

I viewed my skin as dirt.

I couldn't go on with the sorrow and discontent of being dark-skinned. I was tired of the insensitive jokes from kids at school. Gran was aware of the teasing, often sharing tips on how to effectively clean my skin, but she didn't understand the magnitude of my pain. She also wasn't aware of my shenanigans in the bathroom. The culprits of the taunts and teasing? Black kids! Even those with similar skin tones joined the fray – *if* they were considered "light enough" to receive a pass.

Do you see the type of nonsense I dealt with? I was indirectly asked as a child to be mindful of skin color when it should've been the furthest thought. The teasing got to be so bad, that I'd frequently express to Gran how I wanted to be white! My *skin lightening* experiment came to a screeching halt after there was noticeable damage to my face. My natural oils were stripped away, dry blotches were everywhere, and I watched my face turn to a dark ash.

* * * * *

Author's Note: *To the readers with melanin – picture your skin after some noticeable time has passed without applying lotion. As the skin compresses, there's visible dryness and discoloration. Well, that was my face – with or without lotion.*

* * * * *

I was targeted by my own at a time when blacks were unified through song and fashion. It led to a merger with plenty of white and international students. Their friendships felt genuine and my skin tone wasn't the center of attention. *Why was it so easy for them to dismiss this insignificant appearance aspect?*

I found it peculiar how the repeated occurrences of color bashing came from black males. It hindered the chances of ever establishing friendships with them, fearful they would berate and eventually turn on me. Even Fran took a few pot shots at my complexion during playtime (while imitating a character) and though my complexion was noticed, I never felt he did it out of malice like the others. As far as I was concerned, Fran was my *only* black friend.

I had no control over my skin tone, which these idiots failed to understand. My father is dark-skinned, my mother has a caramel complexion, I followed the *Y chromosome*. Simple genetic arithmetic. Of course, there are ways to alter your skin, but why should any child subject themselves to that? If there were any concerns, perhaps they should've taken it up with God!

WHERE ARE THEY NOW?

I used to wonder what some of my former grade school bullies were up to. *Man, if there was only a way to conduct a 'Where Are They Now?' search...* Wait a minute!

w-w-w-dot-f-a-c-e-b-o-o-k-dot-c-o-m...   'Enter'...   'Search names'... Eh, never mind.

Hopefully they've all welcomed in a few *chocolate* babies of their own. For the sake of karma, maybe their children have grown up to some of the vile names their parents unmercifully bestowed on me:

Burnt toast
Crispy critter
Oreo cookie

Doesn't that make you feel all warm and fuzzy inside? If you feel I'm coming across as sour grapes, then I'm afraid you've missed the point. Try to understand the effects of name-calling and what it does to a child's psyche. The long-term effects can be devastating! We've all experienced our share of teasing, but how many children can shake it off? *You shake off a toe stub. I was dealing with repeated stabs to the heart.*

Even some of the best slashers in American cinema have only delivered *one* stab to their intended target. That's all it really takes. A single thrust to the chest and you're usually a goner. But I dealt with kids who wanted to reenact the shower scene from *Psycho!*

Cue the violins

Children are relentless, too eager to find out how many stabs it takes to break you down. It's like the old Tootsie Roll commercial:

How many licks does it take to get to the Tootsie Roll center of a Tootsie Pop? Who the fuck cares! Just enjoy the lollipop... just enjoy my *friendship...*

Today, kids seek affirmation on social media, contemplating suicide if their picture isn't 'liked'! Can you imagine what I'd have been up against if social media existed in my day? Considering my initial battles with emotional distress, I was forced to harbor self-pity because of my perceived *anomalous* appearance. No number of "girlfriends", or "you're so cute" comments made by older women could eradicate the growing insecurities.

To the child apologists, I ask that you do not brush off my experiences as "kids being kids". It is much deeper than that and they shouldn't be let off the hook. I never berated anyone to feel they were beneath me, so why should they? *It's all fun and games until it's your child being put through the wringer by their peers!*

We'll agree that taunting has been a weak spot for children of all generations (and colors), but for a race which has been emasculated for centuries, I must wonder why the black bond isn't stronger. Why do we strip away at each other's confidence? My results could have been catastrophic, leading to ominous meltdowns, self-hate and a lifetime of contempt towards blacks. Worst of all, had I continued the skin lightening escapade, I could have been a future patient on the television show, *Botched!*

WAIT... BLACK IS BEAUTIFUL?!

Pop culture tends to embrace dark pigment these days. There are people willing to tan year-round until their skin finally says, *fuck it* and turns orange and many light-skinned (black women) covet a darker skin tone. We have Idris Elba, gracing the covers of magazines, starring in TV and film – making plenty of women moist with his "charming looks" and "death-defying" features. And he is joined by a cast of brown face representatives who have burst onto the scene over the past twenty-years. All is good in the world and now is as good a time as any to be brown... *dark brown!* In fact, I'm sure women readers are professing their love for chocolate men even as I write!

"I've always liked chocolate guys, what is this fool talking about?"

But many moons ago, you didn't! When the Al B. Sure's of the world whispered sweet nothings in your ear, *we* didn't exist to *you*... and *we* absolutely, positively didn't exist to the mainstream (excluding Sidney Poitier).

CeCe Peniston said it best in her hit 1992 song, "Finally;"
Meeting Mr. Right, the man of my dreams
The one who shows me true love or at least it seems
With brown cocoa skin and curly black hair
It's just the way he looks at me that gentle loving stare.

Okay, so she mentions "brown cocoa skin", but the moment she mentioned, *curly hair,* I immediately took myself out of the running! *I hadn't come across many cocoa complected dudes with her preferred hair texture – unless they wore an S-Curl, so I assumed she was looking for a lighter guy.* Outside of Wesley Snipes, Big Daddy Kane and Omar Epps, there weren't many dark-skinned guys on television. At times, I thought I was on an island all by myself:

Hello! (*hello*) .... *are there any other chocolate brothers around?* (*around... around... around*)*?*

Well, there was that one other guy, you *may* have heard his name: Michael Jeffrey Jordan? But if you weren't a star actor, rapper, or *someone who could levitate from the ground,* you were treated with little regard – subjected to heinous tongue-lashings:

"She's pretty... for a dark-skinned girl."

"You're as black as the night!"

"Stay out of the sun!"

And don't *even* think about playing *hide and go seek*... in a dark room:

"Open your mouth so we can find you!"

Brutal! Dark-skinned people are the targets of insensitive comments that are *never* issued towards lighter-skin individuals. *Biracial kids undergo a different type of hatred, from both blacks and whites.* I can't recall many light-skinned jokes, in fact, there's very little push-back towards lighter complected males.

Teasing someone on how they resemble a DeBarge brother didn't quite cut it. Besides, I'm sure most weren't bothered since the quick rebuttal (towards a dark-skinned person trying to play comedian) was usually something along the lines of:

"At least I don't look like Manute Bol!"

Uh-oh! Not former NBA player Manute Bol! Anyone but him! There's simply no coming back from that. Take your "L" (loss) and walk away. Will this black on black foolishness ever end? Highly unlikely.

* * * * *

Author's Note: *I've noticed an upsurge in confidence in today's dark-skinned male, but nothing upsets me more than the thought of once being uncomfortable in my own skin. My black peers led me to believe that my color was a heinous gaffe by God. How would they react once finding out my full ethnic background?*

* * * * *

"IF YOU WANNA SURVIVE, THEN YOU MUST DENY!"
I was coining phrases long before Johnnie Cochran did it in a courtroom.

* * * * *

Living in America, as an African, can steer you into a state of perplexity. Outside of *National Geographic* and the *History Channel*, America has yet to fully accept African culture and its significance to civilization – continuing to link the continent to *poverty, disease and wildlife*. Additionally, there is persistent mocking produced by black Americans towards born Africans. Their ignorance fosters Africans to act condescendingly towards black America! It's a dead-seated aversion between both cultures that will likely continue for years to come.

Today, I announce my Ghanaian roots with pride. I've even added a tattoo of the Ghanaian flag as an absolution of sorts. But as a child, not so much. During an era when African pride was showcased through music, fashion and film, the form of solidarity had the opposite effect, pushing me towards my *American* side.

It was trendy of black America to resemble Africans through various means, but it never felt genuine... much like white kids who live and breathe hip-hop: There's adoration for the lifestyle, but you *really* don't want black people problems!

While my peers wore African medallions and the colors *red, black* and *green,* I knew they really *didn't* want to be Africans. Why? Because Africans were still the butt of many jokes. Terms like, "African booty scratcher" was as common as a *knock-knock* joke. I had to respond quickly when someone questioned my ethnicity:

"Are you African?"

"Nope, my father is… I was born here!" *Phew! Glad I escaped that one, but how many of them were buying it?*

Shake your head in disappointment, but public-school teasing is nothing to shake a stick at. It's a free for all and only those with *thick* skin are supposed to make it out alive… not *dark* skin. If you wanted to escape further embarrassment, the key was to denounce anything that could potentially be used against you – including your heritage. Only the vigorous types, unafraid to go toe to toe with a bully, would defend their honor or heritage. That wasn't me. I'd shy away from all confrontation, even though I was one of the taller students in school. There's a connotation that tall people are the usual suspects for bullying – but I was part of the *bullied.*

My physical appearance was once gloatingly satirized by America; I read the stories, I saw the images. Historically, America played an intrinsic role, brainwashing the public into believing that *darker* skin was a spoof of the black race. Watch some old films or cartoons from the early to mid-1900s – the last thing you wanted was to be dark-skinned! We were derided for our lack of speaking proper English, mimicked through minstrel shows (in blackface), or shown as monkeys swinging from trees – from where else? Africa!

I didn't *naturally* abandon my roots. America caused this! It was a poignant reminder of the world we live in, but I am a proud dark-skinned African and the true definition of an *African-American* (as much as I disapprove the term). If you choose to study world history, there's a good chance that somewhere along your bloodline – you're an African too!

* * * * *

Author's Note: *The phrase, 'African-American', was created after the terms 'colored people' and 'negro' became dated and outright inappropriate for the modern era.*

* * * * *

African-American implies that the black race is the only race of African heritage and I find that odd. There are black Americans whose roots trace back to the early centuries of America – long before the Atlantic Slave Trade and long before the first white settlers. How should they be defined? How can we tie such a diverse race to one continent? And if we look at it scientifically, shouldn't all races tie to Africa?

Why does America only link ethnic groups to specific regions? African-American, Latin-American, Asian-American – what if the individual is non-white, born in America to American parents? (where perhaps the grandparents were born outside of America). What are they identified as?

Do we identify American-born whites (with American born parents) as "European-Americans"? No, they are simply referred to as Caucasian or white! Notice how citizens of other countries identify themselves by their born country? If you were born in England, you're classified as British, not "African-British" or "European-British" (to distinguish skin color). I'll continue to use 'black' or 'white' to differentiate groups of people in this reading, but I believe the term, 'American' (for born Americans), works just fine.

THE PROBLEM

I am greatly disenchanted by the misrepresentation of black people, considering our illustrious history and impact on the world, which makes it equally hard to accept some of our behaviors today. Before tattoos, hip-hop and gang culture grew into the sensations that they are today, we could detect how battle tested we were through our stories, scars and the indignation on our faces. As bizarre as it is, blacks have an uncanny ability to sniff out the "real from the fake". But today, we take things too far. Some people are truly concerned about 'the city you rep', the 'set you claim' and the 'types of people you know' (I'm sure the Asian community doesn't give a millisecond of thought to any of this). Why do we bother ourselves with such insignificant rubbish?

* * * * *

Under the guise of kids who were living "harder lives", I didn't exude the signs of someone "real" and barring race, I had very little in common with some of my black peers:

- I lived with parents who didn't experience the plight of drugs and alcohol sweeping through our communities;
- Although she struggled to make ends meet, my grandmother resided in an affluent part of Manhattan.

I was living what I perceived to be a "normal life". Our lifestyle didn't fit in with the stereotypes placed on blacks. We didn't go to *cookouts, play spades, or drink Kool-Aid.* There weren't pictures of *tigers* hanging on our walls, or *plastic coverings* found on our living room furniture (well, except for Gran's house). Furthermore, I wasn't allowed to watch movies with profanity, play with toy guns, add designs to my high-top fade (à la Big Daddy Kane), or listen to much rap music. *The latter was frowned upon by my father.*

If I wanted anything to do with hip-hop, the safest bet was to read about it (of course) courtesy of *Right-On!* magazine… or there was always Doug E. Fresh. *Listening to Doug E. Fresh's beat-box for five minutes was considered harmless, compared to the rugged tunes of Ice-T and N.W.A. Regrettably, I missed out on some great west coast music from this era, which I revisited in later years.*

It's not that my family was out of touch from the harsh realities facing the community – we just didn't embody it. But those who are less fortunate can quickly sense the differences in personalities and are usually more than willing to test you out like a sports car. It's a glaring concern facing the black community, but it never gets addressed. Black men are too preoccupied with proving "street cred", from the time we construct our first sentence to adulthood:

"This nigga is soft – let's see what he's really made of?"

Why is proving our manhood so important? We're often shown through visuals, how our women prefer guys who are "rough around the edges" (although that might just be *all* women). But black men are willing to go beyond the limits to prove their authenticity – even if it includes obtaining a rap sheet!

I was mortified when MC Lyte recorded the track "Ruff Neck", when I was growing up;

I need a ruff neck
I need a dude with attitude, who only needs his fingers
with his food!

Wait, let me get this straight… you want a what?!

Evil grin with a mouth full of gold teeth
Startin' beef is how he spells relief...
Is that so, Ms. Lyte?

A lot of our behavior stems from the living environments and lack of parenting (i.e., missing a father in the household). Our bravery is constantly put to the test and we find ourselves persistently *angry* and *over-aggressive.*

"I bet I can slap box better than you!"

Why do we need to play fight? Couldn't we just *play* video games?

You're instantly called out if you choose not to participate in these senseless activities:

"Stop being a fuckin' pussy!"

Whoa! Now, our manhood is in question before we *even* reach puberty! Men and women of these environments enjoy the security blanket of having friends who will go to war (if it calls for such) and the younger generations have found an easier (yet, contentious) way to resolve their problems:

"Who's ready to catch these hands *this bullet?*"

The other races can "talk things out". *I'm unable to pinpoint exactly when this happened to our community, but these are the cold, hard facts. We've become our own worst enemy.* Black men are constantly under the microscope; we continue to be under duress with one another. In a mindless battle of grit, black men will size each other up almost anywhere:

- On the street
- At the job
- At the grocery store
- At the gym
- Even at church, while you're busy praising the Lord!

Our women experience this as well. And don't think about wearing a pair of vintage Jordan basketball sneakers or Christian Louboutin shoes to places like the mall. Some of our eyes will shift directly to the floor, before initially making eye contact. Because strangely, we try to match the shoes with the person in order to formulate an opinion. It's maddening!

Speaking of which, black men have a terrible habit of staring at one another and it is time to speak on it. Perhaps you resemble someone, or maybe it was a form of admiration, but most of the stares are unresponsive – leading to these simple conclusions:

- There's an impending problem (i.e., you don't like the person, or you have an issue with their appearance)
- There's an attraction

Don't be so quick to dismiss the latter. Black men have been emasculated over recent years through fashion and other forms of entertainment, as the number of homosexual black males have increased. Therefore, it isn't inconceivable. But if you inadvertently use *keywords* to insinuate the starer is gay, he'll likely *rip you a new one* … figuratively speaking, that is.

Q: Are you *straight,* bruh – is everything cool?

Translation: Why are you staring at me? Is everything alright?

A: "Straight?! Yeah, I'm straight! … are you?!"

That's not what I meant, dude.

There are still black men fighting earnestly to prove their masculinity, *even* if a same-sex attraction holds true. Very seldom will men offer a compliment (once a stare down is executed), so you're left with these thoughts. Think about it – what reason would a man have to stare into the eyes of a stranger, without uttering a single word?

For simple-minded people who believe *staring* is harmless, I'm sorry to disappoint you. *Glancing* is harmless. Staring is different and can make anyone with a conscious uncomfortable. And I know what some of you are thinking: *How do you know if someone is staring, if you're not staring back?* Let's not play dumb! It's called intuition and you can feel when unsuspecting eyes are on you.

Private eyes

They're watching you…

They see your every move! (sorry, I had an 80s moment – Daryl Hall and John Oates.)

We're taught at a young age not to do it, but adults continue to snub the collective rule, risking confrontation. I've gotten much better at ignoring it, but it hasn't been easy. Besides, I'd much rather ogle women, than have a staring contest with random guys. But if you're a male who *insists* on looking my way, may I ask that you not ignore my *one and a half second rule?*

- *One second* to assess the situation (be it hairstyle or clothing style)
- *A half of a second* to observe my face (while in passing)

Then, proceed to remove your fuckin' eyes from the target! *That is more than enough time to take everything in, no?* If it goes beyond that (without an exchange of words), my *Spidey senses* will tingle. You've boxed me into a corner where I must confront you:

Bro, seriously, is everything alright?

Which in my experience has usually been met with?

"Yeah... why?"

What do you mean, *why?!* Seriously, do people not realize how long they're looking at others? What reason would I randomly ask about your well-being? Moron! For some inexplicable reason their mind goes blank. *I recently experienced a female staring uncontrollably (frowning, of course). When confronted, she quickly apologized. Her explanation? "I thought you were a relative from Alabama". Right, the good ol' "I thought you were a relative excuse". But kudos to her for apologizing. I suppose she wasn't much of a fan of that "relative".*

If I go out of my way to stare, I can assure you, the person wouldn't notice – why? Because staring *shouldn't* be obvious (unless I am seeking your attention)! I don't understand why this simple format can't be followed by all. I'm unsure of how common this is for other races (or if it even bothers anyone), but I've encountered it primarily with black men and it's frustrating. If you're anything like me and would rather not participate in this useless mind game, please take heed to the following:

Never put your head down when passing a Gawker! Hold it up high and keep your eyes straight ahead. Failing to do so means you've been *one-upped* like a game of Mario Brothers, leading the Gawker to conclude what he *probably* assumed all along:

That you're a bitch.

Advantage, Gawker.

* * * * *

Author's Note: *Let's at least work on how we stare at each other if it's going to be longer than 1.5 seconds. Perhaps include a tight lip smile to ensure that all is good, because an icy stare does absolutely nothing. If the smile isn't reciprocated, then hey, consider the polite* *gesture your good deed of the day! And for men who blatantly stare at another man's wife (or girlfriend) in his presence? Tread lightly! Respect never gets old.*

* * * * *

Rounding out the list of disturbing things we do (or at least those with microscopic IQ's) is the continuous passing of judgment. There still exists the ugly notion of darker skin equaling "unpretty", natural, short hairstyles being considered "too ethnic", long, natural hair equaling "that bitch thinks she's cute" and the questioning of black men who speak like Bryant Gumbel! How is speaking like Bryant Gumbel a *bad* thing?

The crème de la crème of stupidity remains the mindless usage of the term, "acting white" (there's no such thing), usually reserved for more *polished, sophisticated* blacks, fully committed to the King's English and ethical living. *We appear to be the only race willing to hold each other accountable for carrying ourselves to higher standards! Have you ever heard of such insanity?*

THE SOLUTION

Make no mistake, the issues at hand are deeply rooted having seemingly become a glaring area affecting black relations. We turn a blind eye towards our own actions – label and sneer at those taking the dauntless task of challenging us to do better, only coming together once an *outside* party desecrates us.

I love *our* history and resiliency, skin tones, hair textures and women, but unfortunately, I wasn't loved back. It caused an adverse effect, where I never felt comfortable being around my own race (outside of family and friends) and while I am greatly bothered by that declaration, I'm not ashamed. I wasn't responsible for these feelings. I don't wish for any pity. The core of this book is about making fun of me and who better than *me* to accomplish this feat? But to fully grasp an understanding of *Ernest,* I must shed light on the areas that greatly impacted me (and others who don't have a platform).

This chapter isn't about "black shaming", but more about *why* we shame one another? We've all been subjected to erroneous and insensitive acts, but who steps up to the plate and mends the damage to prevent our kids from having self-esteem issues? The road ahead is an onerous one, one that will require refinement and plenty of patience. But I hope ~~the current~~ *a future* generation finds enough courage to overthrow our *old* way of thinking – instituting a *new* beginning for the race. Possibly a discussion to revisit down the road.

* * * * *

Author's Note: *Sorry, but the current generation is done. Stick a fork in 'em!*

Chapter Four: Strictly for the Weirdos

This chapter is my 'coming out party', where I'll share a few stories, give an in-depth review of my "abnormal" behaviors, likes and dislikes. Some readers may relate, others, not so much. But it will certainly give you a better understanding of who I am. What's more, maybe you won't feel bad about some of your own idiosyncrasies.

* * * * *

I'm sure it didn't start when I first picked up that *Time* magazine but reading became one of my most enjoyable hobbies. The leisure activity likely resulted from Mom habitually reading children's books to me before bed. While lying in a fetal position underneath my *He-Man* themed bed sheets, I'd listen closely, as she switched up her voice to act out various characters, allowing my imagination to run wild through her narration.

And then, there were the illustrations in the book. I was fascinated most by the alluring colors – watching the leaves turn or the sky changing shades in accordance with the timeline. It proved the illustrator's attention to detail, instantly turning me into a fan of the arts.

From there, I started acquiring books at will – whether through the library, book stores, or the *Scholastic News* catalog distributed at school. The catalog offered a wide selection and it was reasonably priced for students who wished to place personal orders to their home. *What kid doesn't want to receive mail (aside from when the cable bill unexpectedly arrives in their name)?*

Eventually, I upgraded to comic books, biographies, autobiographies, self-help books and newspapers. Before long, I was a bona fide bookworm.

Chris Rock is credited for piggybacking the following quote of a racist in one of his comedy specials. The brainless theory "if you want to hide something from a black person, put it in a book" would not apply to me.

We had four major newspapers circulating throughout the city:

- The New York Times
- New York Daily News
- Newsday
- New York Post

Gran was my newspaper connection. There were plenty of weekend mornings we'd wake up to a McDonald's breakfast, *a cup of coffee and the Daily News*, instead of the intricately worded *New York Times* which my father preferred. After breakfast, I'd lay out on the living room floor, dissecting the sports pages and the funnies, while she focused on the crossword puzzles and horoscopes. There wasn't a paper in town that could duplicate the type of content as the Daily News – especially on Sunday's! Waking up to a *Sports Final* edition of the paper, was equivalent to a child waking up on Christmas morning! The paper was loaded with comics, contests, coupons and a massive sports section with ALL the latest scores and up-to-date stats.

* * * * *

Author's Note: *If the term, 'sports final' didn't appear on the front/back of the Daily News, sadly, you'd wasted your money. 'Sports Final' assured readers that the news and sports information was current. If a shooting occurred at 4:50 a.m., it was likely printed in that edition before the papers were distributed at 5 a.m.*

* * * * *

Since the advent of the internet and the world of *140 characters,* life as we know it has changed. Many people prefer to be on the receiving end of news through various internet sources, as print media dies a slow death. But there was a time when readers combed through the newspaper searching for apartments, jobs or even the start times of their favorite shows.

I love and appreciate what the internet has done – I truly do. Thanks to Al Gore (eye-roll), we have *YouTube, eBay, Amazon, fantasy sports, job and dating sites, work from home opportunities, scores of music and games, online-banking* and most importantly... *free porn!* In fact, I can't imagine a world without the internet. What saddens me about the disappearance of newspapers, is that the younger generation will never experience the feeling of having their fingers covered in black ink after inspecting a newspaper hot off the presses. We're often told by presumed idiots (with a lack of appreciation for the good ol' days), how vital it is that we evolve with the times – but it hasn't been easy for an ol' school guy like me.

* * * * *

Author's Note: *In case you were bewildered by the coffee/breakfast thing, when I said I had certain liberties at Gran's house – drinking coffee was one of them. Whatever she did, I copied!*

ARCHIE & FRIENDS

While most boys were enticed by the courageous efforts of their favorite superheroes (or the conniving ways of villains), I leaned towards a more subdued bunch from a town called *Riverdale:*

> Archie Andrews, Betty Cooper, Veronica Lodge, Jughead Jones, Reggie Mantle, Moose Mason and others.

Ladies & Gentlemen: *Archie Comics. What type of kid did you think I was?* The teens dealt with real life issues (amidst a little fantasy and adventure), but usually stayed clear of superheroes and their stupid *alter egos, death-defying theatrics and mythical superpowers*. Meh!

It was during the latter part of the 80s when I first laid eyes on the Archie cartoon – an animated series that originally aired during the 1960s and I thought it was a worthless piece of garbage! As far as the comic book was concerned? THAT was a different story.

Archie comics were sold at a supermarket on the corner near my home in Hamilton Heights –in sight of the checkout aisle – right above *Readers Digest.* I'd give Mom one puppy-eyed look and that's usually all it took. She'd grab the comic, toss it into the grocery cart and I'd hurry home to get started on my next reading. *Surprisingly, my father even played nice, contributing once in a blue moon to the betterment of my childhood (although I'm sure he'd much rather it been Readers Digest). Has anyone honestly ever read that publication?*

It was quite odd to have been such a wrestling fanatic – the epitome of fantasy – yet turn my nose at superheroes (*Batman* was as far as I was willing to go). But Archie & the Gang were relatable characters, who offered readers a plate of balance without unrealistic *six-pack stomachs, bulging muscles and profound veins.* I got lost in the comic books in constant search of the next adventure. The love quarrels between Betty, Veronica and Archie were compelling, the fights between Archie and Reggie (over Veronica) were fervent, the wittiness of Jughead amused me and the overall friendships were heartwarming. Moreover, I was captivated by the artwork; the splash of colors in the sky, the style of clothing (blending 50s & 60s fashions with later decades) and character traits.

I longed for the day when I would have my very own character added to the mix and would have moved heaven and earth to join *their* world... since *my* world was unusually mean and cruel. I shared an attachment to the fictional cast unlike anything else, desperate to find similar friends. As a teen, I even took a stab at creating my own comic series using real-life friends to imitate the group. No comparison.

Plenty of changes have been made to the cast of Archie since I last picked up a copy, including the addition of a gay character who Archie looks to save from an assassination attempt. Guess who ends up taking the bullet? Archie! *My! Have times changed. Archie took a bullet like a superhero!* I guess the writers had to give the comic a "modern feel" to appeal to a new generation of readers, but they've certainly come a long way!

Honorable Mention: *MAD Magazine*

LIVE AT M.S.G.!

One of the top five Christmas gifts I ever received was a tape recorder and it stayed with me like an untreatable STD. That little gadget was life, itself! I was fascinated by the simple concept of recording my voice and dubbing over it (for hard edits). Fran was responsible for introducing me to that riveting device and to my first *real* girlfriend. *Hey, at least it wasn't a blow-up doll!*

I spent many evenings wearing my broadcaster's hat, inspired by the likes of Marv Albert, Walt "Clyde" Frazier and Tim McCarver. Albert and Frazier often called New York Knicks games, while McCarver was of vital importance to the New York Mets broadcasts. If the Knicks were playing at home (Madison Square Garden), I needed to be in rare form for a show I created, "Live at

M.S.G.!" I was a one-man army, joined by a collection of 90-minute Memorex cassette tapes and a glass of Pepsi to prevent dry mouth.

Ewing calls for the ball on the baseline, posting up Cartwright... Rivers with the bounce pass to Ewing... Ewing dribbles, baseline fall away shot... it's good! Sitting on Gran's living room floor – with a front row seat to all the action – I performed play-by-play, cuffing my hands around my mouth to echo the sounds of the crowd (highly influenced by Michael Leslie Winslow from *Police Academy*).

After the game (if I could sneak in an extra hour without Gran noticing I wasn't in bed), I'd provide post-game interviews with *imaginary players*, feeding the appetites of my make-believe audience. I'm sure the neighbors hated the sound of my pre-adolescent voice, but I was the *only* kid in an apartment building overrun by *senior citizens* and *homosexuals*. What else was I supposed to do in my spare time?

In addition to broadcasting, I used the tape recorder to record music videos (pointless, but certain song favorites didn't receive regular radio play), songs from the radio (pointless, considering most stereos came with tape decks to enable recording), ABC sitcom themes (hello, Jesse Frederick!), commercial jingles and just about anything you can think of. I even took a crack at stand-up comedy, developing a weekly series where I looked to duplicate the success of the *Fran & Ernie Variety Show*. This time, I'd exhibit jokes to a riveting audience... Me!

Mastering the art of double-duty, I'd disguise my voice to play different comedians and hecklers. *Booooooo! You suck!* Often heard after one of my woeful performances. Infuriated by the insult, I'd challenge "the heckler" (me) to a fight, leading to an array of fisticuffs. This is where I'd throw myself around the house, producing punching sounds, salivating at the mouth like a rabid dog and making quite the ruckus. My rambunctious act reached a level of calmness once the heckler was finally escorted out by *security*...oh yeah... I was security! Gran absolutely detested the noise, as we butted heads most nights. A volume greater than *15 decibels* would usually shake her to the core.

The performances captured on tape were scheduled to appear on a Greatest Hits edition someday – until cassette tapes became passé. *For those wondering, yes, I still own the tapes (for my entertainment only!*). The hobby of broadcasting brought out an untapped energy that I probably should have expanded upon. I loved comedy, but broadcasting should have been a serious career choice (more on this topic later).

ALL THINGS WWF

Tapping microphone Do I have your attention? Okay, great...

I played with my WWF action figures until I was fifteen years-old! Pick up your jaw and clean up the wine glass you've impulsively shattered on the floor. Yes, I was a high school student playing with toys – no, I didn't give a damn. Apart from a couple of people, no one knew of this proclamation until now. If you were one of those *too cool for toys* teens, good for you! I engaged in the same activities as all of you, but I still made time for my action figures.

Gran contributed most to my collection (who'd you expect) and I was first exposed to these exquisite *miniature sensations* on Christmas morning – when I was around six years-old. I adored wrestling and the WWF was larger than life.

* * * * *

Honorable Mention: *N.W.A. (National Wrestling Alliance), W.C.W. (World Championship Wrestling), A.W.A. (American Wrestling Association), G.W.F. (Global Wrestling Federation). E.C.W. (Extreme Championship Wrestling) and G.L.O.W. (Gorgeous Ladies of Wrestling).*

* * * * *

The buildup to WrestleMania III is what mesmerized me as Hulk Hogan faced Andre The Giant at the Pontiac Silverdome in Pontiac, Michigan. I remember crying after Andre savagely ripped the gold crucifix off Hogan's neck on an episode of *Piper's Pit*. From then on, I was obsessed!

I usually caught wrestling on Saturday afternoon and occasionally during the late evening whenever *Saturday Night's Main Event* aired. My parents allowed me to stay up and catch a glimpse of "The Hulkster" if they were in a gracious mood, but Gran was the true wrestling fanatic with a collection of VHS tapes that rivaled Blockbuster Video.

One of her biggest hobbies was recording live programming on the VCR, whether it was a big-time boxing match featuring "Sugar Ray" Leonard, a musical performance or something raunchy on HBO. But it was the theatrics of the World Wrestling Federation that usually reeled her in. Cable television was a hot commodity during the 80s and regarding wrestling, the only time viewers could watch some of the top stars competing in meaningful matches. For those living in the New York area, we'd tune into the M.S.G. Network for live WWF events (TBS Superstation for those who watched NWA). Gran usually labeled the VHS tapes in accordance to the wrestlers appearing on the program for the evening:

- King Kong Bundy
- "Macho Man" Randy Savage
- Koko B. Ware
- The Killer Bees
- Kamala
- Don Muraco
- The Hart Foundation

Also featured on the tapes were commercials. She hadn't quite grasped the concept of pausing the VCR while recording a program before a commercial aired. *As I'm sure many of us are familiar with, the pause button suspended live recordings until it was un-paused. Not rocket science by any stretch of the imagination, but if I taught you something new, you're very welcome!*

It was a pain having to sit through yet another *Oxy Cleansing Pad* commercial… until I came across a 30 second ad that changed my life ~~for good~~ *until I was fifteen!* The commercial featured two kids sitting on opposite sides of the floor, hovering over a miniature WWF ring, slamming the figures aggressively. As they geared up for the next bout, the kids erected one of the greatest accessories to a toy collection: The steel cage!

Oh my gosh, what did I just see?! Before the end of the commercial, the LJN collection of toys were strategically placed in the background, including the championship belts, ring *and* steel cage. I endlessly begged Gran, Mom, *Santa Claus… anyone* willing to purchase these objects of beauty. With enough tears (and I'm sure a few spankings), I'd build a strong collection of wrestling figures (with the steel cage, of course) to imitate the matches seen on TV!

- Hogan versus Bundy
- Savage versus Steamboat

I was setting up my own clashes, causing quite the disturbance to the neighbors below. Would you believe I still own these pint-sized toys today? I've heard everything from, *why don't you give them to your daughter? to, throw them away!* My response? No and fuck you! The toys were single-handedly, *the most* important components of my childhood and I admittedly added more to the collection once WCW produced similar items in the mid-nineties: I had to get my hands on "Nature Boy" Ric Flair! *Find an 80s wrestling buff who didn't dream about a Hogan vs. Flair match and I'll personally give him (or her) a chop to the chest and a big boot to the face!* Now, I could create the dream match all by myself!

I played with G.I. Joe's, Teenage Mutant Ninja Turtles and other great toys of that era but couldn't duplicate the same magic. I gave life to these guys and they kept me company on my loneliest days. Who knows, maybe I'll have one more match before it's all said and done…

Okay, maybe not.

MR. TELEVISION MAN

I've always been enamored by television, be it cartoons, sitcoms, game shows, comedy sketches, nature programs, or simply commercials. Aside from animation, some of my childhood favorites included, *Sesame Street, Reading Rainbow, Mister Rogers' Neighborhood, ABC Afterschool Special, Carmen Sandiego* and I always enjoyed the educational mind-fuck, *School House Rock.*

To describe that show in three words: *Came, Saw, Conquered!* The show taught everything – in under *three* minutes – *how's that for your instant gratification, millennials?* From the names of presidents, to the year the United States Constitution was written.

Not a fan of history? No worries! The show taught us grammatical categories – *conjunctions, pronouns and verbs;*

Conjunction, junction, what's your function?
Hooking up words and phrases and clauses...

The producers added a catchy tune and before long, you were on the verge of becoming a whiz kid or if you're anything like me, a *nerd,* reciting jingles some thirty years later.

To round it out, I developed a love for shows where children were the main characters:

- Punky Brewster
- Small Wonder (where I secretly had a crush on Vicki the robot)
- Different Strokes
- The Wonder Years

Just to name a few.

However, hanging around Gran (and Ms. Viola before her passing) caused an early appreciation for programs that catered to an older demographic. Let's talk about, *Little House on the Prairie.* There I was, in front of the tube, ecstatic about Charles Ingalls (Michael Landon) and his wife heading home in a horse-drawn wagon, while the Ingalls girls raced down a grassy hill during the intro. The imagery was serene.

Little House on the Prairie originally aired in 1973, running in syndication through the 80s. I watched the show during the late afternoons following school – especially when Ma-ma babysat. She was hooked on the midwestern drama and though it didn't appear she could understand a lick of English (when spoken to), she'd often blurt out Spanish cuss words targeting the mean-spirited Nellie Olesen;

"Estupida perra!" My thoughts, exactly!

I watched *The Three Stooges* and *The Golden Girls* ad nauseum, but a couple of my all-time favorite comedies were *The Jeffersons* and *Mama's Family.* The snide, insubordinate attitudes of George Jefferson (Sherman Hemsley) and Thelma "Mama" Harper (Vicki Lawrence) humored Gran and it tickled me watching her laugh. As the shows re-aired, I educated myself on the importance of using punchlines to split one's sides. *Whoever said television wasn't edifying lied!*

Here's something that may come as a surprise (or maybe it shouldn't), but I knew who Linda Evans and Joan Collins were, before most boys of my era.

Why? *'Because you were a loser?'* Yes! ... but besides that! It's because whenever Mom watched *Dynasty,* so did I. *I also thought the theme song to Dynasty was epic! Such elegance. Dynasty* evolved to Daytime Dramas – *General Hospital, Days of our Lives, Young and the Restless* and *The Bold and the Beautiful.* It wasn't that I was *trying* to be different – I WAS different! If you're a guy who can relate? **Fist bump**

Make no mistake, I was an absolute cartoon fanatic (we'll go in depth on that shortly), but the information obtained by watching daytime soaps (and other adult content) painted a better picture of reality... even if the programs were based on fiction. For every laugh shared watching *Good Times,* I understood the financial woes of Florida and James Evans. And as much as I craved *The Cosby Show,* I knew it wasn't a reality for *most* urban homes – which is why at a young age... I became a dedicated viewer of *Divorce Court!*

* * * * *

Author's Note: *A little fantasy never hurt anyone and I'm sure I've missed out on some good shows over the years, but there's good reason why I've never watched an episode of 'Game of Thrones' but will watch re-runs of 'The Office'. I need something with good writing and relatability.*

* * * * *

Entering my tweens, I looked to diversify the choice of programming to balance out my cartoon addiction. This would include hit syndicated sitcoms (and TV series) of the 1950s & 60s:

- I Love Lucy
- Gilligan's Island
- The Brady Bunch
- Bewitched
- The Munsters
- The Original Batman Series

Music videos played a key role as well. I'd look to MTV for my rock fix, B.E.T. for the latest in urban and before VH-1 became the *substandard* for black entertainment, the station once fed the appetites for lovers of soft/classic rock, power ballads and 80s. *Right up my alley!* Nonetheless, there was an interactive music channel called *The Box,* enabling viewers the ability to select their favorite videos – all to the tune of a small fee:

The Box! Music Television… you control!

I really have no business remembering their promo, but they were spot on! The Box was also the music channel for explicit hip-hop content, as I tried pulling away from the feel-good sounds of *MC Hammer, Digable Planets* and *Digital Underground.*

Many of the videos featured exhibited women dancing in bikini's, guns, marijuana (hello, Cypress Hill!), with lyrical content considered "too hard" for MTV. But the best of times for a twelve-year-old (at the onset of puberty) was catching racy videos – successively! *I'd like to thank the viewers, who 'took one for the team', maxing out their credit cards to the likes of 2 Live Crew and Sir Mix A-Lot videos!* It was the closest thing to porn and the amount of titty bouncing, hip gyrating and floor humping (by women who are presumably parents to adult children now) was an astounding sight.

Thank you, again.

* * * * *

Ultimately, there were two programs responsible for molding me into a person besotted by fitness and nature. Let us first discuss: *Gilad's Bodies in Motion.* Before fitness gurus flooded the market with "How To…" videos and millennials saturated their social media pages with fitness selfies and snippets of their work-out regimen, there was Gilad Jankiowicz (and a bevy of fitness amateurs) handing out pointers for 30-minutes on ESPN.

The group usually consisted of one ripped guy (identical to rival Gilad) and a couple of petite, *flat butted* women wearing fluorescent leotards. Not only was I impressed by Gilad's grit, determination and ability to stay fit, but he won "cool points" for keeping a calm demeanor during some very strenuous workouts.

"Take a deep breath… inhale…. now exhale out!"

The show filmed on location, at some of the most stunning beaches along the California coast and the island of Hawaii. *There were palm trees, bright sandy beaches, blue water and a sky to die for!* But I was dissatisfied simply being a viewer... I had to participate. After completing a set of crunches, hoping to trim my ridiculous baby fat, I'd lay motionless on Gran's living room floor, anticipating the breeze of the Pacific Ocean through the cracks of the TV.

"Take a deep breath... inhale.... now exhale out!"

What an amazing piece of production.

* * * * *

Author's Note: *I'll say this much – white women have truly evolved in the backside area since the days of this show!*

* * * * *

With the next show a few hours away and Gran monitoring the electric bill like a stock broker on the Trading Floor, I'd give the TV a rest and hop in the shower. When the moment arrived, out came my sketch pad and colored pencils, as I awaited *his* next masterpiece. It was time for *The Joy of Painting with Bob Ross.*

I stared at the TV in complete amazement, as Ross painted some of the most fetching images I'd lay my eyes on. He had an obvious affection for nature and it was harmless entertainment at a time when TV was becoming more risqué. With the stroke of a brush, Ross could turn a white canvas into a myriad of colors. Such breathtaking artwork. Speaking softly into the camera, Ross encouraged viewers to exude patience, providing a little hope for the struggling artist at home trying to keep up... like me. Essentially, his paintings were a presentation of the environment which we often take for granted – God's perfections. I found an inner peace listening to his voice and nature became my new escape from the whirls of life:

- I head over to the beach when I'm in desperate need of some R&R, listening to the waves crashing against the shore.
- I'll watch birds fly in unison before dusk, gazing at the hues of the sky – alone in my car.

- During autumn, when the air is crisp, and foliage is in full effect, I'll drive along an empty back road to take in the colors.
- I often daydream about living in short distance to mountain backdrops, *palm trees* and water.

As Ross so elegantly put it; *there's nothing wrong with having a tree as a friend! The Joy of Painting* opened my mind to an existing world outside of the city and through his work, I learned that nature is one of life's most underrated treasures.

THE EMERGENCE OF SPORTS TALK

I'd wake up each morning to the smell of Folgers and fresh bacon – two of the greatest breakfast smells next to baked bread – and *a monotone voice on the radio.* Gran looked for her morning news fix before stepping out to the hustle and bustle of the city. The portable radio belonged to Ms. Viola and remains one of the many items Gran kept after her passing. The battery-operated device – which survived *six* decades (and a load of cockroach excrement) worked like a charm. I was enthralled by the voices on 1010 WINS, a 24-hour news station on the AM dial that often bragged:

If you give us ten minutes, we'll give you the world!

Pretty catchy and self-assuring. Meanwhile, my parents kept the dial on the FM side which explains my eclectic music taste. While Mom enjoyed the R&B side of things, I experienced an assorted list of artists through my father:

- Phil Collins
- Madonna
- Prince
- Cameo
- Sade
- Paul Simon and Bakithi Kumalo
- Sting & The Police
- George Benson & Dave Koz
- African and Caribbean tunes

There were four FM stations you could count on to deliver great music: WBLS, KISS-FM, HOT 97 and Z-100. I'm unsure why we'd listen to KISS-FM in the mornings (conceivably due to the longevity and success of the station), but it's where I was introduced to Bob Slade:

Bob Slade... Sports Shorts!

I'd usually stop dead in my tracks the moment I heard his signature jingle, as he'd rundown the scores from the previous night. Feeding off the hosts of the show, Slade was very spirited during the short segment, providing much laughter to the audience. *There's nothing like a good laugh first thing Monday morning!* But I wanted more Bob Slade style of radio since my appetite for sports was materializing. Unfulfilled by his short bit, I subsequently added a fifth station to the mix: WFAN 660.

It was the spring of 1989 and I'd just picked up a New York Mets yearbook after attending my very first game with my father. Along with some stimulating features on some of my favorite Mets players, the yearbook highlighted ads from a radio station (only a couple of years in), exhibiting a *slender man* holding a baseball glove, cuffing a basketball and gripping a hockey stick. Truthfully, he gave the appearance of a high school substitute teacher (instead of the *all-sports* athlete he portrayed), but the ad promoted the station's *We Cover All Sports* motto. WFAN was a sports radio station – on the AM dial.

Yes! Oh No! *Not the snooze-fest of AM radio!* I thought. Based on 1010 WINS (and the other calamities on the AM dial), I knew that side of the track wasn't very kid (or music contemporary) friendly. But curiosity got the best of me. My alarm clock-radio was set to go off at six-thirty each morning, as I'd awaken to the sounds of laughter (and an annoying duck sound) on a talk show called *Imus in the Morning*. Unbeknownst to me, WFAN wasn't quite the 24-hour sports radio station that I suspected, but I gravitated towards it quickly.

Quack, Quack! I had no idea what the duck sound implied, but the show starred Don Imus and a cast of others, who blended politics, sports and comedy. Once again, another program catering to an older demographic that reeled me in.

Don Imus is infamously known for making derogatory remarks towards the Rutgers Women's Basketball team in 2007, but I took a liking to the satire on the program long before that. It was a show where politicians were *regularly* ridiculed and when the topic shifted to sports, athletes of *all* ethnicities were singled out. I thought the show was brilliantly crafted and I became a regular listener... at the tender age of eight!

WFAN was also the radio home of the Mets. On the evenings their games aired on cable TV ("Sports Channel" – a separate station outside of the basic cable package that neither my parents nor Gran would pay for), I'd cuddle up to the radio and listen to Bob Murphy and Gary Cohen before bedtime. Soon, I'd find there were a series of hosts on WFAN who specifically covered sports during the overnights (until Imus aired at 5:30 a.m.) and again at the completion of his morning show. Keep in mind, I was usually in school during the day without the slightest idea – until I was home for two weeks... sick with the chicken pox. But from that day forward, I was sold! Fans regularly called in, voicing their opinions and sharing thoughts, but I wouldn't connect with the hosts... not until I was at my wits end with the Mets a few years later.

It was 1992 and the team was fresh off the sorrowful 1991 season which saw them finishing in 4th place... their lowest standing since 1983. Looking for a return to prominence, they spent an exorbitant amount of money on some big named free agents during the off-season. The team started the new season on a high note – but underperformed *considerably* thereafter. The frustration of fans grew to unprecedented levels – no longer would *another* Bobby Bonilla strikeout... with the bases loaded, make me cry. No sir! I wanted to hear hosts who were fully capable of ripping my favorite team a new one. Who would share the same passion as us downhearted Mets fans? Enter Mike Francesa and Christopher "Mad Dog" Russo, collectively known as *Mike and the Mad Dog.*

The hosts became larger than life sports personalities fixtures in my formative years (through adulthood). That "slender fella" who resembled a substitute teacher in the Mets yearbook? That was none other than Christopher "Mad Dog" Russo. Neither host were fans of the Mets (I couldn't blame them for that), but it didn't matter. From that year on, I'd listen to them as much as I could and almost exclusively once I started carrying a Walkman to high school. I'd even elect to *walk* home some days, instead of taking the city bus or subway (like most *normal* students would) – where I feared the threat of a weak radio frequency. Besides, my young legs were more than capable of taking the *hour and fifteen-minute* walk!

The duo made an immediate impact to my welfare and as the years progressed, I became more invested in sports – even calling into the station periodically (I still own the recorded tapes). AM radio wasn't so bad after all. As a teen, I went to sleep many nights listening to WFAN, growing an immediate attachment to the hosts and their frequent callers;

Vinny from Queens.
Eli from Westchester.
Doris from Rego Park.

Fast forward to today and my daily drives consist of WFAN – usually met with a deep sigh by passengers. *You'd listen to WFAN too, if you got a whiff of today's "music" on the FM dial!* Sports radio has blossomed over the years, as we've witnessed many copycats of the Mike and the Mad Dog duo. But lest we forget, WFAN was the original sports radio home and there will never be another pairing like them!

PLEASE PARDON MY WEIRDO...

The unleashing of this unconventional adult-like stance brought me to a crossroad. Due to a haste maturation period, there lived a distinct disconnection from my peers. Aside from that, I became a subscriber to the 'Proper Laws of Etiquette'! It further explains my mannerisms, preference in women, friends and a deep-seated aversion concerning inexplicable human behavior. If you find your blood boiling at any of the vexatious acts below, then you my friend, are a certified "weirdo"! Let's discuss and embrace.

- **Loud TV Volumes**: If I'm not at a movie theater, concert or sporting event, turn that crap down! I grew up under my grandmother and my nerves are bad!
- **Nose Blowing Reminiscent to an Elephant Sound** – Simply uncalled for. Blow your nose like a *normal* human being instead of attempting to shatter every blood vessel inside of your nostrils!
- **Cutting Your Nails in a Public Setting** – That "clip" sound goes through me like a knife. I can't believe the amount of people who do this in public settings. Removing a hang nail is one thing – conducting a full manicure is another.

- **Excessive Dog Barking** – If dogs are good at *voice recognition,* try recognizing the phrase: *Shut the fuck up!*
- **Loud Conversations (in quiet settings)** – Excluding the hearing impaired, is there a logical reason to yell if you're standing (or sitting) within inches of the other person? Why is it important that we all hear your conversation?
- **Open Coughs and Excessive Sneezing** – Sooo, I'm guessing no one taught you how to cover your mouth with the inside of your elbow? Oh, I get it, you find it dumb, right? Listen, common courtesy can go along way… in other words: Cover your fuckin mouth! And if you so happen to sneeze consecutively around me, be advised, you'll only receive *one* courtesy *bless you* (to cover the other *five* sprays of saliva!).
- **Loud Clapping** – There are levels to this clapping thing! Colliding your palms like two crashing cymbals is probably not a good idea. Loud clapping is not a suggestive piece of evidence that you appreciate the event *any more* than the person seated next to you. Clap like a normal person. If you must show *more* appreciation? *Rise to your feet* and clap. Deal?
- **Whistling** – Why do people whistle after a performance? Seriously, are you *that* excited? An applause wouldn't suffice? Why do some of us go above and beyond with *everything?*
- **Hard Walking** – Are you a dinosaur in training? Is your goal to stomp out every living insect on the floor? Are you an angry person and want everyone around you to know it? If your answer is 'no', then why must you walk so hard? "That's just the way I walk!" Bullshit! I've noticed the hardest walkers are about *100 pounds,* soaking wet! You don't have to "tip toe", just walk normally! If you can hear your foot crashing into the floor with each step, then you have a serious problem. There's *stomping* and there's *walking*. This isn't rocket science!

- **Prolonged Handshakes** – *Some* genius thought it was cute to classify the common handshake. We're supposed to believe that a *firm grip* (with direct eye contact) is indicative to being "confident and assertive". Why does this still matter in the age of heightened germs and hand sanitizer? I don't give a damn *how you feel about me during a handshake…* Let go of my hand! Here's an example:

Hi, nice to meet you!

shake (say, "One Mississippi" in your head).

By the time you've finished saying *Mississippi,* release the grip! There's simply no need to squeeze the dear life out of my palm for five and ten seconds at a time. I find it awkward and quite uncomfortable.

- **Incomprehensible Idiots** – A lot of us were fortunate to attend first-rate schools. As for blacks, we're long removed from the segregation laws of the past, where we were denied the educational privileges of our white counterparts. With that said, why are some of us hellbent on butchering the English language?

Am I looking for *13-letter words* every time you open your mouth? No. But would it hurt to *sound* educated at times? I've grown tired of slang terms (and improper English) used on platforms where they shouldn't be used (former athlete turned in-studio analyst and hip-hop artists co-hosting TV shows – I'm talking to you!). How can I take you seriously if you haven't considered taking English seriously? No excuses!

We live in a culture which has accepted the term, "stay woke", because apparently "stay awake" (which is present tense and the proper way to say it) isn't convincing enough. Our culture looks for style points over accuracy and nothing upsets me more than when other ethnic groups mock us in their attempts to sound "cool".

Is anyone else bothered by those who say, 'bling', 'you go girl' and 'da bomb' (the last term being seriously outdated!). It is almost as terrifying, as Morgan Freeman and Harrison Ford wearing earrings at their ages. My brain can't make sense of it all!

- **Attention Whores** – You know who you are, you folks are the absolute worst! There isn't a drug on earth more addicting than *attention*. Whether it's at the gym, with your overt sounds of aggression on *every* machine (*Aaaaargh's!* and *grrrrrr's!*), women who dress scantily to every occasion, bikers who rev up their motorcycle engines for no reason, people who carry on loud cell phone conversations in public settings, those who play music in their cars at levels that rattle my *four-thousand-pound car* (while sitting at a red light) and guys who sag their pants *underneath* their underwear. F.Y.I. – I hate you all! Haven't you heard the adage, *less is more?*

- **Excuse Your Manners!** – If I am holding the door and you refuse to follow my act of kindness with a *thank you,* I'll take it upon myself to shout out, *you're welcome!* (as a friendly reminder). Don't take my kindness for granted, you self-entitled jerk!

- **Kids** – Does anyone else hate them? (especially the *bad* ones?). Yes, people, you can have kids or find them 'cute' – and *still* dislike them!

- **Tailgating Jerks** – Why flirt with death or risk a spike in car insurance? All it takes is a simple step on the brake and both you and your car are goners. You're not going to bully me out of the lane that I am *already speeding in!* Go around, asshole!

- **Odd Male Names** – I am *all* for creativity, but if you're a parent-to-be (specifically a father), please avoid naming your son the following, unless he's going to be a "junior" and you adamantly oppose him having his *own* identity:

1. Bob (Um, yeah…)
2. Chip (cut it out!)
3. LaMarcus (what's the "La" about?)
4. Quentavious (huh?)
5. Dick (are you *sure* about this?)

And for the love of God, can we stop spelling the name 'Sean' (pronounced Shawn) S-E-A-N? I don't care about the name's origins… there is no logical reason to spell it that way. There are two other ways to spell it – choose one!

Honorable Mention: *Children and adults who kick the back of chairs at the movie theater. Cool it, before I break your legs!*
Sidebar: *At least I started off the section saying 'please'!*

* * * * *

My sensitivity levels have removed me from being relatable to humans and I am aware that I belong on my own planet... in another galaxy... far, far away! I have no desire to conform to the ways of you humans and I'll gladly stay inside of my happy bubble! The world that I am about to introduce you to is unusual, but if you can relate, all I ask is that you wipe your feet upon entering... and take off your shoes!

- **Rooting for the Bad Guys in Films** – If you're a crafty, calculated character, who found ways to outsmart the law (i.e.; bank robbers), you have my complete support! Besides, why must the good guys *always* win in film, yet, lose in real life?
- **Do You Remember the Time?** – It's a quirky little thing I do, but if you find a video/song recorded in the 80s and 90s, I can tell you the *exact year and season* it was released. There is always room for error, but I'm pretty damned good!
- **Little Shop of Horrors** – I'm a plant lover who received his official "green thumb" from my father. I'll occasionally play music, providing my "little green guys" pep talks during the cold winter months when they appear lifeless. "C'mon, bro, keep it up! Don't die on me now!"
- **"Take Me to Your Leader!"** – One of my least liked television shows of all-time: *Star Trek.* Least favorite film: *Star Wars* (I find both cheesy). But I am a believer in extraterrestrial life and I am obsessed with UFO documentaries and anything having to do with the universe.
- **Isn't She... Pretty in Pink?** – An all-time favorite film is *Pretty in Pink,* which I watched tirelessly as a kid. I'd cry at the scene when Andie Walsh (Molly Ringwald) confronted Blane (Andrew McCarthy) for blatantly

ignoring her phone calls leading up to the high school prom. Blane, who was born into a rich family, allowed his fellow *silver-spooned* friend, Steff (James Spader), to get into his head about dating a girl below his standards. The couple connected later in the evening and shared an explosive kissing scene at the end.

Sidebar: *If you're wondering where my balls were at this stage? Beats me!*

- **Trix Cereal** – Can I tell you how pissed I'd get watching those snot-nosed, punk kids deny the Trix rabbit a bowl of cereal! For fuck sakes, he's the face on the box! Let him get his sugar rush and get over yourselves!
- **Bathroom Bloopers** – I can't understand dudes who urinate on the toilet seat and floor. I was taught from day one – *lift the seat, stand over the bowl and release.* Once finished, execute the *shake test,* flush and put the toilet seat *down* (even the lid, if necessary). Simple. Don't tell me I was the *only* guy to have been raised this way? Additionally, there is *no excuse* for having to tip-toe in a pool of piss when using the urinal at work (or in public restrooms). Utterly disgusting!
- **Gas Attack!** – I love the smell of gasoline. It ranks up there with the aromas of coffee, bacon and freshly baked bread. Judge me… see if I care!
- **Vinyl** – That hissing, crackling sound at the beginning of a vinyl record is music to my ears. I know what you're thinking: *who still listens to vinyl records?* Well, for your information, I don't. But I vividly remember listening to records as a child – and the sound was hypnotizing.

Honorable mention: *Has anyone else dialed the 'How's my driving?' phone numbers found on the back of trucks? Just me? okay...*

Chapter Five: I Love The 80s!

Maybe I'm a little biased... okay, I'll admit... I'm 'a lot' biased! But there isn't a decade to compare to the 80s. Yes, this is the portion of the book where I'll proceed to brag about my decade being better than yours – so if you feel it will strike a nerve... I suggest you continue reading!

Let's all hop in the DeLorean (how many times have you heard that cheesy 80s reference?) and go back to a time when unshaved vaginas, Jheri curls, mullets and white guys with thick moustaches were all the rave. Let's reminisce about my decade!

* * * * *

Don't talk to me about any other decade – I can't hear you! *La-la-la-la-laaaa!* There was something magical about this era. Okay, so the *crack epidemic* and *AIDS crisis* impacted the population… but *at least* we had incredible music! Our movies were entertaining, wrestling captured our hearts, the fashion was imaginative, porn movies had plots and the cartoons – my goodness, the cartoons! Curse the bastards responsible for destroying Saturday mornings! I wish you all a slow, agonizing ~~death~~ *eternity of reality television* (hey, it's the closest thing to death).

If I could describe the 80s in one word: Epic! It isn't just happenstance, that they've tried to recreate our shows, movies and *even* our music (especially in commercial ads) to generate a buzz. I suppose imitation is the sincerest form of flattery – but get off *our* coattails and create your *own* fuckin' magic!

Through film we had smashes like, *Back to The Future, Teen Wolf, The Karate Kid, Caddyshack, The Breakfast Club, The Terminator, RoboCop, The Goonies, Indiana Jones, A Nightmare on Elm Street, Alien, Gremlins, E.T., Rocky III & IV* (Part IV being my favorite) and the list goes on.

Our cartoons were unrivaled: *The Smurfs, G.I. Joe, Thundercats, Teenage Mutant Ninja Turtles, The Transformers, He-Man and the Masters of the Universe, The Real Ghostbusters, Hulk*

Hogan's Rock 'N' Roll Wrestling, Ducktales, Gem, The Berenstain Bears and *Winnie the Pooh* among others.

Our TV shows – *Miami Vice, Knight Rider, Magnum P.I., The A-Team, Double Dare, The Lifestyles of the Rich and Famous* and *Fame,* to name a few.

There lived *Alf,* MTV, Michael Jackson's "Thriller", *Dance Party USA, Solid Gold,* Rick Astley, "Weird Al" Yankovic parodies, RUN-D.M.C., Cyndi Lauper, Mike Tyson 30-second boxing fights, Luke and Laura's wedding, Who shot J.R.?, Robin Leach, Steven Seagal, Eddie Murphy's "Raw", *Cats Broadway Musical,* Tiffany, Debbie Gibson, The Brat Pack, *Rambo,* Chucky from Child's Play, Billy Dee Williams Colt 45 commercial, Sy Sperling's – 'Hair Club for Men', Life Call – "I've fallen, and I can't get up!" McGruff the Crime Dog, the fast-talking Micro Machines guy, "867-5309/Jenny" (a phone number plenty of 80s children dialed), Lee Press-on Nails, "Just say NO!" Baby Jessica, the Space Shuttle Challenger disaster, "No new taxes!", Garbage Pail Kids cards, Cabbage Patch, Teddy Ruxpin and My Buddy dolls, Elvira…

Sidebar: *I'm forever indebted to Elvira!* (Google images, my friends!).

Panting Okay, maybe I'll desist from listing more awesomeness… except, how do I leave out our musicians? I know, I know, that'll be like pouring salt in a wound. But since I detest the 2000s so freakin' much, I'll be glad to douse you in some sodium chloride… if you'd like?

Here are a *few* of my favorite artists (some of who got started before the 80s) who made a name for themselves in this glorious decade:

- Madonna
- Phil Collins
- U2
- George Michael
- Naked Eyes
- Hall & Oates
- Sting
- Prince
- Bobby Brown
- LL Cool J

- Sade
- Van Halen
- Bruce Springsteen
- David Bowie
- Peter Gabriel
- Robert Palmer
- Bryan Adams
- Huey Lewis and the News
- Paula Abdul
- Tears for Fears
- Don Henley
- New Kids on the Block

Okay, so I got a little carried away. And I need not forget any of the artists who greatly contributed to New Wave, Freestyle and the wizardry of one-hit wonders! I understand if you've gotten choked up reading about such wonderful masterpieces and distinct greatness which will forever live in honor and reverence, but imagine how I feel? Thank you all for becoming a major part of my life – I mean that from the bottom of my heart.

* * * * *

The 80s brought the world *900 numbers.* While men today scour Facebook and various dating sites looking for hookups, we had whores a phone call away looking to get us off. For the tune of *$2.99 the first minute, 45 cents each additional minute*, they'd get physical (cheap Olivia Newton John plug) on pre-recorded lines exploiting callers with dirty talk and fake orgasms. Hey, it was better than being catfished!

If your parents came across the charges – you played dumb! It wasn't your phone bill (to pay) so it wasn't your concern. A little white lie usually did the trick and when informed of the "error", the phone company promptly removed the charges. This was *our* version of saying, "I got hacked!"

There were a plethora of 900 numbers to pique your interest. Some of us called the *Teen Hotline*, others dialed *The Corey's* (Feldman and Haim). I'd occasionally dial Alyssa Milano and Santa Claus. *What?! I wanted to know what I was getting for Christmas!* But there was no better hotline than the following:

So, give us a call, the new line is kinda def, Dial 1 900 9 0 9 Jeff! Yep, that was the hotline for DJ Jazzy Jeff and the Fresh Prince and I take full responsibility for making a now defunct company rich. Sorry about that, Gran.

People didn't take themselves seriously in the 80s, which is why I can sing a thirty-year-old commercial without an ounce of embarrassment. The proof was in our music and through our fashion. We'd wear a pair of *acid-washed jeans* (with rips at the knees – yep, we did it first!), *grubby sneakers* and simply go about our business. Girls wore *big hair, bright makeup with loud colored clothing,* while guys wore *knee-high tube socks,* with unforgettable shorts. *I could've probably done without the men's short-shorts.*

But more important than anything else… Men didn't get their fuckin' eyebrows done! What in the *metrosexual* is going on here?! *I find this to be one of the many downfalls of today's male!*

The world was a better place before selfies and "Instagram fitness models". A world where kids played outdoors, a world where 'pound signs' were called… pound signs, because after all, that's what they are – you can call it a "hashtag" if you want! A world where we didn't make up senseless slang expressions when describing a noun… jewelry and diamonds were called… jewelry and diamonds! *What is this BLING you speak of?*

The 80s were a period when acronyms only existed for music groups, news stations, sporting leagues, wrestling companies, or ABC's Friday night TV line-up titled, "TGIF". (Thank God/Goodness It's Friday). Otherwise, we took the time to *pronounce* the word, without using a shortcut to "sound cool". Can you imagine if movies like, *Planes, Trains & Automobiles* or *Revenge of the Nerds* were referred to as, PTAA and ROTN, respectively? I couldn't either!

Even the cheesiness of the 80s holds a special place within pop culture. Let's face it, the *hairstyles* sucked, *the dancing* was horrid and *skinny ties* and *shoulder pads* were considered "fashionable". Women wore *leg warmers*, we had *fanny packs* and *careless editing* in the movie *Commando* (I still don't know how that film made it out of the cutting room!), then, there was *Full House*. For your information, I loved *Full House!* You can laugh and mock us (or me) if you desire, but the 80s represented a period where *everything* meshed. No other decade compares!

I apologize to today's youth, for waking up to *social media* and *Minecraft* on Saturday mornings instead of the classic cartoons of yesteryear. I'm sorry you'll never know how it feels to watch *Muppet Babies* and *Garfield and Friends* over a bowl of Pac-man cereal. Not your fault. You obviously had no control over when you were conceived.

To the rock fans of today... I'm sorry you didn't experience *our* big hair bands and heavy metal groups in their prime:

- Van Halen
- Def Leppard
- Poison
- Guns N' Roses
- Mötley Crüe
- Bon Jovi
- Whitesnake

You can certainly relive these moments through YouTube and various streaming services, but it isn't the same as watching on the *old* MTV; to those claiming their decade was superior, I ask:

Where is your Live Aid?
Where is your We Are the World?
Where is your Cosby Show?
Who are your Lakers vs. Celtics?
Where is your Return of the Jedi?
Who is your Michael Jordan?

American historians commonly rave over the 1940s, 50s and 60s, but the 80s deserve your utmost respect! Our decade was timeless, I will fight for it every time. Pop culture – You are very welcome!

Chapter Tidbits:

- Three of my all-time favorite musicians made their names in the 80s: Madonna, Phil Collins, LL Cool J.
- My favorite 80s show: *Knight Rider*.
- My favorite TV sitcom theme songs: *Amen, Perfect Strangers, Charles in Charge, Full House*.
- *The Lost Boys* is one of my favorite films of the decade (although it scared the living daylights out of me as a child!).

- I am a proud owner of two Member's Only jackets.
- I still own (and occasionally play) the original Nintendo Entertainment System – which is in pristine condition! Sorry, I have no plans of selling it on eBay!
- My favorite holiday: Memorial Day – It's the kick-off to the summer and many radio stations will devote the extended weekend to an all-80s theme.

Chapter Six: My First Love

Oh, put me in coach, I'm ready to play today
Put me in coach, I'm ready to play today
Look at me, I can be centerfield.
— John Fogerty – "Centerfield" (1985)

Perhaps it was the celebrated history, the stats, the uniforms, the sound of the bat striking the ball, the pop of a mitt, the sunflower seeds or... the stale piece of gum found inside of each package of cards. Baseball was the object of my affection and there wasn't another sport to top it. I was particularly fond of players who chewed tobacco and the visual of grown men adjusting their *jock straps, spitting onto the field* was golden. I yearned for the day of being old enough to purchase a can of *Skoal,* adjusting a jockstrap of my own.

For the kids who wished to emulate their heroes, the closest thing to chewing tobacco was *Big League Chew* (gum). I'd use my five-dollar allowance money to purchase a couple of packages for the guys, in preparation for recess; the time of day when baseball was king! We talked baseball all day long, trying our best to *act* the part by creating a competitive kid's league. This is where we'd record stats and indignantly yell at one another.

Our group was the apple of the other students' eye at P.S. 199, as I'm sure they all wondered why we took things so seriously. It was a strange obsession, but I wanted to be identified as a *baseball player* first, *student* second. My passion for the game was incomprehensible. I was particularly fond of players who wore *eye-black; a tar-like substance placed under the eyes to protect the vision from sun glare or stadium lights.* Will Clark and Don Mattingly, two of my all-time favorite players, wore it best. Not only was there science behind the substance, but from my vantage point, it seemingly intimidated the opposing pitcher.

I searched high and low for this item, figuring it was only exclusively available to professional baseball players. *How can I get my hands on this stuff?* Sounding more like an addict looking for his next hit. *I would eventually find out that it was sold at sporting goods stores.* Until then, I thought of the next best thing: I'd introduced a black magic marker to our arsenal! On the days of our big games, the guys lined up in the boys' bathroom awaiting their badge of honor – courtesy of *Crayola*. With one swipe of the wrist… a star was born.

* * * * *

The eye-black fixation started during Game 4 of the 1990 American League Championship Series. The Oakland A's were looking to advance to the World Series for a third straight year in a matchup against the Boston Red Sox. Aside from being a diehard Mets fan – I was a huge fan of the Oakland A's. Their uniform colors were daring, they were quite the bunch to watch. In addition, they wore white cleats – both at home and on the road – unusual at the time.

The originators of the *Monster bash* (a move where players clashed forearms in the air to form an "X" – usually done as a form of celebration for their homeruns), the A's added flare to a sport known for being unimaginative to the average viewer. Leading the charge for this brash group were "The Bash Brothers", Jose Canseco and Mark McGwire, known for their tape measuring homeruns… and in due time, steroid abuse, the all-time stolen base leader Rickey Henderson, the flamboyant Dennis Eckersley *and* the late Bob Welch, who won a remarkable *27 games* that season (and was awarded A.L. Cy Young).

The only player in the way of another trip to the Fall Classic, was Red Sox Ace pitcher – Roger Clemens. Clemens was the emotional leader of the Red Sox pitching staff. Legend has it, he suggested his teammates wear eye-black as a form of solidarity. Not every player would oblige, but it was do or die and the Red Sox weren't going out without a fight – with or without the eye substance. To the dismay of Red Sox Nation, Clemens was tossed out of the game for arguing with the home plate umpire, as the A's went on to win the series in four games.

Beyond that, it was the first time I'd ever come across a *pitcher* wearing eye-black, and quite possibly the first time it was done in the history of baseball. From that day forward, I became the biggest Roger Clemens fan… *until he accepted a trade to the dreaded New York Yankees in 1999 (following a stint with the Toronto Blue Jays).* I'd always been astonished by Clemens' imposing pitching stats as he was certainly on his way to Cooperstown (until the 2008 steroid scandal). But all it took was a black streak under his eyes to win my heart for good. That was bad ass!

* * * * *

I was fascinated by baseball stats, studying the back of trading cards as if I was preparing for a *baseball exam*. I learned how to calculate a *Batting Average* long before my introduction to division and I personally calculated (and recorded) stats in baseball video games at a time when video games didn't have enough storage to record stats. Furthermore, I answered baseball trivia questions with conviction, usually asked during baseball telecasts or, on *Jeopardy Who holds the record for...? In what year did...?*

Spewing out names and years a black kid *probably* had no business knowing. Keep in mind, during the *Post-War Era* (considered the height of baseball), there was a spike in minority players which increased black viewership lasting well into the 80s. It wasn't uncommon for black children to rank baseball as their top sport. But as the other sports produced more black stars (while growing in popularity), baseball's black viewership declined. Apparently, I didn't get that memo.

Major League Baseball was up against the juggernauts of the NBA during the 80s, as Earvin "Magic" Johnson's *Showtime* Los Angeles Lakers were at their apex, while Michael Jordan was quickly becoming a household name. Baseball lacked the *black star power* needed to garner the attention of the casual black fan, as the generation coming up deemed the sport "slow", "unwatchable" and "boring". Words used to disparage a game where blacks achieved great success:

- Jackie Robinson
- Willie Mays
- Ernie Banks
- Bob Gibson
- Rod Carew
- Hank Aaron
- Frank Robinson
- Joe Morgan
- Willie Stargell

Apparently, that wasn't enough.

Baseball has very little "cool factor" for black kids to identify with, but former two-sport star, Bo Jackson (who played in baseball's American League and in the National Football League for the *then* Los Angeles Raiders), thrived during the mid to late 80s and was the closest thing to "cool". *Not that it should've mattered, but he was an overall fan favorite of white America, especially those on Madison Avenue responsible for dishing out the big bucks for commercial stardom.*

With a course of "Bo Knows" commercials (Nike campaign ads for his cross-training sneaker), a cartoon series *and* his own licensed video game (a rarity at the time), Jackson was probably the first player of my era with the potential to become the "new face" of the game. He had immediate star power! Eventually, the rigors of playing two sports took a toll on his body.

We were introduced to another two-sport star; Deion "Primetime" Sanders, who played several seasons in the Major Leagues for a handful of teams. But baseball wouldn't be the sport he'd excel at. That belonged to football, where Sanders is remembered for his flamboyance and defensive wizardry as an *NFL Hall of Fame defensive back!* Two down, one to go.

The black athlete to crossover into mainstream stardom (with the potential to rival Jordan) was Ken Griffey, Jr. Following the footsteps of his father (who was a successful big leaguer himself), Griffey was primed for greatness from the moment he arrived in the league. With a desirable smile and one of the sweetest swings I've ever come across, *Junior* became one of the top faces in the sport at the start of the 1990s.

One could argue that his preference to wear a backwards baseball cap (during interviews and pre-game warmups) should've propelled him to the top of the lists among young black sports lovers. The style was greatly connected to hip-hop at a time when the music genre was on the verge of flourishing.

Black youth tend to gravitate towards players who "buck the system" (hello, Allen Iverson). The backwards cap was not only Griffey's signature look, but the uniformed appearance for hip-hop artists and its followers. There was even discussion of featuring Griffey's trademark appearance on his hall of fame plaque – likely frowned upon by baseball purists.

Like Jordan, Griffey was raised by his parents, spoke exceptionally well and conducted himself accordingly both on and off the field. The opportunity to eclipse Jordan was there. What hindered Griffey's potential to oust him?

- He played in a small market (Seattle), meaning less viewership in households outside of the west coast (considering the time zone difference)
- Baseball's marketing machine couldn't match that of the NBA

While Jordan was becoming America's darling, baseball relied on its *one-hundred plus* year history as the selling point. It is considered, "America's Pastime" for a reason. Moreover, the sport relies on the *team element* – more than it does individuality, making it harder to market a single player.

The NBA makes a killing marketing their superstars for marquee matchups. There is a notable face on most teams. However, some of baseball's top stars are pitchers: What if that star pitcher doesn't pitch on the night of the nationally televised big game? *In addition, how do you sell a casual baseball watcher on a defensive maestro or a subpar hitter? There isn't much attraction there.*

When most wanted to "Be like Mike", I was convincingly sold on the game played on the diamond (maybe a *quarter* of me wanted to be like Mike). While ratings saw a significant drop in black households, I kept busy through trading cards, video games and TV shows like *Play Ball* – an instructional program hosted by Reggie Jackson, teaching little leaguers the cardinal rule of hitting and fielding. Baseball was everything.

BATTER UP!

My father lives and breathes soccer. It is by far the biggest sport played internationally, but the game didn't resonate with me. You'd figure a global sport could upstage America's pastime, considering baseball didn't permit blacks to play professionally until 1947.

I received a soccer ball long before I threw my first baseball and we'd frequently make trips to Central Park to kick the ball around. This is where my father would emulate the moves of soccer legend Pele. He was a huge fan and frequently shared stories about

Pele's playing days with the New York Cosmos in the 1970s. But I was stubbornly unconvinced.

At fifteen, I attended a sold-out soccer game at the old Giants Stadium to watch Spain – a powerhouse at the time. But that wouldn't work either – I was regularly playing baseball by this time. The stage where soccer captured my undivided attention, was the 1994 World Cup, when the United States hosted the popular world event for the very first time. Disregarding that, I've probably watched more hockey!

* * * * *

I was about seven years old when I watched my first baseball game. It was a Saturday afternoon and the Chicago Cubs were featured on NBC's *Game of the Week.* I can't recall the opposing team, but I remember becoming fascinated by this *unusual beanstalk* growing along the outfield wall at Chicago's Wrigley Field. *What the heck was that?!*

I credit Gran for starting my massive baseball card collection and it was during her Sunday morning newspaper stroll, where she'd pick up a variety of cards at the local Woolworth store (*Topps trading cards* were my favorite in case anyone cared). Shuffling through the cards, I'd commonly come across Chicago Cubs players, posing in front of a brick outfield wall covered in dead vines (presumably photographed during the early spring). But as the weather warmed, those same vines turned into ivy, which ties into the great tradition of Wrigley Field. Just another selling point from the greatest game in the world!

As TV expanded, so did the opportunities to watch teams from around the league. I was astounded by the characteristics of each park:

- **Boston**: *Fenway Park* – Home of the tallest outfield wall in Major League baseball – nicknamed the "Green Monster"
- **Toronto**: *Skydome* – The first stadium to use a retractable roof
- **Los Angeles**: *Dodger's Stadium* – A gorgeous palm tree with a mountain back drop along with an iconic baseball scout – commonly seen sitting behind home plate

(wearing a Panama hat, carrying a radar gun to track pitchers speed)

- **Kansas City**: *Kaufmann Stadium* – A beautiful waterfall sitting atop the outfield wall
- **St Louis**: *Busch Stadium* – The Gateway Arch towers behind the stadium

Honorable mention: Atlanta: *Fulton County Stadium* – Where thousands of fans performed the signature "tomahawk chop", in unison, to rally-on the home town Atlanta Braves. *Quite the site during the early 90s, when the Braves were a baseball juggernaut.*

The backstories of these ballparks (and their teams) are fascinating, but unfortunately, not enough to win my loyalty. That, Ladies & Gentlemen, went to the New York Mets.

LET'S GO ~~YANKEES!~~ METS!

New Yorkers are given the choice of two baseball teams: Mets or Yankees. If I was conceived decades earlier, *at least* the option of the Brooklyn Dodgers and New York Giants would have been available. Unfortunately, both clubs ditched the bright lights of the Big Apple for sunny California in 1957 – leaving New Yorkers in a pickle.

You can't discuss baseball without mentioning the "Bronx Bombers". The Yankees were the prominent franchise – with a history to die for (as of this writing, they are *27-time* World Champions). The amount of success this franchise has reveled in is simply unfair – especially if you're a Mets fan.

Some of the biggest names in the sport donned Yankee pinstripes: Herman "Babe" Ruth, "The Iron Horse" Lou Gehrig, "Joltin" Joe DiMaggio, Roger Maris, Mickey Mantle, Reggie Jackson. The list of names is long, the retired numbers placed alongside *Monument Park* (at the stadium) are abundant.

As much as I envied the Yankees triumphs, I wasn't part of the long list of Mets fans who despised them... at least not until the late 90s. Until then, I'd watch for one player: "The Captain", Don Mattingly.

"Donnie Baseball" was the quintessential 80s baseball player, sporting a mullet hairstyle, eye-black and a Tom Selleck moustache. What I enjoyed most? He wasn't afraid to get his uniform dirty! A defensive wizard at first base, Mattingly used one batting stance (of many) which I commonly imitated and he was lauded as one of the best players of the decade. An almost sure bet for baseball's Hall of Fame, his career took a sudden left turn as we entered the 90s – plagued by injuries, which greatly impacted his Hall of Fame chances. Sadly, Mattingly's prime years occurred during a decade which saw the Yankees at the bottom of the barrel.

They returned to post-season eminence in 1995 – competing in the playoffs (for the first time since 1981) against Ken Griffey, Jr.'s Seattle Mariners in a compelling five game series. It marked the first playoff appearance of Mattingly's career – and he made it a memorable one, putting up terrific numbers against the young, hungry Mariners ball club. Unfortunately for Mattingly and the Yanks, it wasn't enough.

Mattingly called it quits following the '95 season and from there the team took off, basking in one of the greatest runs in sports history – winning *four* World Series titles in the span of five years! A World Series ring eluded Mattingly, but his approach to the game is what I admired most... even while openly rooting against his team.

* * * * *

I enjoyed the Yankees broadcast on WPIX, where legendary sportscaster, Phil Rizzuto, stole the show with his unorthodox approach and famous "Holy Cow!" catchphrase. Additionally, WPIX was the home of two of my favorite programs – which typically aired during weekend Yankee rain delays: *Albert & Costello* and *Godzilla*.

The shows factored into my decision to follow the Yanks while remaining aligned to the Mets – certainly a taboo move among New York baseball fans. But I didn't care. Based on the history lesson, only a fool would choose the Mets over the Yankees. But there was *something* about those friggin' boys in Queens, *yanking* me away from a lifetime of happiness. America, meet your fool!

MEET THE METS!

To placate the old Dodger and Giant fans, the Mets organization came into existence before the start of the 1962 season, adopting *blue* from the Dodgers and *orange* from the Giants, combining it with *pinstripes* (to complete the uniform). *Not a bad strategy, wouldn't you agree?* All that was missing was the success of the three franchises.

The Giants and Dodgers were part of the New York baseball scene from the early 1880s and there lived many diehard fans reluctant to cross over to the Yankees (or further support organizations which abandoned them). Such a defiant attitude can lead to lifelong pain and suffering – as was the case for fans opting to switch over to the *Metropolitans*.

The Mets originally played their home games at the old Polo Grounds – home of baseball's N.Y. Giants (before they departed to San Francisco), in anticipation of a move to the newly built Shea Stadium in Queens, N.Y. It was a long road filled with plenty of losses and inferiority, but in their eighth season, the Mets won the first of *three* World Series.

The second World Series victory arrived in 1973 – followed by a decade of egregious play and baseball irrelevancy. Fans watched the franchise trade away their most prized player, Tom Seaver, while key players from the championship teams were either traded or aged. It wasn't until 1986, when the "Amazin's" hoisted their next and last championship banner – competing in one of the most memorable World Series of all-time against the Red Sox. *It saddens me to say, but I didn't follow baseball (regularly) until a couple of years after their thrilling World Series victory. Ugh!*

While the Yankees struggled in the 80s, the Mets became the toast of the town. They combined the talents of their highly touted prospects, Darryl Strawberry and Dwight "Doc" Gooden, with the savvy production of veteran players like Gary Carter, Keith Hernandez and Bobby Ojeda. The franchise enjoyed a run of National League dominance – which should've led to more ticker tape parades. They were *that* good! But Strawberry, Gooden, Hernandez and others (on the roster and throughout the sporting world for that matter), struggled with off the field drug and alcohol issues, leading to the demise of one of the better teams in baseball.

The core players were eventually broken up and in typical sports fashion, a new batch of players were hauled in by the start of the 90s. Regrettably, this is when I first experienced baseball heartbreak and my tween years (through early adulthood) were dismal! I have a thing for underdogs – maybe because I can relate.

The franchise started out as a laughing stock during their inaugural year – losing *120 games* – and have always been recognized for their follies more than their successes. The decisions made by management have always been head-scratchers and plenty of stars have worn Mets threads only to considerably underperform. The team constantly found ways to stay in the news for the wrong reasons and unfortunately, win or lose, they will *always* be regarded as the "little brother" of the almighty Yankees.

Yankee fans often heckle and sneer at admitted Mets fans: "You're a Mets fan?! Sorry to hear that!" But that wouldn't stop me from supporting the orange & blue. I liked many of their players – my favorite being Gregg Jeffries, a *hot-headed* prospect who hit the baseball better than most veterans. I was also enchanted by announcer, Tim McCarver and his meticulous insight for in-game strategies.

McCarver, a native Tennessean and former major league catcher, added some southern flavor and laughs to the Mets broadcast. I hearkened his every word, where he'd offer great analysis while sharing some engaging baseball stories. Fans and TV critics regularly scrutinized his baseball acumen, but I can make the case that McCarver is the person *most* responsible for teaching me the game from a strategical perspective. He served as a broadcaster for multiple teams and was appointed *lead analyst* during the World Series (through most of his broadcasting career). The networks clearly understood his value, when fans didn't.

I was a frequent viewer of *This Week in Baseball,* which aired on WWOR-TV (the local TV station of the Mets) before Sunday afternoon games. The program was hosted by Sportscaster Mel Allen, featuring baseball follies, interviews and highlights from around the league.

MOVIES

Baseball films have been around for decades, but the first film to grab my immediate attention was *The Bad News Bears in Breaking Training*. There was something special about watching kids take hacks inside of the old Astrodome (former home of the Houston Astros). I lived vicariously through each character – hoping to someday play on a team of my own.

I watched Robert Redford star in *The Natural,* Richard Pryor in *Brewster's Millions and* a promising cast in *Eight Men Out,* (based on the Black Sox scandal of 1919). Kevin Costner starred in, *Field of Dreams* and *Bull Durham* (both are classics), *Major League* is an all-time favorite and *never* gets old ("Juuuussst a bit outside!") and I thought Tom Hanks was terrific in, *A League of Their Own* ("There's no crying in baseball!!!"). Films such as, *Rookie of the Year* and *Little Big League* generated lots of laughs, while *Angels in the Outfield* – a remake of the original 1951 classic – didn't quite live up to my expectations. But the one baseball movie to resonate more than any other was *The Sandlot.* My goodness!

The film was loosely based on a group of neighborhood kids in 1960s California, who were searching for an additional player to fill out their sandlot baseball team. Enter one Scotty Smalls, ("You're killing me, Smalls!") who moved with his family to the rural area. Smalls was not athletically inclined. Due to his shortcomings, most of the guys weren't too accommodating with establishing a friendship – except for the best player on the sandlot team, Benny "The Jet" Rodriguez.

Benny patiently took the time to teach Smalls the fundamentals of the game and they soon bonded. After some growing pains and a little adventure, the group accepted Smalls as their newest member… and that's when the fun began!

About the *only* thing I had in common with the Smalls' character was his passion for baseball and an immense desire to fit in. But what I enjoyed most about the *first-person* narrative film, was how it zeroed in on *fellowship and understanding,* coupled with a nice blend of baseball to get my juices flowing! I grew up with guys who mirrored the characters in the movie, eventually moving to a neighborhood where kids met up at the playground for intense scrimmage games. Thanks to the film, my interest to play on a little league team reached unprecedented levels.

Honorable mention: *Ken Burns' fabled 9-part baseball documentary conveniently titled "Baseball" was sensational! I watched it in its entirety when it originally aired on PBS in 1994 (and I own it on DVD).*

GAMETIME!

I took interest in baseball around the time I was making out with girls in the school library. I always thought I was good enough to play, but never understood why it took my parents so long to sign me up for little league.

Was I a five-tool sensation on the verge of taking the Major Leagues by storm? No. But the potential was there to at least give baseball a serious thought. Missing the final cut for a select traveling team was when I realized I wasn't ready for prime time. The rejection haunted me in the forthcoming years.

* * * * *

I was ten years old when *Josh Levin's* Mom handed Gran an application for baseball tryouts taking place in East River Park. The assembled team would compete against other little leaguers in the Tri-state area. The guys at school insisted I give it a shot. I was psyched but a little apprehensive.

Am I as good as they think? As we awaited the day, Josh and I practiced during recess, but deep down I knew he didn't stand a chance. Josh couldn't catch, his athleticism was heart-wrenching and I felt that he didn't take *playing* baseball as seriously as I did. But he was a student of the game and you certainly shouldn't question a person's heart.

My only concern was making the adjustment from *soft-tossed* Wilson tennis balls and *plastic* bats at the schoolyard, to *fast pitched* hardballs and *aluminum* bats in little league. To get prepared, Mom's new companion, Terrance, accompanied me to various batting cages, where I took a few good swings against the pitching machine.

Man, I've got this in the bag, I thought. I never competed for anything prior to this, but as far as I was concerned, I was the best ten-year-old baseball player in Manhattan – brushing off thoughts of the citywide competition expected at tryouts. *What competition?* My *worthless* school league stats were certified, I was among the "best of the best" according to friends. All I needed was to prove it to these clowns at tryouts.

Game time!

Mom and I arrived at the field shortly after Josh and his parents and I felt the butterflies racing in my stomach. To alleviate our nerves, Josh's dad suggested we toss the ball around to loosen up.

The scene was surreal; packed with hundreds of hopefuls, parents and plenty of coaches. The kids were divided into groups where we were asked to display defensive skills at our desired position – before our names were called to take a turn against the pitching machine. *Pitching machine? Oh yeah... I've absolutely got this!*

I was most comfortable in the outfield and when it was my turn to shag fly balls, I took my George Foster autographed glove to centerfield and caught each one.

"Two hands!" the coaches yelled.

Aaah, Whatever! *I'd watched too many Major Leaguers catch fly balls with one hand – the glove hand – without securing the ball with the non-glove hand. Coaches will stress fundamentals until they're blue in the face and that's exactly what happened. Until you've made it to the pros, you do things the right way. According to my ego, I was already a pro...*

A few kids looked impressive taking ground balls in the infield – firing the ball to first base effortlessly. The outfielders showed confidence as well. I got the sense that many of them were already a part of a little league, not a *schoolyard league,* like yours truly and I was going to get a run for my money.

Finally, it was my turn to bat... the moment I'd been waiting for. I examined the approach of each player before me, but it appeared many struggled to make significant contact with the baseball. There were a few weak grounders, pop-ups and even some swings and misses. I had to make up for the outfield blunder to have *any* chance of making the team.

We were given ten attempts at the plate, while each coach stood by to evaluate our batting stance: *the positioning of our hands while holding the bat, the placement of our chin (advising that we tuck it into our leading shoulder) and our swing follow-thru.*

In retrospect, I'm sure my technique wasn't pretty, but I emulated Cal Ripken, Jr. (the man of 1000 batting stances during his playing days) and proceeded to hit line drive after line drive – to the midst of *oooh's* and *aaah's* from onlookers. *There isn't a better sound than an aluminum bat walloping a hardball.*

I hit a ball so hard, it caused a delay after striking the pitching machine and shattering a piece of the equipment. We watched in awe, as the component flew towards the third base line. One of the coaches raced to the mound – attempting to repair the damage.

"I think you broke the machine!" he laughed.

I was somewhat embarrassed, but there wasn't a smile on my face. I was going to make this team one way or the other. At the completion of my commanding at-bat, I headed towards the dugout and was instantly greeted with a high-five by one of the coaches, followed by a resounding "nice job!"

I'd be lying if I said my confidence wasn't going through the roof. I waited around to watch Josh's at-bats and to my surprise, he did quite well! It was truly a feel-good moment and I couldn't help but think about the chances of us making the team.

At the end, the coaches informed all of the parents that each child would be notified of the final roster – by mail – in three to four weeks. Mom, Josh and his parents were excited, fully convinced I did enough to make the team. For the remaining weeks, I'd badger Gran about the mail:

Did I get anything yet?! "No, boy!"

Is it here yet?! "If you don't sit your butt down!"

Finally, the day arrived. My heart hammered, as I ripped open the envelope with reckless abandon, skimming through the two-paragraphed letter searching for key words. Then, it happened. I laid my eyes on the *two words* that made my heart drop about as fast as the words "I'm pregnant".

"I'm sorry!"

I didn't need to read anything else. The words hit me like a bullet to the chest. In dramatic fashion, I fell to the middle of Gran's living room floor and cried until my eyes begged me to stop. *Fuckin' assholes!* Those in the know of my magical performance were stupefied.

"You should've made it!"

No shit, Sherlock! I thought of every possible reason why I didn't make the cut, until years later when I finally accepted the truth: I wasn't good enough!

The rejection was a true eye-opener and my sorrow carried on for weeks. Playing *schoolyard baseball* wouldn't cut it. I needed to familiarize myself with the *real* game. I can blame my environment

– *I will*. I can blame the climate of the northeast – *I absolutely will*. But the bulk of the blame goes to my parents.

As I've alluded, NYC circa the 80s was not a friendly place. There was always the threat of parents finding their children buried alive underneath some random dirt field. Has there been extraordinary talent to make it to the Big Leagues from the city? Absolutely. But I'm sure they had the right people guiding them along the way. My father was *only* concerned about academics and Mom took a passive-aggressive approach – which led to this:

A grown-ass man who refuses to let go! *I moderately believe I can play in the Minor Leagues for a Single-A team!*

My infatuation with baseball wasn't a secret and it's sad to know that I only lived in short distance from the famous Harlem RBI League – *a non-profit organization, underlying education, specializing in sending kids from urban communities to college*. But *more* importantly – the company emphasized teamwork and togetherness through… baseball!

Harlem RBI commercials commonly featured black and Hispanic kids, in full baseball uniforms, participating in an active league. The sport I loved was being used as a tool to *unite* children – an obvious grey area in my life… and my parents dropped the ball!

The organization didn't come about until the time my parents divorced – a time when Harlem was *vicious*, and genocide was a blip on the radar. So, quite possibly, I wouldn't have joined in fear of my safety, but the opportunity to get involved with extracurricular activities was there. Surrounding myself with kids who looked like me, and shared the same sporting interest, could've been huge! Who knows, maybe I'd be on the verge of having my number retired by the Mets.

Today, Harlem RBI goes by the name, "DREAM". Keeping in tune with their baseball mantra, the company uses the image of a *home plate* as their logo.

WEATHER WOES

Baseball is best suited for the warmer months – bottom line. There's good reason why many American-born players are from warm weather climates, while most foreign-born players originate in countries in the Caribbean and South America. *You can play year-round when you live closer to the fuckin' equator!*

For those of you in warmer climates who desperately wanted to grow up in New York City? We could've made an impactful trade: *My New York City bright lights, for your California sun (minus the earthquakes).* That would've been a steal!

This "Global Warming" stuff is 21st century mumbo jumbo. There may be other parts of the country that no longer experience winter but ask anyone along the northeast corridor about our winter season. One word: Dreadful! Whether it's 50 degrees in December or 15, it isn't easy convincing kids to show up to a baseball field when they're constantly sucking up mucus.

That leads me to another problem: Convincing kids! A standard baseball game requires two teams of nine players – but what happens when you're short a few guys? *You improvise!* Three-on-three games were common (and enjoyable), but will the average kid enjoy an undermanned game? Highly unlikely. Outside of a few friends, I couldn't find enough baseball diehards to play with.

One summer afternoon, I distinctly remember becoming extremely bored. I'd asked Gran to take me to the schoolyard after work – the very same schoolyard where I became a "legend". My only hope was to find a few kids to play catch and maybe take a few swings. After she obliged, we arrived at the park... where I was left standing in the empty baseball field, as I watched a group of kids circle around the basketball court! *For fuck's sakes, it was August – baseball season! Baseball players are referred to as "The Boys of Summer!" What gives???*

Without any other options, I asked Gran if she could toss a few balls my way, granting me an opportunity to imitate the swings of my favorite players. She was my only hope. From about thirty feet away, she'd release high arching pitches (with the tennis ball, of course) that I'd crush over the left field fence, to her amazement. There she was, in the sweltering heat, jheri curl juice dripping from her forehead, appeasing her grandson after an unceasing day. How could I ever thank her? *I still get choked up thinking about it.*

When it wasn't the schoolyard, we'd walk down the block (from the house) where she'd sit on a stationary bench and chat with a few familiar faces from the neighborhood. Next to the bench was the side wall to a high-rise luxury apartment building, which is where I worked on pitching accuracy. I created an imaginary strike zone and practiced aiming the tennis ball into the imaginary box. But once Gran's arthritis flared, it was time to go back inside.

"Alright, boy, that's enough for today!"

I'm reminded of those moments anytime I visit the old neighborhood (and I'm sure my daughter has grown tired of my constant pointing out that wall), but this was my playground... when there weren't kids around to breathe life into a lifeless sport. Nonetheless, I couldn't allow the limitations of the city to impede my dreams.

As years passed, the sexy game became basketball. You can always join a pick-up game around the city and it only takes two people to have a world of fun. Finding a handful of kids to play baseball was demanding, it seemed liked I'd need to make a transition to another sport.

EXTRA INNINGS

I moved back in with Mom the following summer – a little too late in the season to join a little league team. But the goal remained, to stake my claim as someone to be reckoned with – once we narrowed down the search for a little league home. Soon, I'd put on a uniform, attempting to show the world what I was made of. But to my surprise, I'd endure more pain than joy.

* * * * *

Chapter Tidbits:

- I've been known to call out sick on Opening Day.
- I'm an avid watcher of women's college softball and the men's college World Series.
- I was a long-time subscriber to *Baseball Digest*, as a child.
- I'm an active participant in fantasy baseball.
- I still envision crushing a homerun at the field in Williamsport, PA – home of the Little League World Series.
- My bucket list includes visits to every Major League ballpark (I've only been to four, so far) and the baseball Hall of Fame museum.

- One of my goals is to coach a group of little leaguers (ages 10-13).
- The 1991 World Series ranks as my all-time favorite series.
- I hope to build a team of minority baseball enthusiasts to provide funding for baseball academies in select urban cities.

Chapter Seven: Big Feet, Big Roaches: My Teenage Agony

A few things to keep in mind as you read this chapter. I don't claim to be a psychologist, but I take great pride in being a good evaluator. Okay, enough tip-toeing around – I believe my observation skills are freakin' immeasurable! There! It's a skill you tend to master, especially when you've spent most of your childhood alone…

* * * * *

The cooler the season, the humbler we are – which of course is why I love the fall. A chill in the air generally means less bodies outside and more pleasantries as the holidays approach:

"After you, kind Sir…"

"No, no, I insist, after you!"

People are more inclined to hold doors at department stores, drivers will adhere to speed limits (unless, of course, they're from NYC), tempers don't flare as much, and the world is a friendlier place.

The summer, on the other hand, can have a contrary effect on the human brain. The warmth allows for more scantily clad women, conceit and greater attitudes. There are plenty of smiling faces, coupled with the same amount of eye-rolling.

Women are suddenly too good for their own good… and men? Well, we're driven by testosterone, which means conversations are livelier, we attempt to hit 100 MPH on the speedometer – everywhere – and the music volume in our cars is unwarranted.

And lest we forget, urban neighborhoods: *'Tis the season for guns to be drawn at the speed of a cowboy in a western flick!* (I'll never understand this.) During the summer, many neighborhoods are under siege by violence. The residents are hot, hostile and helpless. As we emerge from our winter-long cocoons, the summer allows us to spread our wings for a *mere* two and a half months. Let me take you to my summer in Brooklyn, where I experienced a little of everything…

HELLO BROOKLYN!

On this sizzling late July day, *Carter* and I did what we'd often do on the mornings after a sleepover – *wake up, stuff our faces with the sustenance of Pop-Tarts, play a few hours of NBA Jam on the Super Nintendo... THEN, brush our teeth, before heading outside to shoot hoops. Let's just say morning breath was the least of our worries.*

Carter Brandon Stephens lived a few blocks down from the house – the only other black kid in the predominately Italian neighborhood of *Gravesend.* Living in Gravesend was the equivalent of a white family living in Harlem: You wanted to embrace the diversity, but deep down, it didn't feel right. *To be frank, we had no business living there.*

Carter was the godson of Terrance, Mom's boyfriend; we mingled in the years following my parents' divorce. I'd often attend his basketball games on my weekend visits to East New York, as Carter played on a team coached by Terrance and Carter's dad, *Mr. Stephens.*

Terrance was a childhood friend of Mr. Stephens. The two were inseparable – almost brotherlike. Together, they starred on their Brooklyn high school football team and in due course, took a stab at attending the same college in Virginia. However, a severe knee injury suffered by Terrance forced him to leave school prematurely, moving back into his parents' East New York home – while Mr. Stephens went on to graduate.

Years after a fire destroyed Terrance's parents' home, at the suggestion of one of his Post Office colleagues, Terrance and his folks ventured out to Gravesend, where they found a single-family home with a basement. Mr. Stephens, who didn't have much success on the job front in Virginia, moved back north – with a fiancé and newborn, Carter, in tow.

The young family returned to Mr. Stephens old stomping grounds, where they lived in a tiny apartment until enough money was saved to pursue a bigger home. As the years progressed, the neighborhood saw a spike in crime and at the urging of Terrance, the couple packed up their belongings and moved to Gravesend shortly after their wedding day.

A switch to the quiet, *family-oriented,* neighborhood, was intended to benefit all. The quality of life was peerless and the neighboring high schools – Lafayette and Lincoln, were perfect fits for when the time arrived.

Lincoln had a strong basketball program, as Coney Island legend, Stephon Marbury, was making a name for himself at the time, while former Mets relief pitcher, John Franco, attended the baseball-strong Lafayette during the mid-seventies. Two staple names in New York sports.

Carter hoped to become the next big two-sport star, possessing a quick bat at the plate, incredible speed, poise and a basketball IQ to rival a few pros. He certainly had all the tools to make a name for himself. *I was just over the moon to finally have someone consistently around to play with, sharing my same passion for sports.*

A TREE GROWS IN BROOKLYN

Still set on making the Major Leagues, I experienced a sudden growth spurt over the summer and began flirting with the idea of playing basketball full-time. The sport wasn't new to me, I'd always enjoyed playing, but it *wasn't* baseball… nothing was.

Carter and I practically lived at the park and if we weren't keyed in on a competitive baseball game (where we'd use a sponge ball in place of a hardball – a definite upgrade from the tennis ball), we'd participate in some grueling full court or half court action, with the best in the neighborhood. If the park was dead, that wouldn't stop us either. We'd use the opportunity to work on our two-man game:

- **The Pick and Roll** – An offensive play used by point guards and a big man (made famous by NBA legends, John Stockton and Karl Malone), where the big man sets a screen (pick) for the point guard (who is usually dribbling the basketball) and moves (rolls) towards the basket to receive the pass from the guard.
- **Court Vision** – A game where we'd concentrate on court awareness and using our instincts, without making obvious eye-contact. It required nifty foot work and quick passes.

Carter was shorter in stature and usually played point guard – the position I long desired. On account of our practice drills, I knew exactly where to be on the court when he had possession of the ball.

The constant movement worked to our advantage during some intense battles with the opposition, but oddly, I took exception to my growth spurt. I loved towering over other guys in the low-post, but my interest remained at a position not quite known for taller players.

I idolized the six-foot nine Earvin "Magic" Johnson when I caught him in the latter stages of his career. In the meantime, the six-foot seven Anfernee "Penny" Hardaway was quickly becoming my basketball hero. Their heights were unusual for the traditional *pint-sized* point guard position, but both guys enjoyed much success during their playing days.

That was all the proof I needed. I knew it was possible to achieve likeable success *if* I worked on a few mechanics. The confidence was there, I had the determination to be *good*... not *great* (which I will discuss).

With my agility and height advantage, I had the ability to see the court better than a lot of players my age. And then, there were my passing skills. I could literally make a pass with my eyes closed! The "no-look pass" was a featured move of Johnson (soon to be emulated by many others – particularly "Penny") *and* I was blown away by the players ability to look one way, while passing the ball in the opposite direction and fooling the cameraman in the process. It was... *magical!*

I studied Johnson's passing artistry on VHS tapes, but was fully convinced I'd be the second coming of Hardaway – who was quickly taking the league by storm. Every Saturday morning, I'd watch *NBA Inside Stuff* with Ahmad Rashad and Willow Bay, where Hardaway usually made the highlight reel. *Oooooh! What a pass!* I'd yell at the TV.

* * * * *

Author's Note: *One of the greatest games I ever watched occurred on Friday, December 16th, 1994 as the Orlando Magic visited the Golden State Warriors. The game aired on TNT and was a high-scoring affair with Orlando getting the victory. Penny's performance was one for the ages, executing some of the best passes I'd ever seen. I thought he was the best thing since sliced bread!*

* * * * *

My jump shot was solid, I was a quick, prowess defender with quality ball handling skills. All I needed was to convince the others that I could play the position. But I continued to find myself in the low-post, where I'd stubbornly play like a point guard! Until recent years, the center was considered one of the five positions on the court with the least amount of flare. Centers are typically the tallest players on the floor. Depending on the player, he is often known as the *rim protector.* But as the game evolved, so did the position and there was an upsurge of names who soon became legendary:

- Wilt Chamberlin
- Bill Russell
- Kareem Abdul-Jabbar
- Moses Malone
- Patrick Ewing
- Hakeem Olajuwon
- David Robinson
- Shaquille O'Neal

So, what was my deal and why wouldn't I embrace being the "main attraction" on the court? Because I've never enjoyed being the center of attention!

"He's tall and athletic... so he *must* be dominant!"

Wrong! Can I control a person's thoughts? No. Was their assumption off base? Not completely.

Sure, I could dominate, but I enjoyed being a *fly under the radar* type of guy, taking pleasure doing the opposite of one's belief. Simply put: I preferred the *shock value.*

"Wait, he can dominate *and* pass the ball like a point guard?!"

Yep! But my focus was to simply become a great passer. I was aware that point guards handled the ball 99 percent of the time as they're instructed to echo the coach's play-calling and with that comes a lot of pressure (and exposure), but the point guard's main objective is to get *teammates* involved! That's all I wanted to do.

When you're tall, you become the focal point by default. Playing center wouldn't allow for my desire to keep a low profile, since many of my teammates were trying to take advantage of my height sufficiency against the opposition.

Everyone knew I could score at will, but I got a rush positioning my teammates on the floor or running a fast break and hitting the trailer with an unsuspecting pass. Very few saw the beauty of making the pass (which sets up the play), too concerned with being "the man". That wasn't me.

There has been a metamorphosis of the center position as players today handle the basketball like point guards taking as many three-point shots as the primary shooters on the team. Equally alarming are the centers who take game-winning three-point shots or execute *crossover dribble moves*... à la point guards! That never happened back in the day. It's possible I was born about 25 years too early.

* * * * *

A couple of familiar faces arrived at the park for a two-on-two pickup game. I swear, it was as if the neighborhood had *black radar,* because the park only came alive *after* Carter and I showed up. But it was time for us to put on a show!

We had a thing for keeping the score close – just to make things interesting – before pulling away with the victory. With Carter's finesse guard play and my dominance in the post – *Anthony* and *Joey* were simply no match. After the game, win or lose, we'd come together and slap hands as a sign of respect. There were never any hard feelings, since a game could develop where we'd all be on the same team. Apart from basketball, we played sports according to the season. With football around the corner, there was a chance Anthony and Joey would be a part of a group of guys asked to tackle Carter in the snow. He was as elusive as a young Barry Sanders.

The playground was our field of dreams, serving as an all-purpose stadium far away from where I made a name for myself at P.S. 199. This was "home".

BROOKLYN BULLSHIT

Anthony and Joey went their separate ways, as the sky developed an overcast. Ever eager to improve, Carter and I used the opportunity to work on some more drills. We literally had to feel a rain drop on our brows before leaving.

A cool breeze swept through the playground, as I wiped beads of sweat from my forehead – à la Patrick Ewing at the free throw line. Taking a deep breath, it was time to put my leaping ability to the test and attempt to dunk the basketball like some of my favorite

NBA pros. The playground emptied, and the echo of the ball bouncing against the concrete was the only sound. Carter stood several feet away, egging me on.

I'd been palming basketballs since the age of ten, but I was still too short to execute the fast break *cradle dunk* performed by Julius "Dr. J" Erving in the 1983 NBA finals against the Lakers, where he cuffed the ball and put Michael Cooper on a poster. With the added height and my confidence growing, there wasn't a better time than now. I tightened the laces on my elongated black Nike Air Flights, dribbled some more, hoping to make the leap from the baseline of the court.

Houston, we have lift off... I soared into the air... arms stretched high... legs spread apart – like Michael Jordan in the 1988 Slam Dunk Contest. *Bong!* Rimmed it – taking a hard fall to the ground.

"You missed it by this much", said Carter, describing the distance with his fingers.

The clouds opened, a light drizzle calmly fell to the ground. The precipitation caught us by surprise, so we proceeded to wrap things up... just as a pine green car with four lively teens caught our immediate attention. The teenager seated on the passenger side poked his head out the window, turning my whole world upside down;

"Get out of the park, you fuckin' niggers!"

The comment was instantaneously met with laughter from the group as Carter and I stood there stunned. I made direct eye contact with the teen, unable to convey words before the car screeched off.

Everything was a blur in those ten seconds. What was I to say? We were outmanned, unarmed and it probably wasn't worth the risk. A few years earlier, Reverend Al Sharpton marched through the streets of Bensonhurst, Brooklyn, protesting the murder of an innocent black man – Yusef Hawkins – killed for being in the wrong place at the wrong time.

For those uninformed, Hawkins was falsely accused of an incredulous act, then attacked by a mob of white kids before he was later found dead. The news sent shockwaves through the city, escalating the existing racial tension from the recent Central Park rape charges (where five black males and one Hispanic male were accused of raping a white female) and the Howard Beach murder of an innocent black male. Seeking justice, Sharpton rallied a group of protesters, marching through the streets of Bensonhurst – a *predominately* Italian neighborhood, where their outcries were met with racial slurs and tossed watermelons.

We lived *minutes* away from Bensonhurst!

The actions of the residents proved what little regard they had for Hawkins and his indefensible murder. So, why would anyone care about us? Who would believe our story, had we challenged those teens? *Two innocent black kids, sparring with four Italian guys – in a primarily Italian neighborhood?* We had no chance.

It was the first time being called a *nigger and* it sucked the entire life out of me that summer. I looked at Carter as the car pulled off, but all he did was shake his head. The drizzle turned into a steady rain fall as we walked home.

"Don't worry about it, see you tomorrow", he said in a convincing tone.

* * * * *

The neighborhood was generally quiet unless children were outside playing – or the latest Top 40 hits resonated from passing cars. With a demographic consisting of *working families and retirees,* it seemed like an ideal place to raise kids. However, the lack of diversity was quite bothersome – even for a 12-year-old.

In a varied city such as New York, I couldn't quite grasp an *all (insert race here) neighborhood.* I completely understood how it could've started out that way during the city's early development – when 12 million European immigrants migrated through Ellis Island in the late 1800s. But these were the fuckin' 90s! No way should I walk anywhere to a sea of *one* color.

I formed a few friendships in the neighborhood through my involvement in sports – namely with a kid named *Giovanni,* who I shared a mutual respect for. But for obvious reasons, I was fairly aloof.

Carter lived in the area a couple of years longer (since I was still living with Gran) and had adapted to the ignorance of some of the neighbors. Either that, or he didn't understand the magnitude of the racial slur. But this was new territory for me.

I never encountered such hatred growing up on the Upper West Side of Manhattan where many of the faces didn't look like mine. Maybe a little ignorance from a cashier clerk who *didn't want to place money directly into my hand*, tossing it on the counter instead, or *maybe* an overzealous salesperson *watching my every move in a store,* but most went about their business. After the park incident, my antennas went up. There were plenty of *double take* moments in the neighborhood, where people couldn't believe their eyes!

Black people?! It honestly felt like *The Truman Show.* My life was under surveillance.

Occasionally, we'd spot other blacks in the area (on the weekend, at the grocery store) and instead of exchanging warm greetings... we'd stare (of course). To be fair, I suppose all parties were earnestly trying to figure out what the other was doing in this part of town, but after a certain hour, it was only us and the Stephens family who remained.

I know there's got to be more of us around here somewhere? Where does everybody live? I found my answer soon enough.

"CONEY ISLAND, ASTROLAND PARK FOR A TIME YOU WON'T FORGET!"

You're not a true New Yorker if you don't remember this commercial jingle. The commercial aired on local TV stations throughout the summer, enticing families to head over to Coney Island – one of eleven New York City beaches.

* * * * *

Looking to recover from the park debacle, Carter invited me to join him and a couple of childhood friends who were visiting from his old East New York neighborhood. *Great, now they'll be four of us roaming around Gravesend!*

I'd become housebound since the incident, burning the electricity, playing *Mortal Kombat,* while Mom and Terrance were at work. I wasn't quite ready to get out of this funk, but desperately needed to try.

The heat on this day was intense and the park was as silent as the grave. To beat the temperature, the group had the *brilliant* idea to bike over to Coney Island. Although we lived only 15 minutes away, some time had passed since my last visit and the thought of partaking in something outside of "the norm" excited me. Grabbing my 6-speed bike, I made the five-minute trip to Carter's – where I was greeted by the Dynamic Duo.

I met *Shane* and *Adrian* (brothers) on a few occasions during my weekend summer visits to Brooklyn after my parents split. They were complex individuals: calm and mild mannered around adults, but belligerent when adults weren't around.

Playtime with these two usually meant something physical:

- Wrestling
- Slap-boxing
- Or basketball – where you were bound for a bloody lip, a few abrasions and several "timeouts"!

Calling timeout was the only way they'd show you mercy... but you'd better scream it at the top of your lungs. And if they spotted a single tear on your face, you were called a pussy right on the spot... as blood trickled from your lip. There was no crying allowed!

You had to defend yourself around these guys and they were going to make certain you became a *man*, even if you were still a child and hadn't signed up for the job. That was the East New York in them. Products of their environment and tougher than a two-dollar steak!

Shane and Adrian were the types who'd punch you dead in the chest (or slap your face for the fun of it) if the spirit moved them. I took a few strikes from the guys after making the careless mistake of *bragging* when I beat them both in *Street Fighter II. They were no match for Guile (that was my guy) – but little did I know they'd take losing so hard.*

If you got under their skin, they'd chase you around the house, trying to decapitate you. And if successful? They were generous enough to reattach your head for you. Such gentlemen. It was a necessary evil to surround myself with older, aggressive boys, which is why Mom didn't do anything when I'd go to her bitchin' and moaning about their physicality. She knew how beneficial getting roughed up was. I'd been sheltered for too long.

* * * * *

Carter's parents kept the air conditioner on full blast during hot days – so, we could all look forward to a little R&R afterwards. Before leaving, Mr. Stephens mentioned he'd order a couple of pizzas upon our return. It was hard to resist pizza, but I wanted nothing to do with anything *Italian...* not after the incident.

Tom Cochran's, "Life is a Highway", played in my head, as I attempted a pop-a-wheelie, trying my hardest to be cool. Riding aimlessly through the neighborhood – free as a bird, I'd finally put the park incident behind me. It felt good to be back on my feet. Carter led the way, with Adrian riding his back pegs, as Shane and I trailed. It was quite amusing watching sixteen-year-old Shane attempt to steer Carter's eight-year old brother's bike, yet he made it work. He even managed to throw in a wheelie himself – making it look much cooler than when I tried.

As expected, we caught the eyes of many in the neighborhood, particularly three older gentlemen who were sitting in front of a deli *shooting the breeze.* Their conversation ended abruptly, after spotting us as we drifted through their neck of the woods. It was as if they saw ghosts! *Although, I'm sure their first inclination was to call the Police and not the Ghostbusters!*

Drawing near our destination, I noticed a momentous shift in the community. The surrounding homes and the people in the area didn't look anything like what I'd grown accustomed to. No longer did I spot single-family houses and family owned shops. We were surrounded by *apartment buildings* and people of color! *So, this is where all the black people wandered off to?!*

I was unsure if this called for a moment of celebration... or making a run for dear life! Those *apartment buildings* looked vaguely familiar. Many New Yorkers come from apartment settings, but you *absolutely* know it when you come across the projects! The dynamics are *that* different. There's a menacing look to the buildings and if you're not familiar with the area you become quite unnerved. Of course, there are many great people who reside in the projects, but the tenants look battled tested and ready – as do the neighboring kids. It all appears intimidating from the outside looking in.

If you had a friend who lived in the projects (and sought permission from your parents to visit) the first words out of their mouths was generally: "No!", "Hell no!" or "Be *extremely* careful!"

City projects are usually listed as *Houses* at the front of the property, but upon our arrival, I couldn't find a *white picket fence or manicured lawn* for shit! We'd just bike over to the *Marlboro Houses...*

"Yo, let's cut into this park!" Shane yelled from behind.

But what about Coney… Never mind. It was too hot and I wasn't in the mood to be called a *punk, pussy, bitch* or any other "terms of endearment" from the guys.

Shane spotted a gated dirt field with ramps ideal for bike stunts and that's when a feeling of apprehension hit. But, I didn't want to be the lone person in the group to object our invasion of Marlboro. As we waited for the light to change at the intersection, Carter (always the guy looking to appease the world) turned his wheel into the direction of those *eerie* brick red buildings.

Sigh… an alarm must have set off the moment we touched ground.

*Intruders, intruders! *Loud Sirens**

I didn't even get a chance to attempt a measly stunt. Within minutes we were surrounded, by five thugs who looked like they hadn't bathed in weeks. They appeared to have a hankering for unfamiliar faces and nice bikes. *Where did these guys come from and most importantly, how dare we have fun on THEIR property?!*

Someone wearing a holey grey tank top stood in the path of Carter and Adrian, while another dude circled around and pulled the back wheel from behind them. Adrian tried to put his "East New York hand skills" to work, squaring up as if he was ready to slap box – but the two goons took off with the bike. Carter was a spectator through it all, sitting motionless from the ground. He wasn't equipped for this type of firestorm… neither was I.

While the drama unfolded, I was approached by a tag team resembling NBA players – one guy sporting a Charles Barkley U.S.A. Olympic team jersey, while the other was shirtless – wearing basketball shorts and knee-high socks. The smell of sweat and non-deodorized underarms roamed through the air.

Shane tried to intervene, but the fifth guy (chubby, but nifty) diverted his attention by making a move towards Carter's little brother's bike. Without much effort, the two NBA rejects yanked my wheels from beneath me with *superhuman* strength!

What was all the aggression for? I didn't show any fight and would've graciously handed over the bike had they asked! For all one knows, maybe they expected more bite due to my height. They obviously didn't know me.

Shane managed to escape to the outside of the gated area, while the thieves took off laughing. As for the chubby guy? He trotted across the field, holding up his shorts, shielding what appeared to be a gun. Not only was that fat fuck a decoy – but he was fully armed, I was the only one who noticed!

We were down to one bike – the bike of a 3rd grader. The streamers from the handlebars flapped in the warm breeze, as we walked back home trying to make sense of what had just occurred. Had we *only* stuck to our original plan. I couldn't understand the sudden turn of events, but I was on the prowl for answers. The affairs were just a trailer to the real world and it was time to put on my big boy pants.

TIED UP IN A BROOKLYN BASEMENT

Mom met Terrance at her job where he frequently dropped off mail. They dated for some time, but once the divorce with my father was finalized, she'd transitioned into his parents' basement – which is where I called "home" until I was 18.

The original plan was to tough it out at Joan of Arc Middle School until the end of 8th grade – but that required more years under Gran's roof. With the school not living up to expectations and my teen years rapidly approaching, it was deemed best to part ways. *Besides, I'm not sure how well Gran and I would've meshed with a 9 o'clock bedtime as a teenager!*

Initially, the move to Gravesend was met with great interest. I was prepared to transfer to a school right down the street and Carter lived only minutes away. But with the recent unrest of the summer, I wondered if I'd made the wrong decision.

It was a huge adjustment leaving the confinement of Gran's apartment for a house that didn't quite feel like home. Terrance and I were quite cordial, but it was the first time I'd live with a man who wasn't my father. And, I wasn't exactly thrilled on the idea of living in a basement, even with the assurance that it was *only* temporary.

As one can imagine, we had very little privacy. My bedroom was used as the passageway to their bedroom, and the exit to the front entrance of the basement. We used *a divider* to section off the two rooms in the railroad-styled home. The ceilings were very low, causing a hunch-back posture during my growth spurt and there were those stimulating moments when we experienced the elements of nature:

- Excessive flooding (from torrential downpours)
- Field mice (from the backyard)
- Insects – LARGE insects

They weren't your everyday critters running through the kitchen cabinets leaving excrement everywhere. No! I'm talking water bugs! Nasty looking creatures about the size of a hardboiled egg. Those sons of bitches were faster than anything I'd ever seen – *jet-like speed with the ability to fly!* According to scientists, they make great food supply for birds… but why on earth were they inside my freakin' house?!

Our rooms were within distance of the boiler room (a likeable breeding spot) and there was a drain outside our front door where the bugs congregated during rainfalls. If Mom wanted the kitchen trash taken out, I'd take a quick peek to the ground. *Can I take out the trash tomorrow?*

My main concern was keeping these vermin out of my room and I was usually scared out of my wits, keeping a broom close by in case I spotted one. It took some time to develop the intestinal fortitude to kill them, but after a water bug embarrassingly *chased* me and Mom from my bedroom – it was war! *You read that correctly, CHASED!*

Have I experienced roaches before? Without question. That's a part of life in the big city (the cleanliness of your neighbors has a lot to do with it as well). But these guys were different. Roaches tend to run *away* when sensing danger – water bugs run *towards* you. They are truly an anomaly. Fed up with being a victim in my home, it was time to grow some balls – literally and figuratively. Puberty extended its hand, which I greeted with a firm handshake. I needed to man up.

As a child, I absorbed a lot of information from *MacGyver,* looking to formulate a plan like Richard Dean Anderson. I started building traps around my room (using random gadgets) in case an enlarged insect (or rodent) decided to pay a visit. During the project, I sealed many cracks in the walls using duct tape. I surrounded my twin sized bed with the unpleasant scent of mothballs hoping to keep the insanity away. *Had I known beforehand that none of this would work… I would've saved myself the time and effort.*

Duct tape did absolutely nothing but anger the bugs. Each night, around 1 a.m., they'd participate in what sounded like a track meet, *sprinting through the walls, handing off the baton, in search of Olympic Gold.* Picture the sound of a fast typist, or someone striking their nails rapidly against a desk: *click, click, click, click, click.* I dealt with that *all-night long.* Lionel Ritchie would've been so proud.

The episode ended right around bed time… *their* bed time, which unfortunately was rise and shine for me. I'd just spent the entire night staring at the ceiling and the bags under my eyes were to die for. There wasn't a night more disturbing than when I had my very first *threesome.* Yep, ménage a trois.

From a dead sleep, I suddenly felt a tickling sensation against my leg – hoping to awaken to Reggae artist, Patra *and* the lead singer of the group, Jade, grinding against my leg preparing to snatch away my virginity. Instead, I was in for another treat. I reached over to the lamp and there they were… *two* beetles exposed between my sheets! *For the love of God, I hope I had on protection – or there could be a horde of fatherless half-human, half-beetle babies out in the world, with a beetle mother looking for her child support!*

As the follies continued, I was left with no choice but to sleep with a night light, which I embarrassingly did… well into my high school years! I know what some of you are thinking – *It could've been worse… be thankful you had a roof over your head…* Yeah, yeah, yeah! I get it. But this was absurd, and I wouldn't put up with it much longer.

To combat the disturbances, I started crashing over at Carter's place, almost exclusively on the weekend and nightly during the summer. Thankfully, his family accommodated my intrusion.

Mom had enough. She inquired about a move-out date, realizing Terrance had become a little *too comfortable* with the basement arrangement. He often appeared nonchalant, expressing the desire to finish paying off a few bills and setting aside more money for our next move as a family. Sadly, it never happened.

As for his take on the bug crisis? He thought we were simply overreacting:

"They're just bugs!" he'd say, snickering.

The hell they were!

* * * * *

Chapter Tidbits:

Not only was I robbed of my bike in Brooklyn, but years later I became a victim of another robbery – this time, jewelry. After working as a summer intern, I purchased an expensive gold chain. During an ostentatious act on my part – where I refused to tuck my chain, (because why should anyone have to tuck their jewelry?!) my neck became food for an approaching gang. In typical robbery fashion, the robber brandished a weapon and I paid the price. Naturally, I was incensed and quite rattled, but thankfully, unharmed. Welcome to Brooklyn.

Chapter Eight: The Last ~~GREAT~~ *ADEQUATE* Decade!

Eagerly awaiting the start of 7th grade, I had a moment to reflect on the past school year and the aftermath of the summer. A summer which saw the Mets finish in last place with 103 losses, an ugly hate crime and a robbery in broad daylight! Talk about a cruel summer... Bananarama had NOTHING on me!

September was finally here. A call for cooler weather and hopefully, less contention, as I prepared to transition to a new school.

* * * * *

Transferring schools is never easy, but under the circumstances, it was very necessary. On the first day at Joan of Arc, Mom and I noticed *three* bullet holes staring back at us inside of my homeroom class, as we sat quietly with the other parents and students. I gave her a look of despair – which she promptly ignored.

The school was only a few blocks from Harlem (so that *could've* explained the tomfoolery), but I needed to overlook the fact that I was attending a place resembling Paterson Eastside High (from the movie *Lean on Me*) and shift my focus toward having a productive year. Maybe the school wouldn't be so bad...

"Yo! We gon' fuck y'all up on Friday!"

Then again...

That was *Peaches* and her clique threatening us days into the new semester. Aaah! Good ol' "Freshman Friday" – that *special* time of year where a bullying dyke (and lackeys) threatened to jump underclassmen after the three o'clock dismissal. I don't think I left school any faster than on that day!

Through 6th grade, I was constantly teased by *James Roker,* which eventually led to my first fist fight, having grown tired of his act. Naturally, we went on to become friends (especially since I blackened his eye), but each day at the school felt like my last. *To this day, I still don't know how I made it out of there alive!* Once June arrived, I was on the *first thing smokin'!* – one and done... like a college freshman basketball star making the leap into the NBA. Get me outta here!

NEW SCHOOL, SAME RULES

I.S. 228 was highly rated in the New York City middle school guidebook and based on the calculated photos, appeared to be a diverse environment. The assistant principal was a middle-aged black woman and many people of color taught various subjects. *Sometimes, a picture can be worth a thousand words.* What puzzled me most was how the school sat right in the middle of my Gravesend neighborhood – the same area of the verbal assault that took place a couple of months earlier! How can this be?

As the new kid on the block, I knew making friends wouldn't be easy considering many of the students established friendships the previous year – while I was praying to God to see another day while attending Joan of Arc. But how would I adapt to the new environment? Would the students welcome me with open arms? The anticipation was quite disconcerting.

* * * * *

"There's that crispy critter, over there!"

Welp… it was business as usual! Already months in at the new school and *Patricia McDonald* continued making my life a living hell. I made the blunder of missing my name during attendance, while *Ms. Weiss,* a substitute teacher, struggled to get the attention of the disorderly class. Unfortunately, I was in the middle of a lively baseball conversation with my new pal, *Zepan*.

I genuinely felt bad for Ms. Weiss, who was much older than the regular teachers and obviously soft-spoken… a little too soft. She wasn't equipped to handle such an unruly collection of misfits, but had she *only* announced my name louder, I would've dodged the aftermath of Patricia's comment: Utter laughter!

I was the butt of yet another *black joke* from someone identifying as black. Just another day in paradise. What was her deal?

It wasn't a secret that I was the school "newbie", but I kept to myself and wasn't a part of any circle that rivaled hers. She was always on the verbal attack – as if she was bothered by my mere presence. It's a forgone conclusion there could've been an inkling of an attraction on her end... but try convincing that to 12-year-old me!

Patricia was by far one of the most attractive girls in the school and she knew it. I used to watch her do this thing with her eyes, where she'd squint amid conversation – almost as if she was struggling with her vision. I thought it was the hottest thing! She'd also execute the 'impaired vision' act when flirting with guys, but I knew I didn't stand a chance.

Patricia was into the "rough around the edges" types sporting the latest fashions. I was no slouch in the fashion department, commonly seen in the hottest *big logo* shirts from Hugo Boss, Cross Colours, Tommy Hilfiger and Guess (I also had a shit load of flannel – hey, it was the nineties!), but I'd have to get used to settling as her whipping boy.

What confused me was Patricia's attraction to *Kevinn Kurtis.* The fact he spelled his first name with two 'N's' was disturbing enough, but she was head over heels for this skinny, unathletic dude *of my complexion*, with an uncomfortable-looking gap between his teeth. It was as wide as a football goal post! In addition, Kevinn wore a jheri curl. It was common knowledge that he was only interested in white girls. In fact, he was the *only* black kid I'd ever been around to have white girls fighting over him!

Wait... they're fighting over this Pookie (from New Jack City) - in-the-face looking guy? I'd think. I must admit, he was a legit ladies man with a distinct swagger. As much as I disliked him, he dressed well and showed a pile of confidence. The girls swarmed to this clown like flies to manure. *So, all I needed was an S-curl and a gap between my teeth?? You've got to be kidding me!*

* * * * *

The only person not doubled over in laughter after Patricia's comment was Zepan – my good ol' pudgy friend of Indian descent, who didn't have many friends himself. He was the quintessential "eat lunch in the cafeteria alone guy", usually spotted with his hand against his right cheek and a look of depression on his face. We ran into several students exhibiting that very same look and that's when Zepan and I took notice. *Let's form an alliance!*

Collectively, we were a group of oddities, soon to be known as the "Geek Squad" (ahem! the *original* Geek Squad) – a bunch of bookworms who loved a good joke, TV and sports. *My kind of guys!*

What made us such an amazing group? We were of different ethnicities, with very distinct personalities. My athletic ability may have given me a slight edge in popularity, but together, we were one. Most importantly, there was no room for egos.

* * * * *

As my range of friends broadened, a buzz started going around the school. The piece de resistance? I played sports.

"This new guy, Ernest, can play ball!"

Thank goodness for Phys-Ed! Phys-Ed was scheduled twice a week, as a handful of homerooms shared the gym for an hour. This was my time to shine. As sports thrived on business, replica jerseys became a hot purchase for children. It was the era of Starter hats and Champion jackets, as sports fans wanted to feel like they were a part of their favorite teams. Christmas arrived, and I stocked up on sports attire – namely a Penny Hardaway Orlando Magic Away jersey, which I'd wear during gym class (and occasionally to bed).

A new student arrived in my homeroom – *John Celinski:* a blonde-haired, freckle faced, polished kid, who tied sweaters around his neck. John and his family were well off financially and he wouldn't hesitate to remind you. Not only was he academically and athletically gifted, but he had an older brother who was being heavily recruited by a major university to become their starting quarterback. *Talk about growing up with a silver spoon in your mouth!*

John was pompous at times, making plenty of enemies. The Italian students in homeroom were usually ready to punch him square in the mouth and the girls loathed him on sight. But to his credit, he was smart, athletic and fortunately for the athletic blood in homeroom – good at basketball!

Our paths to the school were similar and likely the reason we gelled. We'd team up with another athlete during Phys-Ed who shared our homeroom class; *Vito Gagliano.*

Vito couldn't stand John; he hated his *parted-down-the-middle hair and* the fact he often bragged about being good at golf.

"Look at ya heeeair!" he'd say in his heavy Italian accent.

And if John attempted to defend himself?

"Get outta heeeeaaa! Go somewhere and play golf!" Vito replied, shooing him away.

Vito often teased John about his older brother being a scrub at football (even though he'd never seen him play), promising to one-day barge through the offensive line and sack him – if they ever crossed paths in the NFL. He was usually very animated during his portrayal, making a booming sound with his voice, with spit flying everywhere!

HAHAHAHA! The comment was usually met with laughter, ending with John turning beet red. The kid was as sensitive as a nipple, refusing to speak for the rest of the day. *Welcome to my world, John!*

I'd always get a good laugh out of the two rivals, but we worked well together on the basketball court. Our skills eventually opened the eyes of one of the best ball players in the school, who asked us to participate in *full court games* from time to time. *Graduating from half court to full court was a BIG deal.*

"Vito! You and the *Penny dude* down?"

Cameron Marshall and Vito were familiar with each other from the previous year, but John and I were the new kids in town. *Besides, I didn't mind being called "the Penny Dude".* I suspect Cameron chose me (instead of John) because of my height.

As I mentioned, with size comes the perception of someone potentially skilled at basketball. I suppose he caught wind of my ability, looking for someone good enough to defend him at point guard. He had a lot of shake and bake moves and the level of competition during gym class was bleak.

Hmmm, so, if Cameron played point guard and I was expected to defend him – Vito shouldn't have a problem relinquishing ball handling duty to me for my showdown with Cameron. Vito was the better shooter in our starting five, but he'd need someone capable of dishing him the ball. My eyes widened at the thought. Who better than me? The point guard position was all mine – finally, I arrived…

* * * * *

"Ewww, Shanice! Why you wanna talk to chocolate boy?!"

Okay, so *maybe* I got a little ahead of myself. After reading the horoscopes for weeks, wondering when my "big day" would arrive… it happened – I managed to trigger the hormones of *Shanice Swanson*, Patricia McDonald's best friend. *Yes, I read the horoscopes hoping to find love.* Maybe Shanice felt some pity for how I was being treated by her friend, or perhaps I wasn't as bad looking as I'd been made to feel. But I wanted to know why she chose me? What was she up to?

We didn't travel in the same packs – Shanice hung out with Patricia and a group of rowdy Coney Island girls who liked "bad boys", while I attached myself to kids who carried *baseball almanacs* in their backpacks. Yet, there she was – in all her beauty, approaching during recess with a *perfume-scented* folded letter that if I smelled today, I would promptly link to her.

It was your typical *do you have a girlfriend? Yes or No* letter, but Shanice was brave enough to include an essay. *An essay?! Was this a girl after my own heart?* I read the letter repeatedly that evening to the point where I could recite it word for word, answering *'no'* to her girlfriend question, handing it back the next day.

It was official – I had a girlfriend! After receiving the news, Patricia informed her ghetto friends, ribbing me during lunch.

"Ernest why aren't you sitting with your *gurlllfriend* at our table?"

Oh, so ~~this bitch~~ *she* knew my name after all. I was too ashamed to face a group of kids I had nothing in common with – even if it made Shanice feel bad. I sat at one table, she sat at the other and we broke up in roughly three weeks! Hell, we never even kissed. It was my shortest "relationship" on record.

PICK A SIDE

The two groups didn't interact much, but I spent an equal amount of time with the *Jocks* and *the Geek Squad.* Vito and I bonded through our interest in sports, but he'd commonly question my loyalty since I primarily sat with Zepan and the guys, during lunch.

"Don't sit with dose guys, sit ova heea!"

You'd have to give me a good reason why. One thing is certain; I am loyal to the one-hundredth power – unless something catastrophic happens in the relationship to cause a shift. Collectively, the guys all meant a great deal to me and I wasn't going to pick sides.

Vito invited me to his home more times than I could count, where we'd collide in some very intense games of NHL Hockey on the Sega Genesis. His backyard was also the sight of some epic one-on-one battles, where we'd attempt to find out who could reign supreme in basketball. We were relatively close in distance and strangely, I was comfortable strolling through *his* predominately Italian Gravesend neighborhood more than my own.

His dad was highly respected, and Vito was the popular jock in the neighborhood who kept a very small circle. To my surprise, his family generally rolled out the red-carpet upon my arrival. *Imagine that?*

Sports was life for Vito. He was an exceptional little league player with enough trophies and newspaper clippings throughout his home to prove his legitimacy. There wasn't a sport he couldn't play… except for golf (although it wouldn't surprise me if he hit a few hole in ones).

We had some amazing times talking shit to each other – but never anything personal. He'd clown me for liking the Mets and Jets, because, again, who would choose two historically losing franchises over the conquering Yankees and Giants? Vito also played for a little league that rivaled the one I soon joined.

"Why would you play ova dare?!"

I'm uncertain if we would've remained friends over the years, as the social climate on race has taken a turn for the worse. If we're being honest, how many black and Italian males grow up as best buds? But for what it was worth, Vito was a good dude and I'm still amazed to have not heard his name mentioned on ESPN over the years. The kid was extremely talented and I thoroughly enjoyed our friendship.

GEEK SQUAD

- Zepan was often two-fold; witty, with great one-liner comebacks, but quiet as a church mouse.
- *Gerald*, kept to himself, but enjoyed reading and sharing a good laugh.
- *Slavik* was a ball of energy and quite skillful at telling jokes (another buddy who welcomed me into his home).

- *Conner* was the wise-ass of the group, with a strong desire to be hip – but couldn't help receiving A's on every test.

And then, there was *Harry*. We probably had the most in common – tall, quiet, fans of the arts *and Married with Children* junkies. Harry usually sat in class drawing pictures of fictitious heavy metal stars, while teachers bored us with their spiel.

Our entire group was a bunch of bright guys, but I was dumbfounded at Harry's level of success while being inattentive in class. His thick Russian accent and fear of being teased, usually kept him away from participating. *Again, welcome to my world, brother!*

Harry spoke and understood English just fine, but he used the language barrier as an excuse to escape being called on. Just when the class expected him to be a complete failure – he'd have another trick up his sleeve.

"Harry, 98 percent – nice job!"

Teachers only announced the names and grades of the students who passed, while the unlucky ones *only* heard their names:

"Zepan…"

I couldn't understand Zepan. He was honestly one of the brightest guys I knew, but he wouldn't study to save his life! I watched him wing it for the whole semester, settling for *barely passing* grades. He simply didn't care. At times, Zepan had test scores rivaling the speed limit of a school zone neighborhood! In comedic fashion, he'd crumple the paper and fling it to an isolated area of the classroom. I'd roll in the aisles! But one thing is for certain, if you'd ask him *how many complete games Jim Palmer had for the Baltimore Orioles in 1975?* he'd answer convincingly:

"Twenty-five!"

Through Zepan, I learned you can be smart *without* being book smart.

* * * * *

Harry's ability to retain information was impeccable and I tried picking his brain as much as I could. *How can I scribble in my notebook for a whole period and still have a near 4.0 GPA?* There were whispers that he was older than his listed age, as Harry was the only guy in school with a full moustache. But that didn't concern me. We were tight and I had his back... except for that one afternoon during lunch when tensions arose in the cafeteria.

Our good ol' friend with the two N's, Kevinn, accused Harry of skipping him on the lunch line – which Harry vehemently denied. The two jawed back and forth, before Kevinn went on the personal attack... *after all, what else would you have expected?*

"Get the fuck outta here with that stank ass breath! – you weren't in front of me – you KNOW you were skipping the line!"

Admittedly, Harry's breath did smell like a combination of *cheese and Lipton tea,* but the rest of Kevinn's claim was preposterous. Henry wouldn't have skipped anyone. Moreover, that was my pal – and nobody talks about my friend!

Now angry, I took a deep breath and raced over to the vending machine... to purchase an Arizona Iced Tea. I needed to cool off with a cold beverage – before the fight started. *Surely, you didn't think I was joining in on the fight, did you?*

The two squared off – Kevinn in a *slap boxing street-style position* and Harry... in a *Fighting Irish Stance* (à la the Notre Dame Fighting Irish logo). Oh boy.

Harry couldn't evade the teasing this time! The students in the cafeteria snickered wildly, pointing at his unorthodox pose, while Kevinn took a few uncontrolled swings. Harry, standing about a foot taller than Kevinn, showed some nifty footwork, backpedaling from Kevinn's haymakers, throwing a quick jab of his own. Finally, the school officials rushed to the scene, breaking up the melee. The odds were heavily stacked against Harry. No way was he supposed to pull through against the chick magnet!

In the end, Harry proved to be the Geek Squad member with the biggest heart. He was a man's man, with or without the moustache. If I had the cojones, I would've put down my drink, raced over and sucker punched Kevinn for the ridiculous spelling of his first name. Instead, I watched Harry, like a proud dad. Way to represent!

BACK IN THE SUMMER OF '94

We ran laps around the park, in preparation for the upcoming season, as snow flurries dropped from the sky. It was late February, but the Little League season was rapidly approaching. Carter was already a member of a traveling team which competed across the borough.

Typically, the team with the best record moved on to the playoffs, with a chance to win the conference championship. If victorious, the said team entered the out of state *Babe Ruth Tournament* to compete against the best teams in their selected age group across the region. I hoped for the same opportunity, but first I needed to prove that I belonged.

The idea of making a traveling team is rewarding – it gives you bragging rights and a chance to thump your chest in the little league circuit. Tryouts were a few days away and I knew the participants would be combative and raring to go. *The alternative for the traveling team was the 'In-house squad' – usually the group of kids deemed "not good enough".*

I was full of nerves that evening, as Mom, Terrance and I drove to the indoor facility where tryouts were being held. I replayed the fundamentals in my head during the thirty-minute drive, trying my hardest not to get overwhelmed. *Just relax.* I needed to redeem myself from the debacle at the East River park and couldn't blow this opportunity.

All eyes were on me, as we arrived at the indoor hub, where I was surrounded by more white faces than I'd ever seen in one place at a time! Disturbingly, there wasn't a black person in sight, I allowed the setting to intimidate me from the moment I walked through the door.

Were there any other black kids willing to play baseball?! Mom and Terrance wished me luck before walking off with the other parents, while the coaches paired the traveling team hopefuls into groups. Each "soft toss" was met with an astounding *pop* in my glove. I'd never caught warm-up throws at that speed and my hand paid for it dearly. I was up against kids who were more seasoned with something to prove!

After a couple of embarrassing goofs in the outfield, it was time to take some hacks at the plate – where I hoped to recreate the magic from a few years ago. Instead, I fell flat on my face, completely forgetting how to hit a baseball. I found everything to be too fast-paced that evening and I was quiet during the car ride home. But rather than sob like a child, I was unbelievably thrilled at the thought of playing with a group of perceived scrubs on the In-house team. To take part in my own version of the *Bad News Bears* was better than not playing at all.

* * * * *

It was Friday, June 17th and I was in the basement, sitting on the corner of my bed watching Game 5 of the NBA Finals. The Knicks were looking to take the lead in the series against Hakeem Olajuwon's Houston Rockets. I had jitters leading up to the game, praying for a win that would inch us one step closer to an NBA championship – the first since 1973.

The game started late that evening, but it was the beginning of the summer and I had all the time in the world. Typically, on the night before a little league game, I'd try to get enough rest, hoping it was the difference between having a big performance or going 0 for 4. *I could've been Rip Van Winkle – absolutely nothing was going to break me out of my season long slump.*

The raucous crowd at M.S.G. inspired the Knicks to take an early lead, as both teams looked geared up and ready to go. Though the series was missing the *oomph* of past NBA Finals matchups, it appeared the viewers at home were in for a treat that evening. *Knicks fans weren't concerned with ratings – we just wanted a damn championship!*

Unexpectedly, the unthinkable occurred. The game went into *split coverage* – on one side of the screen were the Knicks and Rockets and in the bottom corner, a white *Ford Bronco* speeding along the freeway. Why would NBC attempt to interrupt an NBA Finals game for a high-speed chase?! Can anybody tell me what the heck is going on? *Maybe the makers of Grand Theft Auto configured this brilliant idea to reinvigorate the video game series (previously played on the 8-bit system). Sony PlayStation was a little over a year away from making its North America debut. Maybe the company was prepping video game lovers and in cahoots with NBC to increase the NBA Finals ratings. Yeah, that's it!*

Or was this a gaffe made by an NBC intern, who inadvertently previewed an upcoming Fall premiere show – *America's Most Inconvenient Television Interruptions?* I was wrong on all accounts. I watched in awe, as police cars were in hot pursuit of O.J. Simpson.

Wait, Officer Nordberg from The Naked Gun movie? The guy who raced through the airport in those corny Hertz commercials? One of the greatest NFL running backs of all-time? The Juice???

It was the infamous Bronco chase, as motorists gathered along the California freeway cheering Simpson on. His buddy and personal driver for the evening, Al (A.C.) Cowlings communicated with the authorities, as O.J. sat in the back of the Bronco aiming a gun at his head. Millions of Americans watched, the NBA Finals were an afterthought. By now, we are all familiar with the events leading up to the chase, but this was a pivotal moment in American television history – making 1994 a year to remember!

For what it was worth, the Knicks won the game but eventually lost the series to the Rockets in seven games. At least there was the New York Rangers, who hoisted hockey's Stanley Cup for the first time since the 1940 season.

* * * * *

Minnesota Twins starting pitcher Jack Morris pitched 10 scoreless innings against the Atlanta Braves in Game 7 of the 1991 World Series – arguably the greatest World Series game I'd ever seen. The Metrodome was alive as Twins fans waved their *hanky towels* in unison. Gene Larkin's game winning bases loaded single put the team on the board, giving the Twins their 2nd World Series victory in four years:

"The Twins are gonna win the world series... the Twins have won it! It's a base hit... it's a 1-0 ten inning victory!"

That was the call of legendary sportscaster Jack Buck after captivating the baseball world the night before with his phenomenal Game 6 call of Kirby Puckett's game winning homerun:

"Into deep left center (for Mitchell) ... and we'll see you tomorrow night!"

That was baseball at its finest hour. The 1992 and '93 seasons saw the Toronto Blue Jays win back to back World Series', in what appeared to be the forecast of a *dynasty team.* By this point, baseball had a plethora of young stars who would carry the sport for the next decade. And then... the 1994 baseball strike occurred. The game was shut down for the first time since 1981, due to a fervent war between baseball owners and the players' union – in a classic case of *capital structure...* or in layman's terms – *principle and greed.*

August 12th was the start date of the season-long strike and for the first time since 1904, the labor tussle caused baseball to cancel the World Series. *The game I loved turned its back on me and millions of other fans. It was truly turning out to be the summer from hell.*

I never paid attention to the business side of baseball – I didn't think I needed to. It's a simple game, one which required *very little* to earn my trust. In fact, my trust came at no cost. Yet, I was expected to understand the dollars and cents aspect of it? I couldn't fathom the day baseball would tell its fans to fuck off, but it happened. *If that's what you want, that's what you'll get!*

It was the first time I realized the sport was a business, so I followed suit, creating a protest of my own which lasted three-quarters into the shortened 1995 season, where I'd *only* tune in for the World Series. I couldn't find it in my heart to take back my *first love* – after she left me during one of my darkest hours.

* * * * *

The highlight of the summer ironically started on the same day of the baseball strike. It was the 25th anniversary of the first Woodstock event – *a festival promoting peace and music.* With baseball in the back seat, I focused on MTV's wall-to-wall coverage of rock's biggest performers. I was long removed from my father's neglect of hip-hop, as the genre was my preferred choice, but overall, 1994 was a big year for music.

Since moving to Brooklyn, I had a nice collection of hip-hop cassette tapes – artists like, Das EFX, Wu-Tang Clan, Craig Mack, K7, House of Pain, Kriss Kross, Da Brat, Masta Ace, 69 Boyz, Domino, Dr. Dre, Snoop Doggy Dogg, Notorious B.I.G. and Tupac Shakur. In addition, there was Dionne Farris, Ace of Base and John Mellencamp – proving once more that I was a music enthusiast. But it was Harry and a kid named *Danny,* who introduced me to a new sound before the end of the school year: *Alternative rock.*

I was naïve at first, figuring alternative rock was nothing but "collective noise" – usually the label given by cynical listeners of hip-hop. Boy, was I wrong. The euphonious sounds of guitar riffs and drums by groups like, Stone Temple Pilots, Green Day, Soundgarden, Collective Soul and Nirvana, seized my brain that summer, becoming a major part of my life soundtrack. Connected with the weekend-long celebration of Woodstock '94, I would have missed out on the spectacle taking place in Saugerties, New York, had it not been for the guys. Almost 25 years later and I continue to play songs from these artists regularly!

PARTY LIKE IT'S 1995!

Marred by the Knicks missing a chance at their first title in over 20 years, a dreadful inaugural little league season and the ugly baseball strike, 1994 couldn't end soon enough. The new year brought hope and the shift in the climate happened almost immediately.

The economy was booming, gas was cheap, hip-hop music was scorching hot and I reached a new level of popularity at school. Shanice asked me to the school dance shortly before graduation and we did our best that evening to make up for the debacle of the previous year. Above that, I was absolutely tearing the fuckin' cover off the baseball in my second season of little league. About damn time!

* * * * *

There were moments during my first year where I'd step up to the plate to the sounds of encouragement:

"Come on, E! You can do it!"

But those at-bats usually ended in strikeouts followed by slick remarks:

"Can this kid even play?"

I grew tired of being labeled as, "the black guy who couldn't hit". Actual comments uttered in the stands. For some reason or another, I couldn't make the adjustment from schoolyard to real baseball, leaving doubt on whether I should even go on. Every coach in the league knew I was lousy and opposing players snickered after each out.

Being the lone member of a group – whether on a job or a sports team – can really make for some trying times... especially when underperforming. No matter how hard I tried to fly under the radar, I stood out like an NBA player in a room full of horse jockeys!

Before the start of each season, In-house league officials commonly integrated coaches and players from the league. I wasn't a fan of that strategy, having built a few friendships on our last place team, but I needed a fresh start and coaches who knew what they were doing. Thankfully, I was introduced to a new coach, *Coach Marrone*.

Coach took the time during practice to pull me aside with his son (who was also new to the league) and work intensely on our mechanics – specifically hitting. He advised that I make a few adjustments with my swing, which unbeknownst to me was of uppercut form. Unfortunately, my previous coaches were particularly dumb and inattentive... either that, or they enjoyed watching me make a fool of myself.

"Lean on ya back leg, E!" Coach Marrone instructed.

That's when the light switch went off. Little did I know, something as simple as *leaning on my back leg and leveling my swing* would result in an MVP-like performance for our first-place Cardinals team. I went from being a stooge who once batted last in the line-up, to becoming the lead-off hitter (and conceivably our best player) on my new squad. And one Saturday morning, with Mom sitting in the stands, I hit my first homerun... a blast to straightaway centerfield into the railyard off *Joey Damato* – the best pitcher in the league (who should've been on a traveling team). I floated around the bases with a boyish smile, as my gold *number 21* chain (which Mom bought prior to the season since it was my favorite number) dangled from my neck. Players around the league were flummoxed! *I swear, I wasn't on steroids.*

The hot streak continued while attending baseball camp held at a Brooklyn high school. My production impressed *Coach Senegate* so much, that at the end of the six-week camp, he awarded me a trophy for *Most Outstanding Player.* Later that day, Coach offered me a spot on his high school varsity team!

"You're too good for JV (Junior Varsity), if you attend the school, I can put you on varsity easily. There are a lot of juniors and seniors on the roster... so you may not play as much, but I think you're good enough for the team."

Say what?!

* * * * *

While America was on pins and needles awaiting the verdict of the "Trial of the century", my father was on the verge of making his biggest move since arriving in the states – uprooting from our old apartment in Hamilton Heights to the Garden State.

For many New Yorkers, a move to New Jersey signifies success. Say goodbye to the bedlam of the big city and hello to the sound of crickets and lawnmowers. He was through with city living, looking to enjoy the fruits of his labor with a move to the suburbs. The move would also signal the end of my visits to the Tomlinson home.

I spent a couple of weeks in Jersey, seriously considering a move of my own. Despite the success of little league, summer camp and the possibility of playing on the varsity team, my despair over the water bug infestation grew. The relationship with my father wasn't convincing enough to make the move outright, but I bonded well with his new companion and her boys, to at least consider it.

Her sons took me under their wings almost immediately – sharing fashion tips and breaking down the steps on how to grab a female's attention. They were an assertive and confident bunch, while my shy spells were ongoing (still kicking myself for blowing a chance with *Vicki Santini* and *Josie Pendleton* the previous year).

I desperately needed a boost of confidence – if I had any chance of getting a girlfriend. With the upcoming freshman year several weeks away, I took in all the information I could – listening intently to the latest slang, watching every rap video and memorizing the words to the hottest hip-hop songs of the summer. I needed to carry this momentum… even if it meant altering my character to fit in.

* * * * *

Chapter Tidbits:

- My father had to console me after watching Mike Tyson get his ass kicked by James "Buster" Douglas on February 11th, 1990. I don't think I'd ever experienced that much pain (in sports) outside of the Mets 1993 season and the lousy Jets 1996 team which finished with a woeful record of 1 win and 15 losses.
- As Saturday morning cartoons drifted into the sunset, I made up for it by becoming an avid watcher of the teen sitcoms, *Saved by the Bell* and *California Dreams.*
- Elton John's "Circle of Life", remains one of my favorite songs and was sung by my eighth-grade graduating class.
- I listened to Dave Matthews Band's "Ants Marching" every day during freshman year of high school.

- "Only Built 4 Cuban Linx" by rapper, Raekwon the Chef, is my favorite Rap album of the decade.
- *The Real World: Hawaii* remains my favorite season of the 90s reality series.

Chapter Nine: School Daze

After watching my first 'Back to School' commercial, I was overcome by a feeling of despair. In my mind, summer was officially over. I inauspiciously elected to stay in Brooklyn, sticking it out with Mom, Terrance and the bugs, but I couldn't shake off the "Summertime Blues" – or better yet, Seasonal Affective Disorder (SAD); a debilitating depression affecting sufferers in the fall and winter months. This was serious stuff!

On the bright side, fall looked promising. There was a much-needed, new cast scheduled for the upcoming season of Saturday Night Live, the O.J. trial was on its last legs, Minister Louis Farrakhan was gearing up for the First Annual Million Man March and Jay Leno had a ton of new material to split my sides.

Finally, with early mornings becoming a troubled spot, I needed a swift attitude adjustment if I wanted to obtain success in the upcoming school year. That meant zero tolerance for water bugs! I couldn't allow these creatures to disrupt my sleep in one of my most important years to date. Now a freshman at Edward R. Murrow High School, my days required plenty of energy – keeping up with the 4,000 nerds enrolled at the academically acclaimed school. Plus, I had a girlfriend to find. I didn't go through that summer drill for nothing!

* * * * *

On an unseasonably mild autumn morning, I surprisingly woke up feeling like a million bucks. The school year had kicked off just a few days ago and I was fully charged. My body was still readjusting to a new sleeping pattern – after eight long weeks of late summer nights, but I was psyched.

I had a little time that morning to catch the previous night's recording of *The Tonight Show,* as Edd Hall introduced the cast and featured guests for the evening. I always preferred Leno over his late-night rival, David Letterman. His personality and witty humor were relatable, he appeared to be a good guy. Not to mention, he was the clear underdog!

Leno took a lot of heat as Johnny Carson's replacement on *The Tonight Show,* when the legendary host bid farewell in 1991. Letterman, Carson's understudy and a late-night connoisseur of his own, was the odds-on favorite as his successor. The perfect match, so to speak… except, NBC had a different idea. The critics had a field day, often joking about Leno's squeaky voice and profound jawline. Naturally, I took every jab personal. Many felt Leno was "unfunny", lacking the credentials to carry-on such a prestigious program. How would America warm up to a *struggling* actor-comedian when Letterman was the household name? *Ooooh, the suspense…*

The selection of Leno over Letterman spearheaded an HBO produced movie (*The Late Shift*) which documented the comedians rise to stardom and icy relationship. In the end, NBC's decision turned out brilliant. *The Tonight Show* grew into a ratings juggernaut and both comics went on to have outstanding careers in late night television. The turn of events triggered Leno to pen his autobiography, *Leading with My Chin,* which I immediately asked for once it hit the shelves.

Speaking of which, Mom was easygoing with a bedtime hour on school nights – as long as the TV timer was set. So, I promptly stayed up each night to catch Leno's opening monologue. It was *must-see-TV!* (cheap NBC plug). In case sleep got the best of me, I'd set my VCR to record the 11:35 p.m. talk-show – a routine I'd perform regularly throughout the school year.

I'M CUCKOO FOR COCOA PUFFS!

Disclaimer: *The following story is not intended for the weak-hearted (or stomached).*

Mom wouldn't treat me to her mouthwatering pancakes until the weekend, leaving my breakfast choices slim: Pop tarts, cereal, or *foolishly skipping* "the most important meal of the day" were the options. I frequently opted for the latter since I was such a procrastinator.

Gone were those effortless *five-minute* walks to I.S. 228. My days started early, and it was important that I supplied my body with enough carbs to get through it. But like most teenagers, I thought I knew everything, foolishly depriving my body of food until the afternoon.

I spent too much time watching Leno that morning, leaving little time to pull out the frying pan to make an egg sandwich. I was also out of my cereal favorites, declining to pollute my mouth with the sugars in a stick of Winterfresh gum to compensate for food.

What would I eat while lusting over Jesse Spano on Saved by the Bell? There was a half-empty box of Cocoa Puffs sitting alone in the cabinet, next to an unopened container of Old-Fashioned Quaker Oats oatmeal. Two terrible choices at the time, but my stomach was growling uncontrollably. I wasn't sure if I'd ever eaten Cocoa Puffs... but I found Cocoa Pebbles quite enjoyable. Moreover, I wasn't much of a chocolate cereal guy, but the blending of chocolate milk was always enjoyable, so Cocoa Puffs was the victor by unanimous decision.

Over the summer, the guys informed me to hold off wearing new school clothes until the late fall (to create *shock value* to those paying attention to my outfits), but my new sneakers and gold chain (which I'd only wear during little league games) could no longer sit on the sidelines. My outfit for the day was ironed out and prepared the night before and it was time to break out my new Charles Barkley black Air Force Nike's to go with my black jeans.

I made a pit stop to the bathroom, dabbed my mouth of the excess milk, patting the top of the mini afro I'd grown over the summer. Somebody was getting a girlfriend today! It was time to meet my friends.

"I'm out, Ma!" I announced.

Mike, who attended I.S. 228, arranged to meet me in front of Connor's house in the morning before school. Together, we'd walk to the nearest bus stop – a *mere* thirty minutes from his house, before taking the twenty-minute bus ride to Murrow. Of course, there were other means of transportation that could've gotten us there quicker, but we trusted our legs. Besides, we had a collective fear of taking the subway and getting lost.

There were certain parts of the borough where three kids – *Asian, black and white,* didn't want to find themselves as a unit. That was simply a death wish. In addition, there were scores of unruly teenagers standing at bus stops en route to school – usually the cause of major delays.

It wasn't unusual watching passengers enter the bus through the rear doors – in fear of being late. When at capacity, bus drivers pleaded with commuters to wait for the next arriving bus – forgetting one very important thing: This was New York City. You don't ask New Yorkers to 'wait' for anything!

* * * * *

I had a lot of adrenaline going that morning, producing a bit of a sweat by the time I arrived at Connor's house.

"Is it warm out, or is it just me?" I asked Mike, who arrived minutes before. Mike was seldom affected by the warmth, usually sporting dark colors year-round. But today was a different story. He removed his black flight jacket, while we awaited Connor's arrival.

Now walking, a conversation ensued about our new classes and teachers. It was early, the guys were a bit too animated for my blood, so I kept my words to a minimum. On top of that, it was uncomfortably warm, I couldn't escape the beads of sweat on my forehead.

"Yo, Ern, you're sweating like crazy, man!" Conner blurted out, with his high-pitched voice.

The sweat was an unusual sweat and my temperature switched from hot to cold – like the shower temperature after the toilet is flushed. I spent the better part of the walk trying to make sense of it. Did I have a fever? Something wasn't right.

Conner alluded to receiving a *500-hour disc* in the mail from *AOL* (American Online), which for a teenager was the equivalent of hitting the lottery – but the remainder of the conversation was hazy. Suddenly, my stomach made a disturbing sound – which could have easily registered a 7.0 on the Richter scale!

We've all experienced it – that moment when something doesn't particularly agree with your stomach… and your insides start talking to you. Well, *the weapon in my intestine* needed attending and we were too far from home. What was I going to do? Assuming it was just a little gas, I figured I'd give it a good push out into the atmosphere. No one will suspect a thing.

When we arrived at the bus stop, I decided to sit on the park bench – which was in walking distance of the bus once it came along. The crowd was light, but most of the commuters elected to stand with hopes of grabbing an available seat. Perfect! I excused myself from the guys, making up a fib about having to finish a "homework assignment". I opened my backpack in search of non-existent homework, putting on a show for the ages. *Now, where are those doggone papers?*

* * * * *

Author's Note: *Murrow had a terrific drama program that I should have seriously considered after this performance.*

* * * * *

Alas! I was on the bench. The calculated move allowed enough time for my body to let 'er rip! I unbuttoned my pants far enough to expose my backside, using my backpack as a shield for my mid-section. Almost immediately, my stomach went from zero to one-hundred! *Maybe my brain subconsciously thought I was on the toilet?* For the love of God, I had the shits!

To make matters worse, I didn't have any wipes, napkins, or paper towels... because, who honestly expects to shit themselves? The only thing in my possession was a travel sized bottle of Speed Stick Ocean Surf deodorant that I brought for gym class. I was assed out... literally. And just when I thought it couldn't get any worse?

"Ern! the bus!"

For fuck sakes I wasn't finished! No way was this happening to me – no fuckin way! Where did I go wrong? Until the thought occurred... Cocoa Puffs!!! I'd *never* eaten chocolate on an empty stomach – was that fuckin' cuckoo bird responsible for this? Perhaps the milk was rotten. My mind was playing tricks on me.

Thinking fast, I tried diligently to wipe away the evidence using several pieces of loose-leaf paper, before discarding them to the ground. I proceeded to pull up my pants, wisely rubbing the stick of deodorant over my jeans... about *one-hundred times* – hoping to conceal the odor. As the bus approached, I *uncomfortably* powerwalked to the guys, trying my best to play off the calamity in my pants. Apparently, there must have been an episode where I lost a little control on the bench and inadvertently made a mess on the *outside* of my clothes...Oy vey!

"Ewww, it smells like shit in here!" yelled one girl.

The scent of Ocean Surf deodorant wasn't overpowering enough. The seated passengers opened the windows at once, with the air conditioner at full blast, while others promptly fanned themselves. The expressions on board were priceless. The smell was so bad, the bus driver drove a good stretch of the ride with the front door open! (probably a code violation – but understandable).

Shitting on yourself not only humbles you, but it opens the line of communication with God! I asked the Lord to forgive me for my sins at the *first* sound of my stomach showing it had an attitude... because after all, He is a *forgiving* God: *Please, Father, don't let this happen to me! I beg of you! I promise not to watch anymore Janet Jacme videos... I promise!*

All for naught.

On the bus ride, I boldly gave the appearance of someone disoriented by the stench, *even* questioning the guys. "Did someone shit themselves?! Who would do such a thing?" They laughed hysterically, but I was in total disbelief that I dodged this bullet.

Thankfully, the smell subsided just before we touched school grounds, but the damage was done. I rushed to my homeroom class (instead of making a dash to the restroom) in fear of being marked late for attendance. It wasn't until minutes into first period when I excused myself to get cleaned up. I'll spare you the details.

If that wasn't an Oscar-worthy performance, I don't know what is.

* * * * *

So, the question I'm sure many of you have is this: *Why didn't I turn the heck around once my stomach performed a backflip?!* Here's why: I was completely scared and embarrassed! Too scared to miss a day of school so early into the year, concerned about making a good impression as a new student and downright embarrassed having to explain to the guys that I wasn't feeling well.

Could I have played it off to make it appear like something else was wrong? Yes. But I wasn't *that* savvy at 14. Even if I made a U-Turn, I would've found myself shitting somewhere on a street corner! There wasn't a nearby restaurant to run off to and we were still walking through an all-Italian neighborhood! *Can you imagine the look I would've received knocking on a random homeowner's door, asking to use their bathroom?!*

If a similar stomach disruption occurred today, I would have made an immediate *exit stage left*. But prior to freshman year, I only missed school on three separate occasions:

- The chicken pox
- The Flu
- The time Mom turned me into an *alopecia patient* while attempting to cut my hair

Let's just say high school started off on the wrong foot!

* * * * *

Author's Note: *Taking a risk that morning was easily one of the five dumbest things I'd ever done in my life. I bet you're just dying to know the other four!*

* * * * *

CHECKMATE!

Well, let's not waste any more time! – here's another dumb decision.

* * * * *

Turning down the offer to play varsity baseball – to attend a school *without* varsity sports, being better known for their *chess team*, tugged at me every day. My confidence was at an all-time high, where I'd experienced a summer for the ages, but I couldn't let go of some inescapable factors:

1. **The school's location:** *Bay Ridge, Brooklyn* – I'd grown familiar with certain parts of Brooklyn and the black population of Bay Ridge was a *meager* 0.1 percent (that may be a bit generous). I wasn't interested in going to a school where *maybe* a dozen black students, likely members of the school's basketball team, made up the populace (as of 2017, there were 68 black students out of 1000 students). I was still shaken to the core from the incident in the schoolyard and sought a diverse atmosphere to thrive in.
2. **Was I good enough, or was the summer of '95 a fluke?** Deep down, I always knew I could play baseball, but it was a matter of proving it to others. I dominated the In-house league for *one* season and had an exceptional *six-weeks* of camp, but was that truly enough to earn a spot on one of the city's top high school

baseball teams? Probably not. I needed more work. Additionally, how would I have handled the pressure of being the only black kid on a team full of *older* white, Italian kids? Based on what I've shared thus far, probably not too well.

Several coaches at the time were grooming me to make a serious run at basketball (with hopes of becoming a two-sport athlete), but I shied away. I didn't think I could live up to the expectations, didn't trust being around my *black peers* (with an attempt at basketball) and I didn't want to be singled out on an all-white team. Furthermore, I wanted *writing* to be a part of my immediate future and Murrow featured a highly favorable Journalism/Mass Media program.

Here we go again! I knew the chances to crack into the writing industry were greater than playing in the Majors, but did I want to be a journalist that badly – to give up on a life-long dream? Probably not. Unfortunately, I couldn't overcome my concerns.

The moment anyone asked about the school I attended, I responded with a three-second delay…

"You go to Murrow?"

… Yes.

"Isn't that the school without sports?"

Sigh… Yes.

I was a tall, athletic kid, going to a school full of nerds. How in the world would I fit in? For the record, I strategically placed Midwood High School above Murrow during the high school application process. Midwood was highly ranked academically, they participated in varsity sports and the racial breakdown was favorable. Based on my academic excellence at I.S. 228, surely, they'd accept me? *Not only was I spurned expeditiously, but I knew a couple of kids who were accepted with subpar grades! How do you get turned down by a school ranked lower than the one which accepts you?*

Lucy! You have some 'splainin' to do!

Murrow was the far superior school academically, but what did their staff see that Midwood didn't? In protest, I'd mumble a few words under my breath, as the football team headed to practice… at their beautiful, *all-turf football field* conveniently located across the street… from our school! Talk about adding insult to injury!

Just look at these fuckin' clowns – standing proud, with their stupid equipment bags and ugly helmets, like they'll REALLY make the NFL. Ha!

As the kids say today, "stop hatin'!"

I LOVE GIRLS, GIRLS, GIRLS, GIRLS...

My contemporary attire and gold chain were methods used to inform students that I was a jock – with a sense of style and not a *geek...* like one of them. It wasn't that I was trying to hide my intelligence, but I was utterly embarrassed attending a school whose main objective was producing the next Bobby Fischer! I desperately wanted to be a chick magnet.

* * * * *

Author's Note: *Sadly, I never became a "chick magnet" at any point in life. I had a few nice runs through my twenties and early thirties, but never did it turn out like I'd hoped.*

* * * * *

Murrow's female to male ratio was 2:1 and I received their attention rather quickly. Education was a priority and I was coming off some admirable academic years, but it wouldn't supersede my lust for attention. I knew I could get farther than most – simply by coasting along and "getting by" (a clear recipe for disaster), instead of striving to be the best. I figured, *why evoke senseless study habits on subjects I had little care for?* What's wrong with *B* or *C* grades? Is that not passing?

I'll admit, I was a changed man through high school and what hurt most was the understanding that if I wanted *any* success with the ladies, it was critical I make black friends. Going into a state of seclusion, from the perceived "oddities" I became accustomed to, wouldn't be easy. *Who else could I talk to about Seinfeld?* The notion of aligning myself to one race of friends went against everything I stood for, but black and Hispanic girls were in abundance and I was at their mercy. If they were drawn to "problematic personality types", I'd have to rub elbows with a few.

* * * * *

Author's Note: *For those wondering, the idea of dating outside of my race was equally titillating, but unfortunately, not reciprocated. In what was the sign of the times, most of the ethnic groups stayed within their own and I was forced to take heed of the school's racial divide.*

"JUST PULL THESE BITCHES BY THE HAND, E., THEY LIKE THAT!"

For the record, I am mindful of how this can be perceived as *borderline* harassment, but such lucid words (instilled over the summer) worked effectively over the four years at Murrow. In a matter of time, *hand pulls* grew into *hugs, hugs* turned into *cheek kisses,* graduating to *corner mouth kisses.* Before long, I thought I was the black Zack Morris!

An uninterested female will never allow her mouth to get too close to yours – unless there's an attraction. So, it was safe to say, I was "in the door" with those that I encountered. Through high school, there lived a couple of short-term relationships, a few make-outs sessions and some tough rejections along the way. I even had my fair choice of prom dates, which I elected not to attend, due to my concern with hurting the feelings of the person I would ultimately reject. But like most teenage boys, my thoughts concerning girls were impudent and I wanted action.

I was still a virgin, but I was more interested in finding out whose breasts were going to be engorged in my mouth... than making the Dean's list. I wanted to keep up with my peers and their eye-popping sexual stories. They couldn't have all the fun!

There was enough porn in my collective memory to feel comfortable in the act (if it ever surfaced), but through my girl infatuation, I went through high school without getting laid, watching my G.P.A. drop lower than Enron stock! The sad part? I didn't have a sense of urgency to fix it. I trusted my brain to get me through the troubles, unaware of how quickly high school years flew by.

* * * * *

Author's Note: *I spent most of my time at Murrow going through the motions, trying to figure out who I was, instead of recognizing where I wanted to go. In addition, my obsession for skipping Spanish* *class (one semester) was downright unacceptable. If Murrow kept records of students "hooky history", I'd be in the Top-Five for most cut classes in a single semester. The arduous journey of putting on a front (and not giving a damn about where to place accent marks – in a language I figured I'd never speak), led to six-weeks in summer school where I missed out on a paid internship, working at a major bank. All for the love of acceptance.*

* * * * *

"YOU DOWN WITH S.A.T.'S?"

Becoming a *Straight-A* student required too much effort, very little time to live a normal life and I was satisfied receiving a 'B' if I passed the exam. As school became more challenging, the B's quickly turned into C's. I continued to embrace the lower grades – instead of striving to do better. The feeling of *just passing* was exhilarating and I was usually happier than a *Maury* guest after being told – "You are NOT the father!" *Woohoo! Well, at least I passed that motherfucker!*

I got an early taste of academic success, winning a bunch of certificates, medals and trophies (which have since dry rotted), but as time progressed, I found school *too* demanding and unrewarding. *Yes, I was practically searching for a school/life balance as a teen. Studying for two, three, four days a week wasn't fun.*

I wasn't up for the challenge of learning *useless* subject matter anymore, but I wouldn't adopt that attitude until the 10th grade… which is when I realized my dreams of finishing at the top of my class were nothing but a *pipedream.* Everyone knew I was smart, but becoming a *Brainiac* wasn't intriguing. Brainiac's didn't get ass. I only wanted school to teach me the 'necessities of life', rather than undertake a world of stress.

* * * * *

Make no mistake, up until 10th grade (and thereafter), there still lived a natural fear of failing. So, I developed study techniques to enhance my learning experience (especially for weaker subjects) and improve my grades overall. One idea was to thoroughly study science and history text books, recording the answers to questions that could potentially appear on exams on my tape recorder. I'd follow the routine for weeks and on the night before a big exam, put on my head phones and listen intently to the recordings. I wanted my brain to soak in all the information to ensure I'd pass, figuring the repetition would pay off. Guess again. Not only would I *barely* pass the exams, but at times, I'd fail… and fail miserably! *How was this strategy not working in my favor?*

Troubled by the results – I tried the next best thing… If you thought tutoring, you thought wrong! It was a game I called *20/20 vision* (particularly in math and science class), where I'd arrive early to strategically place myself next to a Brainiac – because I could always count on them showing up to class first. It was my *only* hope to avoid a possible repeat of the two subjects responsible for collectively putting their feet up my ass! *I knew those students paid little attention to wandering eyes (usually too concerned with finishing the exam before the rest of the class). Rather than copy answers line for line, I'd attempt to answer a few questions on my own. I also knew that I'd provide enough 'wrong answers' to prevent a teacher from growing suspicious. The key was to answer at least three-quarters of the exam correctly.* Desperate times called for desperate measures and instead of using my brain, my academic fate was in the hands of… *my eyes!*

Teachers were cognizant of the widespread cheating at school and swiftly reorganized the exams. *You can always count on teachers playing spoiler.*

Question #1 on my exam was likely question #10 on the exam of the persons seated to my left and right. You needed the vision of a hawk to pull that one off – without making it obvious you were cheating. Sadly, it would spell the end of my vision game, but I'd soon get by – thanks to *my pen* playing the hero.

* * * * *

The focus shifted to the S.A.T. exam: The *most* overrated piece of junk I'd ever come across. Yeah, I said it. It's useless! I remember Sasha Dawes carried an S.A.T. study guide throughout the 5th grade prompting me to ask, *why in the world are you reading a book about Saturday?!* The expression on her face was jaw-dropping. Perhaps Ms. Glynn should've re-thought the whole class valedictorian thing.

So, this is what universities got their panties in a bunch over – the impractical piece of garbage known as the S.A.T. (Standard

Aptitude Test). Not only are students expected to maintain a superlative G.P.A., but they're told to rack their brain some more, vying for *university acceptance* – in a game of "who exudes more intelligence". To try my knowledge (plus see what all the hype was about) I took the P.S.A.T.'s (Practice Standard Advance Test) during my junior year.

"Hey, Ernest, you get *two-hundred points* just for writing your name!" Hooptie damn doo!

Not sure how true that story was, I don't think I ever cared enough to find out. But I figured if I cracked a score of 1000 (out of 1600) I'd be okay once that "big boy" arrived. At my first and only attempt... I scored a measly *eight-hundred!* I recalibrated, picked up an S.A.T. study guide and tried to familiarize myself with the format of the exam. By the time senior year arrived, I was sure I'd nail it!

Senior year arrived... *Sorry, but the score has been permanently removed from my memory, courtesy of the Neuralyzer device used in Men in Black.* It was that bad.

When you're constantly put on a pedestal by teachers – with the accolades to go along with it, a poor S.A.T. score can leave you wondering if you're truly an idiot. In addition, I was confused at how some of the misfits I hung around with managed to produce higher scores – while being academic duds. Were they really a bunch of Einstein's putting on an underachieving act for acceptance, or was I the *real* halfwit?

I nearly lost my mind when one of my buddies informed me of his S.A.T. score. *What did you get?* I'd ask.

"A ten-fifty" (as he handed his test results to me).

A ten-what?! My ego couldn't accept the embarrassment – no way was I dumber than this dude!

* * * * *

Author's Note: *Somewhere out there, lives a student possessing a 3.9 G.P.A., who just scored a 1599 on the S.A.T., looking to jump off the nearest bridge! I loathe you. There's nothing wrong with aspiring to be the best, but don't be fuckin' ridiculous!*

* * * * *

COLLEGE DROPOUT

Murrow provided its seniors the opportunity to receive credits through an internship, with the chance to work off-site for six months. This was perfect for students who already possessed enough credits to graduate (and really didn't need to be in school until June), or those who were looking for an "easy way out" ... instead of re-taking chemistry for the *one-hundredth time. Guess I'll give it the old college try!*

To apply, students were required to write *a thousand-word* essay explaining why they should be chosen. If selected, the internship would be treated like a full-time job. Meaning: *A display of good working habits, including punctuality and excellent attendance.*

Credits were *only* awarded if students sustained a high approval rating at the completion of the program. But all I kept thinking about was the *one-thousand-word* essay requirement. *A thousand words?! I can do that in my sleep!* As expected, I was accepted to the program in the forthcoming weeks.

I worked at a well-known bank in the Wall Street area, where I was exposed to beautiful career women and the *repulsive* nine-to-five grind. I successfully completed the internship and come June, my name was called with the rest of the graduating class at Madison Square Garden. Again, there was no way I'd pass chemistry on my own and I couldn't fathom the horror of not graduating on time. My pen came to the rescue once more...

* * * * *

It was college or bust, because after all, society has brainwashed us to believe this. Despite my *piss poor* S.A.T. scores and *mediocre* G.P.A., I applied to over a half-dozen schools – and denied acceptance to *most* of my list! I was down to four choices – two of which accepted me, the other two which were Godsent.

First, a local community college. If I had done my homework – and not allowed pride to get in the way, I would've simply gone to "thirteenth grade" in a heartbeat. That was the running joke for students electing to go to a two-year college, but rather than attend, where I could've excelled before transferring to a four-year college, I completely snubbed the school altogether, too concerned with 'perception'. *Ignorance is truly bliss.* We're now down to three.

I realized how little I enjoyed waking up on Saturday mornings braving the summer heat – waiting for a *fly ball* to come my way. After enjoying a nice season at a new league (this time in Manhattan, where I was finally able to experience diversity on a baseball team), I felt it was time to put baseball to rest and shift my focus to basketball. It was the sport of choice with friends at Murrow and more importantly, I was good at it.

Around college application time, I brought a disposable camera to the basketball court, which is when I asked the player sitting out to act as my personal photographer. *Snap away! Just make sure you focus on ME.*

The plan was to create a portfolio to present to the athletic boards when visiting campuses, or when mailing off my college applications, as I was looking for an advantage to compensate for my subpar G.P.A. and lack of varsity sports participation. It was a dramatic plea of: *I know my school didn't have varsity teams, but don't hold that against me – look! I can really shoot a basketball!*

Along the way, a four-year college in Connecticut caught wind of my athletic background, offering a scholarship to play basketball for their Division II team. Seemed odd, considering I only played two seasons at a rec-league, but through word of mouth (of the various coaches I'd surrounded myself with) anything was possible.

I was grateful for the chance; my father and I paid a visit to the school – where we sat with the coach for nearly an hour. I took a liking to the environment and after a complete walk-through of the campus, I informed the coach that I'd decide in the upcoming weeks. It pains me to admit, but after much thought… I rejected the offer. Here's why: *Separation anxiety!*

In retrospect, I should've attended the school. The campus was roughly an hour and a half outside of New York City, but I wasn't ready to detach myself from childhood friends and Gran's well-being was still a priority.

Sidebar: *Childhood friends who ironically aren't a part of my life anymore.*

Though Gran was quite active, I was her primary errand runner and to be frank, she was my best friend. I felt compelled to stick around due to my uncertainty on who would fill the void. We're down to two schools.

During the spring of junior year, my father and I took the *six-hour* drive to Hampton, Virginia to witness one of his best friend's daughter graduate (with honors) from Hampton University. She was a born African, who upon moving to the States as a teen, excelled without blinking an eye. In fact, she was graduating from Hampton a year early! *Because that's just what us Africans do... well, except for your author...*

Throughout the trip, my father insisted that I "build a relationship" due to her academic ties. In doing so, she could put forth a good word and I'd be in the door at Hampton without much trepidation. *Good ol' fashion nepotism. A common practice in this country. I can dig it.*

Rather than take his words of wisdom, I was lost in translation – trying to "build relationships" with every girl in my line of sight at the ceremony! My goodness! I'd never been surrounded by such beautiful black women. There I was, fantasizing about bedding virtual graduates. Ugh.

It was a joyous occasion to witness aspiring students inch closer to their dreams, as proud parents and siblings cheered them on. I wanted to experience that feeling. In fact, I wanted to experience it *there*, at Hampton! I knew once my moment arrived, I'd bask in all the glory... until reality struck me between the eyes: Hampton was an all-black school! *Have I lost my everlasting mind?!*

Though I was far removed from the teasing of my elementary – middle school days, when it came down to the application process, regrettably, Hampton was an afterthought. *People can't talk you out of experience and I was scarred.* Now, we're down to one.

I chased prestige rather than choosing the school(s) that made sense, but St. John's University was the winner. I can honestly say that St. John's was the *only* New York school I wanted to attend, as it is considered one of the top universities in the city, and I dreamt about playing for their men's basketball team as a kid – during the days of Malik Sealy and Felipe López. Plus, I'm sure they were over the moon with my kick-ass college essay! This was a match made in heaven. Being accepted, after underachieving all through high school, was a major boost to my ego. The school's acceptance letter was fate... but, I really had no business going. I wasn't prepared for college life.

This wasn't *A Different World* or *Saved by the Bell: The College Years* – two TV shows which inspired me to partake in the college experience. This was the real deal. But for some reason or another, I went to St. John's expecting to be the big man on campus... when I was simply a small fish in a big ocean.

I managed to amass the attention of girls in high school under false pretenses and thought the scheme would work in college. Not a chance. With approximately 20,000 students, a men's basketball team that appeared on national TV and freshman arriving on campus in nice cars, I honestly expected to stand out with *zero* credentials? Who was I kidding? The joke was squarely on me! And why was I still so caught up in attaining the notice of girls? Was I only electing to go to college for the allure of a cute face and nice booty? *Well, kinda...*

So, why wouldn't I join any clubs or fraternities to try and fit in? Because I didn't think I needed to. In fact, I find frats pointless and unbecoming. I longed for acceptance, but at 18, I wasn't concerned with making lasting friendships with "new people" or connecting with students for future employment advantages. Aside from that, I thought it was quite lame of frat brothers (and sorority sisters) to shield their vehicles (specifically, the license plate holders) with *Greek lettering* – and the whole 'look at me, I'm a *(fill in the frat/sorority)*.' Seriously, no one cares! Besides, the activities I heard about weren't all too enticing. I couldn't imagine *drinking* random frat brother's toothpaste water (among other things for hazing), pledging, hooting & hollering, or throwing up hand gestures for acceptance. ME? Never in a million years. It wasn't that serious.

My college experience was met with *zero* "drunken nights and wild orgies" (like how it's portrayed in movies), Atlanta's *Freaknik* was about to become obsolete and the closest I'd get to any spring break adventure was courtesy of Carson Daly and MTV – on-site, in Cancun, Mexico.

My fondest college memories? Taking a ridiculously long daily train ride from Brooklyn to Queens, staring at girls on campus, watching a few of them embarrassingly throw themselves at random members of the basketball team and spending hours in the school library writing songs – hoping to break into the music industry as a songwriter. Maybe, *my pen* could rescue me once more.

* * * * *

My senior year of high school (through college) remains one of my biggest gripes with school. I find too many times, students are made to feel incompetent – if they aren't ranked among the best. Why should *anyone* feel that way at 17? Literacy and understanding basic math is all the average person needs (excluding those working in specialty fields). How can *science grades* and *S.A.T. scores* determine my position in life?

We'll all agree that a 4.0 G.P.A. can potentially earn you a six-figure income (or more) down the road – but does that define success? The quick answer for most is *'yes'*, but is *your* perception the reality for everyone else? No! Success is solely based on perspective.

Once flourishing in school, the widespread proclamation is the increased probability of landing a *good* job. Define "good job?" Society ties "good job" to money – no matter how you spin it.

Q: How many people with degrees detest their jobs, but love the pay that comes with it*?*

A: *Plenty!*

Q*:* How many people with degrees detest their jobs *and* the pay?!

A: *I wouldn't know where to begin.*

Q*:* How many people with degrees *truly love* what they do and are equally satisfied with the pay?

A: *Plenty – but suffice it to say, not an overwhelming amount.*

Does any of this sound "good" to you? We've all encountered the high school dropout, short-term college student, or that individual who *didn't attend* college at all, who found their lane and surprisingly make a decent living. But there's an existing narrative that *money* is relative to "good living" and I find it illogical.

Money creates greater financial opportunities – but that's all it does. "Good living" should be defined under *financial freedom* (which *truly* creates opportunities, if you were to ask me) and not through income alone. Depending on location and inflation, a $50,000 annual salary can be equally satisfying – *if* you've dodged the traps of society:

- Elaborate living (i.e., expensive cars, top-tier cable and cell phone plans)
- Debt (student loans and excessive credit card spending)
- Kids (as "cute" as they are, kids are traps – especially if there isn't any pre-financial planning involved)

Due to a baffling educational ploy, capitalism and the obsession for lavish living (where many seek validation through large purchases), somehow, a $50,000 per year income (or less) has been deemed "inadequate", and quite possibly laughable to those reading.

Here is my other problem... college! College is often celebrated, when it should be condemned for being a fallacy that completely misinforms students. Outside of studying the required courses pertaining to one's major, students are asked to learn utter nonsense. And if they fail in succession, guess what happens? They are essentially expelled from school! Whether public or private institutes, how does one get kicked out of school for failing on their own dollar, excluding those receiving free money?

For those who graduate, you enter the real world seeking big salaries, to compensate for the accrued college debt, because after all, your degree signifies *how great you are* (as per employers).

"I deserve this income because I paid my dues!"

Have you?

What about the employee who hasn't finished school but has a shitload of work experience in the same field?! Why are they less valuable? Our economic system is insistent on college being the pathway to "success", so, I suppose you can't fault students for sharing this privileged attitude. But I find degrees are the catalyst to a false sense of entitlement.

Presuming the graduate hasn't landed that "terrific paying job", now what? They're left to feel like failures because their whole existence was based upon making top dollar! Why must you make top dollar? Are you trying to compensate for the accrued student loan debt? *Isn't $50,000 a livable income (depending on location, of course), or are you that obsessed with becoming a well-to-do individual?*

Society tells us, that if we wish to make $100,000 per year in our selected fields, a *bachelor's degree* won't cut it! We must contemplate graduate school (cha-ching!) and before long, our student loan debt will spiral out of control. When is enough, *ever* enough?!

There's a famous saying: 'The richest person is one who has no debt!' Truer words have never been spoken.

* * * * *

Author's Note: *Don't confuse 'schooling' with education. There is a difference. Be diligent through life, study independently and you can learn just about anything.*

* * * * *

I know there are plenty of college advocates out there; "You won't amount to anything if you don't have a degree... a degree is everything!"

If you say so. For those electing to go to college, just be mindful of your selected major – with hopes that it pays off.

Pay offs: *Finding a subject you share a deep passion for, where it doesn't feel like a "job". Or majoring in something 'financially rewarding', if making big bucks is your main objective!*

Disclaimer: *Don't go to school just for the sake of going, where you'll amass a ton of debt without the means to pay it off! Have a plan! And you absolutely shouldn't major in a subject that isn't financially rewarding – if your immediate plan is to start a family.*

I understand 'things happen', but if your major pays a maximum salary of thirty-thousand per year, you reside in a big city and you've come out of the gate impregnating everyone in sight, or you're a female whose overly-concerned about a "biological clock" ... at 22! ... I can only wish you good luck! Lastly, don't look for your significant other to make the bucks for you. Make your own fuckin' money!

For those who feel college isn't for them, it is imperative you become *extra* attentive and calculated regarding personal and financial dealings. Try your best to avoid life's ploys! Remember, life is what *you* make it... not what society tells you it should be.

I've been fortunate to meet people who have experienced what I consider "rich living" (without a handsome salary), through three keys of basic survival:

- Good Credit
- Efficient saving habits
- *Money management*

Money Management: *Saving, investing, remaining debt free.* It can take you a long way.

Once you've accomplished these feats, while honing a skill and learning how to profit from it, the rewards can be beneficial. Valuable lessons learned – no thanks to school!

Chapter Ten: Ass, Tits, Porno Flicks...

Pornography gets a terrible rap. Has it greatly contributed to the demise of society? Unquestionably, it has. The industry is filled with smut and demeaning acts and if you're a parent of one of these actors... you've completely failed! (when your daughter's face gets ejaculated on – on camera for a living, there's just no coming back from that). But porn has certainly been a useful tool for those of us who can look beyond the filth. There is an obvious art form to it and we can have a serious discussion about the industry without being crass. Let's talk about it!

* * * * *

I'd like to think we've all seen a naked body before. And if you're a disgruntled married or single man, I'm sure you've seen a naked body *everyday* courtesy of the internet (just kidding)! But for many men, the obsession to look at naked women starts relatively young. We're mesmerized by tits the moment we come out of the womb, eventually graduating to ass. Males, young and old, all love a nice ass!

Nudity is highly celebrated in other countries and it is quite common to find a bare ass on commercials. In America, not so much. If you were anything like me as a kid, you'd do anything to catch a glimpse of a naked body; whether it was *screwing around with your vision* (trying to spot those Double D-cups through a scrambled cable channel that your parents didn't subscribe to), or it's possible you came across a dirty magazine buried somewhere in your father's closet. If you had a friend with unlimited access to X-rated material in their home – even better! *I've been reduced to wearing glasses as an adult, so you can pretty much figure out what I did.*

I was *seven* years old when I discovered my first *Penthouse* – locked away in one of Gran's trunks in the closet... and there was no turning back. The trunk is where Gran kept my toys and on one Saturday afternoon, while searching for something to play with... BAM! There she was, Ms. Vanessa Williams! The magazine was a few years old, but I was intrigued by the graphic material, frantically turning each page to see what else was in store. Some of you may be wondering what Gran was doing with a copy of Penthouse in her home… here's the answer: She was a grown-up – that's why! *I got out of the habit of questioning adults… once becoming an adult* (*plus, the magazine was a Collector's item*).

Gran was responsible for teaching me about the birds and the bee's, pulling *no* punches concerning casual sex talk:

"You put the pee-pee in the coochie mama – and make sure the coochie mama is clean!" Simple and effective.

Penthouse opened my eyes to many things; *That split opens?! Why is it so pink when she exposes the inside? Why is she sticking her fingers in it and looking at the camera seductively? What is this movement in my pants??* The latter observation was the indicator that females were something special.

I was a subscriber of *Sports Illustrated* at the age of ten. Near the end of the subscription, I received an exclusive offer for a free six-month trial of *Playboy.* I don't recall the specifics on why we accepted the offer, but I certainly remember Gran tossing a magazine covered in black plastic wrapping onto the living room table each month after retrieving the mail. I'd rip the plastic apart – like a Hulkamania t-shirt, browse through the airbrushed beauties and read each article like it was good literature written by Ernest Hemmingway. *What, none of you read the articles in Playboy?*

However, one of the major problems concerning the magazines? Not enough women of color. I loved the sight of blonde hair and big boobs – like any other man, but as I got older, I wanted *color* and *curves*.

Terrance was a collector of *Jet magazine* (among other things), usually keeping a stack of copies on the floor next to his bed. I'm *positive* they were kept for "educational purposes", as Jet made for an outstanding read – commemorating black excellence. But to the delight of male readers, there was one page you could count on each month: The Jet Beauty of the Week! Finally, curves!

Amateur models, with different shades of skin and hair textures, dressed in bathing suits – with unpretentious poses. *No purple and blonde wigs allowed!* I conducted my own "personal research", seeking the model with the cutest face and Coca-Cola bottle figure – to add to my 'Wall of Fame'. But the female body was too desirable to stop there. I needed more.

* * * * *

The schoolyard kissing in 2nd and 3rd grade and the ass gawking of *Geritza Osuna* in the 5th grade – jump-started my attraction to females. But it was my reaction to Patra *winding her hips provocatively in music videos* that did me in. There wasn't a woman alive who could command my brain and make body parts move on their own. But just as much as I savored every moment of her hip gyrations, it was the allure of Cindy Herron's beauty that often made me melt. My crush for the En Vogue singer was ridiculous! I could sing, "Giving Him Something He Can Feel", word for word. Why? Because I wouldn't miss a chance to watch the video – two, three, sometimes *four* times a day! *The way that red dress hugged her petite frame... well, it absolutely made me feel something...* I was secretly plotting on marrying this woman – even if she had me by 20 years!

My behavior wasn't any different than your average boy, but my lust for women was forceful and I desired sex a little too soon. Still years away before my first encounter, I had an idea of what sex was, without a girlfriend to feed my appetite. I wanted *more* raunchiness and *less* forced smiles and methodical poses found in magazines. Unfortunately, I'd have to make do with my celebrity crushes until something better came along.

* * * * *

During those late summer nights as a 'tween, I got acquainted with the corny *saxophone tunes* of Cinemax After Dark: Soft-core porn at its best. I was usually front and center, as a Fabio look-alike finessed his way into the silk sheets of a hot blonde in an erotic drama. On Saturday nights, around 11 p.m., I'd head to the living room – unwilling to look away from the screen. There was a lot of skin on skin *and* the actors were fully elated.

Is he really penetrating her? I'd think to myself. The action seemed all too real. This is exactly what I needed! Years later, I'd learn about the secrets of camera angles. *I knew something was peculiar when the actress was commonly positioned a little too far from the actor's waistline during a blowjob scene.* Like a good student, I'd take notes on what stimulated the female's body – paying close attention to movement, sounds and bed chemistry. I figured this much; with all the knowledge I was obtaining, I was gonna completely knock the socks off the person I'd lose my virginity to!

The deception of Cinemax After Dark was much ado about nothing; I had exposure to breast, ass and the occasional glimpse of a groomed vagina. If you would've asked me – this was as good as it got. But my entrance to the *world of sex* broadened once my household was introduced to the *hot box*.

For the new generation of readers, a hot box was an illegal cable box, enabling subscribers total access to every cable and pay-per-view channel. Cable providers (along with the authorities) grew wise to the growing trend and through advance technology could detect the households "stealing cable". If caught, you faced a hefty fine and jail time! Thankfully, we were in on the hot box frenzy during its early stages and to my delight, I had wrestling pay-per-views *and* two additional channels in the palm of my hand: Playboy and Spice!

I didn't have cable in my room, so I'd have to wait until the coast was clear (usually after Terrance left for work). But I knew there were a few hours to spare before Mom got home, therefore, I'd take my homework into their bedroom and flip a coin:

Heads: *The grace of Anna Nicole Smith's boobs on Playboy?*
Tails: *The indecency of Jenna Jameson in a hot orgy scene on Spice?*

I loved Anna Nicole, but Spice won unanimously... even when the coin landed on heads! Both channels were obvious upgrades from Cinemax, but rather than take notes, I started recording on the VCR – looking to build a collection of movies from a few of my favorite porn actresses: Jenna Jameson; Asia Carrera; Jill Kelly.

Spice was hardcore, commonly highlighting vaginal, anal and oral scenes, girl-on-girl action, threesomes, gangbangs, movie spoofs and more! The stuff 'tween boys dreamt of ... or, perhaps just me.

* * * * *

Terrance kept a crate at the bottom of the closet, which I spotted from the corner of my eye when the closet door was ajar. The crate was usually covered with clothing and I never thought anything of it since the closet space was small. *Surely, the crate was for extra storage.*

The sliding closet doors were usually shut and if I noticed a slight opening, I'd close it. It was the least I could do, considering my invasion of their room. But I'm guessing Terrance was in a rush on this day.

When I got home, I entered their room to find his side of the closet wide open – and the crate *very* much visible. Strange. In my usual after school fashion, I powered up the TV, browsed through the channels, before ultimately landing on my *two* new favorites. Suddenly, my conscious started to talk: *Ernest, close the damn closet door! ... now!* Okay.

My conscious was right. It's not that I was a sufferer of OCD (Obsessive Compulsive Disorder), but if there is anything I cannot stand, it's a half-way closed door... in a dark room (I've awakened many times for a quick bathroom break, closing my bedroom closet door – if fully opened). It was unusually dark that afternoon and the lightbulb in their room must've blown out. Without a replacement bulb in sight, I took a few steps to the closet – attempting to close his side, until I noticed something jamming it below. *That could've explained why he hadn't closed it all the way.*

I went down to one knee to figure out the cause of the stoppage, when I noticed a *scandal bag* laying on top of the crate. *Hmmm, what is this?* Mom typically hid Christmas gifts on her side (of the closet) when it was that time of year, so I assumed Terrance was doing the same... but it was *only* October! *Did he complete some early Christmas shopping?*

I opened the bag and there they were... *dazzling* VHS tapes – with big, bold, blocky lettering. I pulled out a tape, reading the featured names: Ron Hightower and Janet Jacme. The actors were on the front cover – naked. Eureka! Porn!

I locked both the basement and living room entrance doors, scurrying back to see what else was in this crate. Voila! Porn here, porn there, porn everywhere! *It was Christmas in October!* Terrance had an obvious attachment to black adult films, with a serious collection of videos from the 70s, 80s and early 90s. It was time to do some *research*.

Contrary to popular opinion, I found 70s and 80s porn unappealing. The actors were apparently allergic to razor blades, the makeup was horrendous and the storylines? Ugh! Many of those stars paved the way for more modern-day names, but I couldn't help the feeling of wanting a STD checkup and a hot shower afterwards. *I swore I once saw a crab fly out of the television!*

The 90s videos looked "cleaner", *and* on many afternoons, while finishing homework, I found myself watching a ton of material. In fact, when Terrance brought home the amateur sex tapes of Tonya Harding and Pamela Anderson (featuring Tommy Lee), I watched them before *he* did after finding the un-played tapes hidden behind his dresser – in what else? a scandal bag, of course!

If you're wondering whether Mom was a fan of his collection? She wasn't. But I was so locked in on making my debut in San Fernando Valley, CA (the one-time home of the adult industry), I came up with my own stage name... just in case: Malcolm Harden (see what I did there)? Anyway, thanks, Terrance... *I think?*

* * * * *

To tickle my fancy, there was MC Hammer's, "Pumps in a Bump" video which was bliss, excluding MC Hammer frolicking around in a speedo and *Luke's Peep Show,* starring the one and only Luther (Luke) Campbell (from 2 Live Crew fame). The show featured uncensored videos, explicit talk and the occasional in-studio interview, where he'd ask female guests to remove their tops. Quality Friday night television (and a cheap thrill), as far as I was concerned.

Does anybody remember *The Robin Byrd Show?* If you were an inquisitive kid growing up in Manhattan during the 80s and 90s, you know exactly who I am talking about. The program aired on public access cable TV (channel 35 on Time Warner cable) *and* I found out about it accidentally.

As Gran skimmed through the channels one late evening, my quick eye came upon breasts. But these weren't your average boobs... they were 38 Double F's. *Wait! Turn back!* We'd chuckle for a few minutes, as Robin fondled the bosom of the hot redhead, but Gran knew the content was inappropriate and quickly turned the channel...

"Alright, boy, I'm going to bed. Don't you stay up too late!"

Okay... Right back to channel 35 I'd go. The TV was all mine and I'd treat myself to this wonderful (yet, unbearable) production. The show was filmed in a low-budget studio, using some of the tackiest television graphics I'd ever seen. But for a half-hour, I witnessed random women stripping their clothes and dancing to some egregious tunes. It also marked the first time my young eyes came across a transgendered woman!

At the end of the program, Robin typically took calls from viewers who wanted to speak to guests. One night, I attempted to call, after Heather Hunter took my breath away with an amazing performance. I fell in love with her beauty and wanted to share my appreciation for her work... until a graphic flashed across the screen: *This show was pre-recorded.* Son of a bitch! Not sure if I would've gotten through – considering my voice sounded like Mickey Mouse... but it was worth a try.

* * * * *

From there the nudity continued; we'd reached the mid-90s, the internet was taking off and so were the hormones of teenaged boys and girls. For those with computers, pornography was at your fingertips and there wasn't a thing your parents could do about it, except enforce parental restrictions *if* they knew how. The only thing standing in the way was a slow dial-up connection.

Slavik had superior internet speed at the time and there were plenty of days during high school where he'd invite me to his home. We'd giggle like a couple of school girls watching images of women sticking obscene objects into their vaginas. And for the first time in my life... I watched a dog give a chick oral. *Sadly, my eyes can never un-see that!*

The acts were considered extreme (and inhumane) until more grotesque material started making its rounds on the web. Thankfully, I had my limits. I wouldn't own a personal computer until the turn of the century, which is when a few old buddies advised on the one and only, Heather Brooke.

One word: *Keeper!*
Two words: *Extremely talented!*
Three words: *I love you!*

There was B.E.T.: *Uncut* – a late-night music program, which aired uncensored videos from a few lesser-known hip-hop artists and the imagery was enough to keep many of us awake in the wee hours of the morning. Finally, for my 21st birthday, my buddy *Courtney* treated me to an *all-inclusive* stay at an X-rated shop in midtown Manhattan. The store was nice and empty, the owner gave two young men the liberty to roam around – which we did, for about forty-five minutes.

"Go, go, look at whatever you like – nice birthday gift for you!" he exclaimed in his heavy middle eastern accent. We proceeded to grab quite a few VHS tapes and DVD's to add to our collections.
Honorable Mention: *The Howard Stern Show* on E! television and *Black Tail* Magazine.

* * * * *

Many growing up on porn, likely experimented with masturbation earlier than expected. Not me. In fact, through the hundreds of hours of X-rated material, I honestly didn't know masturbation was a form of pleasure until I was around 21! That's how seriously uninformed I was. I figured, if you had a partner, you had sex. If you didn't... well, you waited until one came along.

I was unaware of one's sexual appetite, didn't know a thing about "pent-up sexual frustrations" being tied to one's emotional state and certainly didn't think people were hard-pressed to pleasure themselves – whether they had a partner or not.

As a teen, if at any point I felt "hot and bothered", I knew the feeling would subside. Besides, who has time to drain their nut sack all day long? *You make time!*

While in school, there was a running joke how the "unpopular guys" went home to "beat their meat" – usually followed by a silly hand gesture. *You know of the gesture I'm referring to.* I always thought the term was used figuratively – something along the lines of calling someone a "loser" (the students conjecture was embedded in my mind, likely the reason I shied away from "the palm experiment").

T-Boz from the group TLC, released a single in 1996 entitled 'Touch Myself'. I was seriously angered when I first heard it played on afternoon radio! The gist of the song was T-Boz showing appreciation for her partner – whom she often thought about when she was alone and sexually aroused... I suppose it's better than cheating *shrugging shoulders*

On top of that, I never believed the masturbation theory from these uninformed students applied to me – especially since I had my fair share of female onlookers. But since they ignorantly linked *self-pleasure* to *teasing,* I wouldn't "touch it" with a ten-foot pole.

Heaven forbid if the thought ever crossed my mind and somebody found out?

Seeing that I wasn't sexually active, pornography was the closest action I could get. I'd withstand the repetitive, 'Plumber coming over to fix the pipes' storyline – if it meant catching a hot girl with her legs spread apart like the Air Jordan logo. I simply admired the female body – imperfections and all and it was all the satisfaction I needed.

* * * * *

Author's Note: *I'm an advocate of safe-sex, but safe-sex in adult movies? No Bueno!*

* * * * *

Chapter Tidbits:
Tonya Harding's amateur sex tape was the saddest celebrity adult film I ever watched... until I came across '1 Night in Paris', featuring Paris Hilton. I don't know why I was so excited about the latter, but it absolutely sucked!

Honorable Mention: *Kim Kardashian and Ray-J. One thought: Somebody tell Kim to shut her pie-hole! You're being penetrated, not murdered!*

Chapter Eleven: Control Your D**k, Control Your Life!

I've paid very close attention to women over the years. I haven't begun to figure some of you out and I'm certainly not about to waste anymore brain cells attempting to, but I have a good understanding of how a few of you operate. I'll play nice, for now, because I want the reader to make the connection of women being just one of my downfalls – but don't get too comfy... I'm coming for you!

* * * * *

God knew exactly what He was doing when He created females. They are our kryptonite. Men have risked their lives fighting over women, fighting with women and will go to great lengths for their immediate attention. In addition to a nice sunset, there is nothing more satisfying to the eyes than a female who is well put together.

Such women will commonly cause us to break character, where we go from *admiring the view*, to having a sudden urge to start a conversation. What about when an attractive lady walks by – and you realize you're a natural contortionist? *Because, who else but a woman, can make men turn their neck like the character from the Exorcist?*

Finally, has anyone swerved their car in the middle of the road – because they couldn't keep their eyes off that incredibly beautiful attraction? If it sounds like I'm speaking from experience... guilty as charged! *No one should possess that type of mind control!*

But there is something amiss about today's female and we need to talk about it: Social fuckin' media! Women have an immense obsession with themselves today and I find them vain and self-centered as ever.

The camera phone is killing women slowly, as millions of photo galleries are filled with gratuitous poses – that are ready to be showcased to the social media world or, for their own viewing pleasure. Women are found aggressively competing amongst themselves with inexcusable "challenges" found on the internet:

- Who can arch they're back the furthest in a doggy-style position?
- Whose butt looks biggest sitting on the bathroom sink?
- Who can fit into the tightest jeans?
- Who looks better in their Calvin Klein undergarments?
- Which pair of leggings reveal the most (or least) camel toe?

There are all types of pictures posted online, leading to scores of *new followers* and *self-assurance*. As appealing as it may seem – the whole act has gotten old. Here is a list of items that need to perish for *any* hope to be restored (concerning the male-female alliance):

1. Social Media
2. Leggings
3. Butt injections

Honorable Mention: *Colorful wigs and fake eyelashes.*

Due to the implosion of the listed items, the *Average Jane* seriously believes in her own celebrity, making it harder for the *Average Joe* to strike up conversation. Men are commonly met with uninviting faces – or women who will simply avoid making eye contact altogether (which I highly recommend if you're involved). It's gotten to the point where men are unsure of what to do next –*if* there's an inkling of interest: *Do I smile back at her? Is she interested? Shall I start a conversation? Do I simply look the other way?*

Some of us have gotten so used to being publicly ignored, we'd rather take a glimpse, gather a thought and look the other way to avoid possible rejection. I'm even guilty of rolling my eyes at women, because today's self-assured man has been conditioned to behave *just as* self-centered as our female counterparts. *There's only so many times a man of my caliber will allow you to give me your ass to kiss. Since I'm already anticipating the eye-roll, allow me to beat you to the punch!*

But gentleman, tread lightly! Just as we make assumptions – so do women. If you choose to ignore a female (who is admiring the view) the thought is:

1. You're involved
2. You're conceited
3. You're a homosexual

Why is the third option never considered when the shoe is on the other foot? I'm sure plenty of women have mistaken me for all three, but I've never cared. I didn't become this way by myself.

Sometimes I'll throw out a compliment – something along the lines of, "I like your hair" and promptly go about my business. Women have gotten used to our predictability after a compliment and I find many of them dread the follow-up: *Can I get your name? Can you add me on social media? Can I take you out? Are you from around here?* The latter being too intrusive. *Ladies, I pay attention!*

So, I found another route. Instead of being "typical", I'd rather make your day by keeping my words to a minimum, allowing *your* mind to wander (for once).

"Wow, that's all? Why didn't he say more?"

Because I didn't need to! A compliment can *stay* at a compliment. I'm simply uninterested in the cat and mouse game that adults play, I certainly will not force conversation if the vibe isn't right. If you don't wish to speak, neither do I. However, through experience, I found that women can be *just as* aggressive as men if there's interest. *If you're a good reader of body language, you'll notice how sly some women are.* Only then do you make a move. The problem today? Women who are 'involved' are notoriously known to send signals as well! Especially in the workplace!

* * * * *

Author's Note: *There's being 'extra friendly' and then there's 'flirty'! Use your own discretion in the workplace. I don't want to be held liable for future relationship woes.*

* * * * *

In the age of social media, where the number of followers appears to confirm your desirability, women find solace in their *1000 male followers* (who comment on their every picture), yet, handle random male public acknowledgment as poorly as Donald Trump handles criticism! Social media has tainted our minds, obliterated interfacing skills and the feeling of exclusivity has died.

SHE'S GOT LEGG(INGS)... SHE KNOWS HOW TO USE THEM!

We can talk about *comfort* until we're blue in the face, but leggings have given women with disenchanting figures the look and feel of a million bucks. Why? Because leggings restore confidence – no matter the shape or size of the woman. If you are one of those fortunate *B.B.W.'s,* what I like to refer to as *Booty Blessed Women,* leggings will further inflate your ego, as drivers inadvertently slam on their breaks – causing more rear-end accidents due to your... *rear end!* See what I did there?

Leggings have become the go-to weapon for *comfort, confidence and control.* They feel good, you're proud of how your ass looks and you've managed to make a man (somewhere) lose his train of thought. That's fuckin' power!

Witnessing a nice booty can truly make our day. It's almost like watching a car accident – we just can't look away. *Spotting a nice backside is about the only time a man will show mixed emotions. We're usually happier than a pig in mud, yet, heart-broken because we know our chances of bedding you (on the spot) are slim to none.*

I don't know what changed over the years, but *even* white women have joined the fray. Black and Hispanic women have a little competition on their hands, as white women with asses have become the *new* phenomenon. Whatever it is, let's tip our hats to places like, McDonald's *and* the makers of processed foods. Without them, there would be an invasion of "ironing board backs" like in olden times.

Ironing board backs: *When a woman's lower back overlaps the booty.* No Bueno!

As an observant of the 80s and 90s, shapely booties weren't in abundance as they are today. Now, *every* race has their share of "butt phenoms". Due to mainstream media's ass obsession, we have jeans that are designed to specifically target this area for women with butt defects (or those looking for a little *oomph* back there). In the meantime, spandex has quickly replaced the common female pant:

Winter: Leggings and Uggs boots
Spring: Leggings and sneakers
Summer: Leggings and flip flops
Fall: Leggings and knee-high boots

The world has seemingly gone *legging/yoga pants/spandex* crazy! You laugh because you *know* it's true. *All I ask, is that you don't wear the same pair five days a week... I know you're out there!*

But here is where we need to draw the line – my place of serenity: the gym! The gym would be the appropriate place to wear leggings, but you're putting men in a pickle when there's midriff, visible camel toe *and* embroidered designs on your backsides (usually in the shape of a peach). When you're dressed in this manner, you're indirectly (or purposefully) inviting our eyes to your body. Let's call it what it is: You want attention!

Ultimately, men are left with two choices to avoid coming off as perverts:

1. Look down to the floor
2. Look at each other!

Oh boy... Because the moment you catch us ~~staring~~ *glancing,* we're met with eye-rolls and attitudes! *What exactly would you like for us to do? I'll wait...* I understand common sense *isn't* always common to all, but can we at least try to use it?

Ladies, in all seriousness, be proud of your curves. Curves are fantastic! But you've got to play fair. Let's fuse comfort with *principle* (if both genders are sharing close quarters – excluding the beach). A nice figure walking around the gym – in spandex, is the equivalent to a well-endowed man walking around in biker shorts; it's an annoying distraction! And we all know the reaction if *that* occurred:

"He's sick in the head!"

"Ewww, that is completely gross!"

"I'm sure he's gay!"

"Gurllll, I wonder if it's as big as it looks?"

The focus should be on our individual bodies at the gym – not my body – and yours! *If I didn't pay enough attention in school, I certainly made up for it by becoming a butt expert! Now, if I can just find a way to get paid for it! How does 'Booty Specialist' sound?*

* * * * *

Author's Note: *The state of the modern-day female is equally as alarming as today's male! We've got to collectively figure out how to get back to the basics.*

* * * * *

HOW IT ALL GOT STARTED

*My first kiss occurred in **Kindergarten** and by now, you've all learned about a few of my escapades during grade school. But, what were the events that fostered my women itch – particularly, older women?*

* * * * *

Yancy double locked the front door, hurried back to her room to check on "the kids", before straddling me, as she crashed her braces against my gums. Once the uncomfortable make-out session ended, she removed her pants, placing my hand on a *fuzzy area* between her legs. Before long, she was "sound asleep" – we had an early day ahead of us.

I was an *innocent* eight-year-old playing "house" with my babysitter's teenaged daughter, not having the slightest idea why I was being humped and puzzled by that fuzzy area that I caressed, fingered and pressed my lips against. *I didn't have any hair on my private part, so what was her deal?!*

Though I'd already feasted my eyes on my first vagina in Penthouse, I really couldn't make the connection between the magazine and real life. Yancy was aware of how promiscuous our behavior was, as the slightest sound startled her.

"What was that?!" she asked, launching out of bed to turn on every light in the house.

I'm sure her nerves were rattled at the thought of an ensuing ass kicking (if we ever got caught), but she couldn't help herself and I was simply following her lead. We were a "married couple", just doing what married couples do. We'd play "house" from time to time – when the *actual* house was empty, but our most memorable moment occurred inside of the family's *Astro Van*.

One rainy afternoon, we joined Carmella and Ma-ma as they ran a few errands in the Bronx. Due to the precipitation, rather than exit the van at each stop, Yancy suggested we stay inside – as they wandered about. Carmella concurred.

We knew they'd be awhile and that's when Yancy proceeded to kiss and hump the life out of me – fully clothed – on the floor of the van. I suspect it was the *act* of sex that satisfied the concupiscent teen and though I didn't have a clue on what I was doing, I played my part accordingly. *Happy wife, happy life!* She'd get up momentarily to look out the window, only to return and repeat the act.

Kissing Yancy was like trying to kiss barbwire. She was sloppy, and my mouth paid for it dearly. Once we finished our raunchiness, ~~I'd puff on a cigar and kick my feet up~~ *her hair was entirely disheveled* – almost as if someone rubbed a balloon on the top of her head! Upon Carmella's return, she questioned the flustered appearance, but Yancy, always a step ahead, blamed it *on the rain* and humidity. *Way to tap into your Milli Vanilli!* Hold your pity, folks. I was having the time of my life!

* * * * *

Every so often, Jeanette would pick me up from the bus stop, standing there in full catholic school girl attire – à la Britney Spears, "Hit Me Baby One More Time" video. She was the "guy magnet" of the sisters and I always sensed jealousy from Yancy when boys looked her way. They were both attractive, but Jeanette's physical appearance stood out. She had quiet tendencies, but I knew there was a wild side. I'd usually overhear the conversations she'd share with her boyfriend, as she'd put on her best *bedroom voice* – followed by a goofy giggle. Little did she know, while chatting with her boytoy, this inquisitive little kid frequently peered through the cracks of her bedroom door – as she undressed.

Jeanette tied her *Rapunzel-like* hair into a ponytail, removed her bra and stared into the mirror with a look of confidence. It was my first time witnessing breasts up-close and more importantly, I didn't have to go to Times Square and pay for indecent exposure. This was free of charge. Thanks, ladies.

* * * * *

One evening, my father picked me up from Carmella's and unbeknownst to me, Savannah Gill left a *friendly* message on our family's answering machine. During the twenty-second ~~Phone Sex Line audition~~ *message*, she moaned for what seemed like hours, shouting my name at the top of her lungs. I wasn't familiar with those sounds, but soon found out that her act was unacceptable. *What would possess her to do such a thing?*

Okay, so, we kissed a few times, but what would make her infringe on proper answering machine etiquette? This was a family house phone – not a personal one! When we arrived home, Mom met my eyes with a look of disgust. I was completely mortified when she asked that I listen to the message. She wanted answers, but I didn't have any....

"Take off your clothes!"

My parents weren't going to perpetuate the nonsense and I was immediately used as collateral damage. *You're welcome, Savannah!* The ass-beating would live in infamy and I was on solitary confinement for weeks!

GLUED TO THE TUBE

My feet were wet (so to speak) and I was more than convinced as the years progressed, I'd be swatting the ladies away like flies! Until then, I grew exceedingly attracted to white women and there was something about the names below that had me on notice:

- Julie Newmar
- Tina Louise
- Nicole Eggert
- Christina Applegate
- Kathy Ireland
- Elizabeth Berkley
- Rena Sofer
- Krista Allen
- Jenny McCarthy
- Carmen Electra (born: Tara Leigh Patrick)
- Jennifer Love-Hewitt

White women have always been abundant on TV and film – and if it matters any, the first actress to give me a *tingling sensation* portrayed a "cat"! (Julie Newmar's *catsuit* awakened me more than Eartha Kitt's seductive voice). But at a time when guys were going batty (and reaching for the Kleenex box) for the likes of Pam Anderson and Cindy Crawford, I placed my eyes on more unconventional names – because I never quite understood the obsession for A-list celebrities.

Thankfully, as television evolved, so did the addition of women of color with plenty of names who would soon become worldwide sensations. While black men dropped their jaws (and grabbed a bottle of lotion) to Janet Jackson, Naomi Campbell, Halle Berry and Rosie Perez, here are a few names that I paid attention to at the brink of stardom:

- Robin Givens
- Cree Summers
- Jada Pinkett Smith
- Aaliyah
- Stacey Dash
- Tyra Banks
- Alysia Rogers
- Aisha Tyler
- Nicole Ari Parker
- Kerry Washington
- Mari Morrow

Again, prominent names in the entertainment industry – whose careers hadn't quite taken off at the time I spotted their beauty. *How many of you had pictures of Cree Summers on your wall…? Don't all raise your hands at once…*

I found a shitload of "B-listers" flying under the radar – on the news, commercials, soap operas, sitcoms and "straight to DVD" movies. Here was my simple logic: I never dated the "popular girl", so why set myself up to believe I'd have a chance with an A-lister? While you all shoot for Beyoncé, I'll mingle with the likes of Denyce Lawton – who shares a similar beauty. *If you're unfamiliar with Denyce, even better!*

I get it, there's the "fantasy element" which the common fan orchestrates in their head, but if you haven't learned by now – I'm not common! A man's arousal is all the same. Kim Kardashian won't cause a blood rush to my penis any more than the hot, flirty *salesgirl* at a department store. Why consume energy on *unrealistic* expectations, when there's beauty everywhere? I'm a man who understands his limits.

* * * * *

Author's Note: *I'll put my favorite female weather/traffic reporters up against any of PEOPLE® Magazine's Most Beautiful Women list!*

* * * * *

EYES ON THE PRIZE!

I've always known there to be a distinct difference between my peers, but the thought really kicked in during high school, when I'd stare intently at the eyebrows, sideburns and *forearms* of girls I'd communicate with. *You read that correctly.* While most guys are drawn to normal body features, I was too busy trying to put two and two together hoping to make four: *She's intelligent, pretty, her eyebrows, sideburns and forearm hair are profound... that probably means she's got a bush 'downstairs.'* And I wasn't talking about George. Yep! I was *that* guy.

Meanwhile, in Ms. Vega's class, I'd daydream about clearing her desk of papers, placing her on top and acting out a scene from Cinemax After Dark. She was what I referred to as "a snake", or S.S.S. (the *"sssing"* sound of a snake): *Sexy, sophisticated and stylish.* All she had to do to get my tongue wagging was show up to school in a pencil skirt. Damn, was she hot!

I attended high school during one of the biggest teacher-student scandals in history (see Mary Kay Letourneau and Vili Fualaau for those who are interested), but it was still somewhat taboo. In today's climate, where teachers are seducing students at an alarming rate, I probably would've found myself on the evening news. There is very little requirement these days – a generous text message, with a *smiley face* emoji should do the trick. Before long, your sexy, unhappily married English teacher is taking the risk of flushing her career down the toilet, sending nudes to your phone, arranging to give you a blowjob in the backseat of her car, while becoming a registered sex offender in the process! *Where were these teachers during my day?!*

Okay, so pornography (and my teen babysitters) facilitated the distinction that I'm sure most teenaged boys weren't attentive to, but I can assure you there was a method to my madness. My goal was to make certain I lost my virginity to someone mature, both physically and mentally. In other words – I wanted a *woman* and not a *girl*.

It was a given that I was attracted to brains and maturity before beauty. Any guy who has ever lusted after a fuckin' *robot,* Jesse Spano (who's character was a compulsive study freak), a high school computer teacher and *Female Business Correspondents* on FOX News – can attest. *What man doesn't want a woman who can thoroughly explain the S&P 500 live from the floor of the NYSE... in a pencil skirt, of course?*

But through high school, I searched for the total package. The longer I went without a serious relationship, the more meticulous I became. My future girlfriend had to be *the one;* the one I'd consider marrying, have ~~children~~ *a child* with and "live happily ever after". I was certain I'd find her with ease.

A SUCKA FOR LOVE

Sasha Dawes made a random call to a mutual friend – inquiring about my phone number. For some reason or another, she wanted to contact me, after many years had passed. As expected, my antennas went up. *What would she want all these years later?*

I was confused, yet excited, when I saw a *New Jersey* area code appear on the caller ID that evening. Our first conversation was a success – lasting well over two hours, as we discussed life and future goals. The conversations continued through the week. Before long, we were speaking regularly. No way was this coincidental, Sasha was back for a reason.

She made quite the impression on my parents while we were kids. My father often teased how she should've been my girlfriend. But I was intimidated by her wit, condescending tone and *sophistication* – the latter becoming a top requirement for a significant other as years progressed.

Sasha came off as snobbish, usually thumbing her nose at child-like behavior. I mean, the girl was studying for the S.A.T.'s, at a time I was *only* concerned with going undefeated in Tecmo Bowl! Her parents were successful, so her taste was exquisite... too exquisite for my blood at the time and her entitled attitude was unbecoming. There were whispers of an attraction, but our academic rivalry usually kept us at bay. The thought never occurred that we'd meet again. *Perhaps God was answering those solicitation calls for a mature girlfriend.*

Once we established our relationship statuses as single, I couldn't wipe the stupid smile off my face when she suggested we meet up in the city. *Yes! No!*

The NBA Playoffs were scheduled for the upcoming weekend and the Knicks were the first game of a tripleheader. Fuck! I can't miss this game. I *never* missed Knicks games! "What time do you want to meet at the bus terminal?" I asked.

Well... that didn't take long! (the things guys will do for a piece of ass). For the record, I was still a virgin and wasn't expecting sex, but it was my first official date. With the constant ups and downs I'd encountered with the girls at Murrow, I couldn't miss out on the opportunity to mingle with someone I was very familiar with. The Knicks would have to wait.

I showered, got dressed and left the house in a haste, making the subway trek into the city. As I arrived at the bus terminal, there she was – *a tall, brown-skinned, model-like figure, wearing a jean-jacket, black spandex and knee-high boots* – fitting the exact description she'd given me. My heart raced uncontrollably, as she looked in the opposite direction. I freshened my mouth with two squirts of Bianca Blast and marched right over to the one I'd imagined would carry my last-name. To add to the suspense, I tapped her on the shoulder...

"Oh my God! I can't believe it's you!" she shrieked. We hugged for what seemed like hours. She didn't have to say another word. Sasha and I knew what we'd known all along; we were meant to be. Our meeting was destiny. We spent the day walking around the city, hand in hand, laughing, browsing through clothing stores. We even caught a few minutes of the game – standing outside a restaurant:

Knicks 48 – Hornets 47 at the half.

I was missing a good one, but Josh kept me informed with occasional score updates to my beeper. *The good ol' beeper days!* (Google it, Millennial!) Sadly, we reached the end of the date, but all I could think about was how we'd make the perfect couple. Though we lived far apart, the allure was obvious and our families were cordial. A relationship made sense.

I thought about kissing her on the way back to the subway – but didn't want to come off overzealous. Instead, we embraced with a deep stare and another drawn-out hug. I threw in a kiss on the cheek – for good measure, just to send her home with something to think about. *I became a pro at the calculated cheek kiss and a quick licking of the lips afterwards – LL Cool J style – once locking eyes.*

It was tough watching Sasha go, but I loved watching her leave. Those hips were talking to me – as she disappeared into the crowd. *If you spotted a UFO over Manhattan that evening – it was me, floating all the way back to Brooklyn.*

Following the date, we continued communicating in hopes of meeting again. Over the next few weekends, Sasha had prior commitments, while my Saturday's were tied up – in what was my final season of baseball. I was still kicking myself for not kissing her (I felt she wanted to as well), but my objective from day one has been to maintain a *gentleman's* modus operandi... even if my mind is in the gutter. I was positive that come date *number two* – we'd swap spit! Unfortunately, there wouldn't be another date.

In a sudden turn of events, Sasha started to play the "phone game" – that men are often accused of. I got my first real taste of heartbreak – outside of the 1994 baseball strike.

Phone game: *When phone calls go unanswered, unreturned, or when someone abruptly stops calling.*

Okay, so now we're going to play with my emotions?!

Keep in mind – cell phones hadn't saturated the market yet, so there was no such thing as a *text message,* nor could you leave a message on someone's social media account... because there was no such thing! A clear sucker for love, I continued reaching out, while spacing out the calls, hoping to get in touch with her. But the mental mind-fuck proceeded.

"Oh, Hi Ernest, Sasha's not home..."

Suddenly, she'd forgotten how to call back. Just when all hope was lost and I was on the verge of waving the white flag, she decided to call. Sasha and I spoke at length, where she apologized profusely, blaming her disappearing act on "being busy". *Aaah, the good ol' "I was busy" excuse!*

Upon asking about my availability for the following weekend, I immediately shoved any ill-will to the side and like a sucker who was hard-pressed for love... I agreed to a "second date". Thankfully, the Knicks weren't on the sports calendar that day. I arrived about an hour early to the landmark at Central Park – on what was a beautiful spring afternoon. The birds were chirping, the flowers were in full bloom and love was in the air.

Sasha was the punctual type, but I was thrilled to have gotten there first. I wanted her to pay attention to how serious I was about taking our friendship to the next level. I grabbed a dozen roses from a nearby vendor – *one o'clock* would be here soon. I grew tired of shooing away bees, so I decided to take a stroll through the park. My beeper showed *one-fifteen.* Maybe her bus was late. But one-fifteen turned into *one-thirty* and eventually... *two o'clock.* Something was wrong.

I walked over to a pay phone and called her house. No answer. Perfect! Why would she be home anyway? Duh! But I wanted to be certain. I kept the beeper in the palm of my hand, hoping to hear the roaring sounds signaling her arrival. As I made my way back to the landmark – still, no sign of Sasha.

Three o'clock. Maybe we'd missed each other? But Sasha would've informed me of her whereabouts. No way would she have taken such a trip, only to head back across state lines without trying to communicate. What was going on?

I called her house a second time, when her dad answered. This was the straw that broke the camel's back:

"Hello, Mr. Dawes, this is Ernest."

"Oh. Hey Ernest."

"Do you know what time Sasha left? We were supposed to meet a couple of hours ago."

"Sasha was just here a minute ago... I think she may have stepped out."

Stepped out?

"What time were you guys supposed to meet?"

"Around one o'clock – I've been waiting, but I haven't heard anything."

"Oh boy – no, she was *just* here... I'll have her get in touch with you."

"Thanks."

Sasha stood me up. I honestly don't know what went wrong. Maybe she had a boyfriend, or perhaps she wasn't as interested as I thought – but it was an apparent wake-up call. The magnitude of hurt was overwhelming, she never did call back to explain her actions. In fact, a *few years* would pass before she'd call again.

I recognized the number on the caller ID that evening and was tempted to answer… until common sense intercepted my curiosity. She wasn't going to make a fool out of me a second time. It took several months to fully recover from the sting and I was numb for weeks, missing out on plenty of meals, giving the silent treatment to friends. I didn't deserve that type of hurt, but the incident triggered something inside. A light switch went off. No more Mr. Nice Guy!

From that moment, I developed a narcissistic attitude towards women, tolerating very little. I turned into the asshole who *wouldn't* return calls when promised, I detached myself emotionally after *one* simple argument and I made a promise to never chase pussy again… until I innately chased it again! But things would be different this time around.

CHANGE OF HEART

I was clearly having difficulty attracting the types I envisioned, so I turned the tables around and settled for those below my standards. Instead of holding onto my virginity until marriage – which admittedly was never the plan, but it would've been nice to save it for another virgin, I figured it was time to relinquish it. So, at 19, I gave it away to a girl – known for her talent for giving blowjobs in the stairwells of my high school – after inviting her to my 'House of Horrors', better known as the Basement. Thankfully, during our escapade (which lasted for hours, where I'd experience blue balls instead of a nice release), we weren't greeted by any *uninvited guests.*

I also committed one of my most insensitive acts – *leaving a date early* with one of the sweetest girls I knew, after growing tired of her visible cracked heels and dirty fingernails! *If proper hygiene is a requirement for guys, you'd damn sure better be clean as a whistle. No exceptions!* Her calls went unanswered following the date.

Finally, the day arrived where I crossed paths with Patricia McDonald once more – this time, at a local Foot Locker. She proceeded to spark up a conversation, making weak attempts to flirt as I contemplated purchasing a pair of Nikes. In what was my best attempt at portraying someone bipolar, I changed my mind at the register – inviting her to my mid-section in an *unpleasant way,* before promptly walking out of the store. Patricia stood there… stunned! We weren't amicable, I didn't need to pretend.

Maybe it was time for something new. I wasn't happy about the number of rejections I received, I outwardly rejected anyone who shared compatibility – *if* there was a fragment of a non-attraction. I had a bad taste in my mouth concerning black girls – especially the ones from the city. It was time I turned my attention towards another ethnicity.

* * * * *

Through my experiences and observations, I found white women easier to communicate with; they were *very* welcoming, cheery and their voices provided comfort – even if they came off phony at times. But oddly, white women (in the city) turned the other cheek towards black men unless you dressed like Lenny Kravitz and spoke like Carlton Banks from *The Fresh Prince of Bel-Air.* I've always articulated myself well, but with hip-hop fashion becoming my style of choice, I wasn't going to make compromises for their acceptance.

I was intrigued by Asian culture, but our races collided. I made several Asian friends over the years, but Asian families are commonly known to look down on blacks – particularly, black men. No way would they approve of someone of my caliber with their daughter (I found out many years later that Filipino women have a strong regard for black men). So, there remained one dominate ethnic group left in the city. In a town swarming with *Puerto Ricans* and *Dominicans,* it was time I test the waters.

I watched *Telemundo* and *Univision* like there was no tomorrow, hoping to become fully immersed in the culture. Their women were all the way sexy, giggly, relationship minded, I had some experience thanks to Yancy, plus, I was informed by Latin male friends, that once you've made a connection, they're *much* easier to bed. Maybe that was a bit stereotypical of them, but who was I to argue? It was time to find someone to sleep with!

I was a hopeless romantic, who at this point wanted nothing more than to hit & run… like a drunk driver racing from the scene of an accident! I wasn't going to allow anyone to get close to my heart again.

* * * * *

Author's Note: *Racial Breakdown of the city:*
- Black men – black women
- White men – white women
- Latin men – Latin women
- Asian men – Asian women
- **White men – Asian women**
- **Black men – Latin women**
- **White men – Bi-racial women**
- **Black men – Bi-racial women**

* * * * *

Additional Author's Note: *This isn't of popular opinion, but my encounters with black women validated the reasons to at least explore other options. In no way does it imply women of other races are without flaws, but the notion that black men only wish to pursue white women (and others) "because they're willing to put up with our crap... and give us oral all day long", is asinine!*

I am certainly not a "male-apologist" (or a "black-male apologist", for that matter), as I find a lot of our behavior inferior. But has it ever occurred, that maybe 'good black men' are equally tired of putting up with the same shenanigans we're often accused of? Perhaps some of us simply find comfort dating outside of our race! The question is, why are black men lambasted for this? Do we continue to eat the same meals if our bodies react poorly? We shouldn't, yet when it comes to something as simple as dating, we're expected to stick to one type – good, or bad. How is that ethical?

Chapter Twelve: Chatlines and Hard-On's: My *Roaring* Twenties

It was easy to observe my frustration at the local bank branch that day, but her deep stares and playful humor erased my ire. The bank representative gave the impression of someone interested in pursuing a form of a relationship and I was at attention.

She did enough to supplement the dress code of her employer – but grew visibly tired of closing her suit jacket. Her 'girls' were busting out of her cherry red top and my eyes were locked in on the target. To her credit, she tried her best to be professional, handling my banking matter to the best of her ability – but the more she left her seat... the more I'd stare. It was as if she was purposefully flaunting her body and the thoughts in my head - at that very moment – should have been illegal!

I managed to leave the bank with a cell phone number (which she intentionally circled with a red sharpie on her business card) and a hard-on – that could've taken someone's eye out! Soon, I received a phone call, where she updated me on the status of the banking discrepancy. Then, the unthinkable occurred. The conversation intensified to a more personal level. She went from exhibiting professionalism, to asking whether I had a significant other. Regrettably, I did and so did she. In fact, she was a newlywed! Yet, she suggested we 'hang out' and meet up for drinks. Suddenly, I was drawing the attention of women who were involved. Was this a cause for concern, or celebration?

* * * * *

Pandora's box was opened, my virginity days were behind me. I was in search of a pretty face and a sexual lust greater than mine. As I mentioned, I had a few Latin friends, but we didn't travel in the circles of their women. I knew if I wanted to attract them, I'd have to get out of my comfort zone and make some appearances at the club. I was aware that Latina women enjoyed moving their hips on the dance floor… but the club scene wasn't my cup of tea.

There were too many women at the club, only interested in "looking cute" and worse – *only* frolicking with each other, instead of intermingling. In addition, I was uncomfortable with the number of guys hunting the same girls. I really didn't have the courage to ask anyone to dance – especially after watching her dance with another dude. *Could I handle being openly rejected? What if I spend money trying to make a good impression and she walks off with someone else?* I understood the mentality of most clubs – it's fair game, but my heart couldn't handle any more rejection. I had too many questions and not enough answers – so I talked myself out of going most of the time.

Next was the bar. Unlike most teens, I didn't have a desire to be *under the influence.* It wasn't important to me, or the company I kept – so I steered clear. I took pride in remaining vigilant and never carried a desire to expose myself to poisons that could hinder my awareness. But those days were over. Different from night clubs, I wanted to be around a "controlled environment", with less ego and more laughs. So, I leaned towards bars and "Happy Hour". A few drinks on a Friday evening following work was harmless and the possibilities of a one-night stand – greater!

There were a few casual drinkers within my group, but apart from a couple of people, most weren't in a rush to find "Mrs. Right", (or sleeping with as many women as Wilt Chamberlin) like I was. *Clearly, they were "the brains".*

Consequently, there wasn't anything "happy" about the bar scene. While in pursuit of a nightlife, rarely did we find a group of single women sitting alone – giving us the 'let's fuck' bedroom eyes commonly seen in movies. They were usually tipsy, having a good time by themselves, or coupled with male friends. If any of us dared to look in their direction, they'd typically respond with conceit or excessive eye-rolling.

Soon enough, my nightlife consisted of bowling, beer and *boobs,* where we integrated fun, laughter and drinks entertaining ourselves at the bowling alley or strip club.

* * * * *

I was completely turned off by the noticeable scars on the breasts of a couple dancers. I turned my attention to *Raul* and spent more time cracking jokes than placing dollar bills into the G-strings of these hard-working women. Once I got over the eye sore, it was time to experience my first lap dance. Little did I know, I was supposed to remove the items from my pockets before a dancer hopped aboard my crotch.

As she danced to Ludacris' "What's your Fantasy?" *Storm,* (who was black with natural boobs) was clearly bothered by the thingamajigs in my pants. Expecting to grind against a hard-on – she was rubbing her *lady part* against my wallet... and set of *janitor-styled* house keys!

"You have to take out your keys, baby!"

Such an amateur move on my part and sadly, I left the club without a hint of an arousal that night.

* * * * *

The internet was a growing trend in most households and *AOL* chatrooms were all the buzz. Many were lucky to find love, others hooked-up and a few people took the risk of meeting strangers and were disturbingly murdered! Naturally, I decided to roll the dice.

The web was a welcoming platform for meeting women, without the hassle of chasing them in the club – praying they'd *back it up,* teasing your dick all night. *What fun is that?* No matter how hard I tried to limit my search to "no strings attached", I was back on the prowl for a relationship.

As a stickler for love, I combed through the profiles on *BlackPlanet* and *Mi Gente* without a clue on how to upload a picture through a dial-up connection, eventually becoming pen-pals with a girl from California; the niece of an actor from one of my favorite childhood TV shows (don't bother trying to guess). We'd talk on the phone, send photos *via U.S. Mail* and write lengthy love letters to one another... but was I *really* going to travel to California for love? Had I become that hard-pressed?

Yes!

She had family in New York, but they didn't communicate much, so the onus would be on me to make the trip if I wanted to make a love connection. I'm a firm believer in long-distance relationships... *if* the participants are willing to make the necessary sacrifices: *communication* and *alternating visits.* But how often would I travel to the west coast?

I stayed up to the wee hours of the morning to hear her voice, awaiting her customary goodnight call. I didn't care about the stinking three-hour time difference... even if most of the time I could barely keep my eyes open.

Hello...

"Hey baby. I just got home from work. I wanted to say goodnight."

Baby??? Yessss! For all my *Pee-Wee Playhouse* fans, "baby" was the *secret word of the day!* The lights in the house flickered, the alarms went off and I gained a burst of energy! But as expected, we couldn't keep up the momentum. Months went by without any flight arrangements and soon the frequency of the phone calls diminished. We were too inexperienced to carry on such a demanding relationship.

* * * * *

I scoured outside the city because locally things were a mess! What I presumed was only a "New York City thing", turned into a cultural affair. The era of the classy female was on a steady decline. Attitudes increased, women walked around with uninviting faces and there were *plenty* willing to expose the most sacred areas of their body through fashion. No longer did I have to play the guessing game – wondering if *the woman in front of me had on underwear –* when the Victoria's Secret thong peeked from the average female's low-rider jeans!

It was the *new* norm *and* young men had to adapt quickly. Women looked to embrace their "sexy", no matter how flagrant it was, further validating my stance on staying far, far away from relationships. It was: Get laid – *again*... or die trying! *How could I give my heart to any girl who thought it was cute to publicly show her ass crack?*

The focus was still on Latinas (or an Aaliyah look-alike), until a buddy informed me of how strict fair-skinned Latin parents were concerning their daughters dating dark-skinned guys.

Here we go! I thought to myself. Thankfully, I had a good run, escaping any race drama, but I wouldn't necessarily escape the drama...

* * * * *

Author's Note: *Not only is dark skin mocked in black culture, but deemed 'low-class' in other cultures? Good grief, Charlie Brown!*

* * * * *

On my last day at the job, I grabbed a newspaper from the newsstand as I made my way home. Reluctant to commit full-time to the prominent role on Madison Avenue (after initially filling in for a woman on maternity leave), I thought it would be wise to take a little breather. I'd been working diligently since leaving St. John's, saving enough money to help Mom with a few expenses, if necessary, or take time to explore better job opportunities. I didn't have many financial obligations aside from a monthly credit card bill, so there wasn't much of a hurry to get back to work.

I directed my attention to the *help wanted* section – in search of a job, when I caught a glimpse of the personal ads on the next page. There were several *18 to 20-somethings* searching for "casual dating and relationships". Hmmm…

I got a kick out of reading the *great* literary works of others in my age bracket, who were looking for the same things relationally. At the bottom of the page was a featured ad for a toll-free line – where *singles searched for love*. The company was promoting a free trial – so I figured I'd give it a try:

Hey fellas, what's good? It's ya girl, Precious. I'm twenty-two years old, five-seven, one forty-five, black and Indian, cute in the face – slim in the waist… I've got long black hair, a fat ass, I live in Bed Stuy – do or die baby!

Ehh…

Hi guys, it's Ashley… an attractive, down to earth – white female calling out of Manhattan… I'm sweet, funny, I enjoy movies, walks in the park…

Okay, I like what I hear! … carry on, carry on…

I'm on the line today, looking for older white gentlemen!

Son of a…

Dis Monique! I'm twenty-five, calling outta Jamaica, Queens… I'm thick in all the right places! … I'm lookin' for a nice guy who has sum'n going for himself… I got two kids, so you must like kids…

screaming babies in the background

She has way too many damn commands and has kids?! *Oh, hell no!* I thought to myself.

Hey, I'm Lizette, I live in Brooklyn, I'm twenty, Dominican... five-five, one-twenty-five... I have a peanut butter complexion, brown eyes, long hair – a little past my shoulders... I'm pretty – I have nice lips, with a cute ass (giggle). I work and go to school... I'm looking for a nice guy – preferably black and tall... he must look good... I'm on the line looking for a relationship... please, no head games. If you're the one, hit me up!

I hurried off the toilet in search of my credit card.

Callers were required to add *a block of time* – if they wanted to continue with the service, so I did just that, creating an ad of my own to join in on the fun. Within minutes, a flood of lonely girls sent messages to my personal mailbox, complimenting my voice, stating how I "seemed like a guy with a good head on my shoulders".

Very good observation, ladies. As you can imagine, my confidence was through the roof! In my best Barry White impression, I amassed 20 messages in the span of fifteen minutes. No... fuckin'...way! I weeded out the uninteresting messages... until I heard a familiar voice with a Latin accent.

*Hi, I'm Lizette (giggle)... I just came across your ad... you seem like someone I'd like to get to know. I'm really feeling what you had to say and I'm looking for the same thing. Listen to my profile and let me know if you're interested. I hope to hear from you soon... *muah!**

God, I know you hear me. Please, let this be the one! I replied within minutes, assuring Lizette that I wasn't looking to play games. To prove it, I left my phone number in her personal mailbox to avoid exchanging messages on the line. Time is money and I wasn't going to fall for the trap of maxing out my credit card by adding more minutes, once my free trial ended. This was only meant to be an *experiment* ... and I *think* I found "the one".

We hit it off quickly and after a week of conversations, curiosity got the best of us.

"When do you want to link up?" she asked.

I informed her on wanting to take things slowly, but we couldn't get enough of each other – sometimes speaking two and three times a day. This was before picture messaging, so I only hoped she was as hot as described. We arranged to meet and I couldn't look away. *Wow! Did I hit the jackpot?*

Lizette looked amazing; pretty face, long hair and her jeans looked painted on. But she smelled like a mixture of Victoria's Secret body lotion... and Newport cigarettes. *She'll do,* I thought.

Mom was at work, so I had the apartment all to myself. It was freezing outside and since we hadn't made any plans, I figured we could watch a little TV and get to know one another. Apart from the bedrooms, the rest of the apartment was unfurnished, hence the immediate 'let's watch TV in my room' idea. We'd only been living there for a few months – since Mom and Terrance split, but I wasn't looking to be a *grand host.* Besides, there was plenty of entertainment in my room. We spent a few hours making small-talk, skimming through channels and music magazines, before she laid out on my bed asking if I had condoms.

Wow, that was quick! "I absolutely do", I said. My attraction to her was fierce – never mind it being the first-time meeting. My Latin buddies were right – we connected... and I didn't even have to break a sweat. This was the moment I'd been waiting for!

* * * * *

Author's Note: *A buddy advised me of a condom trick, after ejaculating – fill the condom about three-quarters of the way with water, tie a knot at the opening of the condom and squeeze the bottom portion to ensure there is no breakage.*

* * * * *

Since losing my virginity, I'd been completely paranoid about the risk of contracting an STD or impregnating anyone. I was young, with a promising future ahead and wanted to play it safe – no matter how I felt about adult movies! Even more important, I had *zero interest* in becoming a parent – especially in my 20s. There was sure to be plenty of traveling ahead and I needed to mingle with as many women as I desired before truly settling down.

No matter how much Mom teased me about 'not wanting to be an old grandmother', having kids wasn't the be all – end all to my life. I didn't have a "biological clock" to speak of and I valued freedom – like the oxygen I breathe. In fact, I *only* entertained the idea of kids… *if* married. And that was a *big* 'if' (considering what I was up against).

* * * * *

As far as Lizette goes, my swimmers were safe and sound. I disposed of the condom and headed back into the room as she quickly placed my wallet on the night stand.

"Why were you in my wallet?"

"I just wanted to make sure you are – who you say you are… because people are crazy these days!"

I walked over to retrieve my wallet, as she pulled me towards the bed trying to seduce me with her beauty. Lizette had a 'never mind that I looked through your personal belongings' expression on her face, placing my hand on her breast – attempting to rile me up. That bullshit *almost* worked. Thankfully, I manned up and proceeded to get dressed. It was time to put an end to this day. We walked back to the subway and kissed goodbye at the site of her train.

"Yo! You better call me later!" she demanded.

Right. Unexpectedly, her "ladylike" command turned me on. There was a laundry list of violations – starting with inviting a total stranger into my home. And I couldn't shake off Lizette rifling through my wallet. I didn't carry much cash, but my identification cards were obviously tampered with. What was she up to?

In the coming days, we'd speak more – almost too much, as the girl who *worked and went to school,* seemed to have a ton of time on her hands. She was really pushing for a relationship, figuring another visit to the house (a week later) was the best way to prove it. *The way to my heart has never been to seduce me, but at that point in life… she got an 'A' for effort.*

There weren't any wallet stunts this go around, but I eventually gave into her relationship demands as Valentine's Day rapidly approached. Now, the phone calls were coming non-stop. *It felt good to be 'wanted', but her vibe from the start was very suspicious.*

During a night out with friends, I took a break from bowling – where I scored a personal high of 180 – to check my cell phone which was sitting inside my bowling bag. I glanced at the phone and to my surprise – *41 missed calls…* all from Lizette! *Is this chick fuckin' insane?* This was the type of stuff that *only* happened in movies, it dawned on me that I was experiencing my own *Fatal Attraction and* I was visibly disturbed.

On the voice messages, Lizette inquired on my whereabouts, but taking an indecorous approach was certainly not the way to go about it. I planned on chewing her out.

"Don't be mad at me – I was worried about you!" she shouted.

"But I spoke to you a short while ago!" I answered back.

"So, what! I already said I was sorry… What the fuck! I'm your girl… I love you!"

Oh boy… Whatever you do, dude, just don't tell her you love her back…

"I love you, too – but that doesn't make it right!"

Idiot!! We'd have tiny arguments from time to time, but the back and forth made me want her *even* more. I was galvanized when she'd call back to see if I had cooled off.

"*Papi*, I like when you get angry… it shows you ain't a punk – it's sexy!"

Good grief… well, *at least* I wasn't a punk in her eyes! Almost a month had passed since our last meeting, but Valentine's Day was in a couple of days. As much as I considered the holiday *worthless,* longing for the day it would be wiped off the calendar… for good, I figured it wouldn't hurt to make amends and buy roses. We were officially an item, *surely* I'd see her on Valentine's Day…

Valentine's Day Arrives:

You have a collect call from the Metropolitan Detention Center! What? I'd never received a collect call in my life. What could this be about? Lizette calls me hysterical, claiming she'd been arrested after getting into a fight in her neighborhood.

"Wait, what is going on?" I asked.

"These bitches are jealous of me!" she replied.

Jealous of what?

Furthermore, why was she getting into random fights and why on earth was she calling me from a facility known for holding *prisoners with pending cases?* As far as I knew, she wasn't a prisoner. We spoke for a few minutes before the operator proceeded to interrupt the call.

What had I gotten myself into? It was the second time I'd been stood-up, wasting money on roses. In the days following the mysterious phone call, there was more unsettling news:

"Ernest, I'm pregnant!"

"Yeah, okay! Get the fuck outta here!" I replied.

"(Giggle) I'm serious! I'm… I'm tellin' you the truth!"

I knew I passed the condom test (on both accounts) and she was fully clothed – right until the point of intimacy, acting shy, claiming to be "ashamed of her body". So, unless I had *super* pre-cum with the magical prowess to impregnate through denim jeans, I called bullshit on her claim!

"Who's the father?" That set her off.

"What do you mean?! You're the fuckin' father!"

Somehow, she managed to sway my initial thought. Did I really get her pregnant?

Sidebar: *When the pregnancy news broke, I was so distraught, I allowed myself to get drunk with a group of friends, before attending my overnight job. It was the first and only time I'd ever gotten drunk, and I missed falling onto the subway track before an arriving train by just a few feet! Once boarding the train, I sat in a corner seat, leaned my head against the side wall and dozed off until I reached my stop… which I nearly missed.*

Now on pins and needles, I broke the news to a couple of buddies who were more experienced when it came to these types of women. I gave them the rundown of our encounters, receiving a vote of confidence.

"Man, she's bullshitting! Don't fall for that!"

How would Mom take the news?

"Go over her menstrual cycle, but if you're saying you wore a condom – and there weren't any accidents, you should be fine."

I paid attention to sex-education during school, but a lot of time passed since then, and I needed a refresher. Every woman's cycle works differently, so I looked to Mom and Gran for advice. When Lizette attempted to count the days in her cycle (from our last outing), the numbers weren't adding up.

"I don't have to count the days, you're the only person I've been with."

I pulled the phone away from my ear as doubt crept back in. Mom was naturally disappointed by the news, yet convinced I was being fooled and offered to speak to Lizette. Two heads were better than one – maybe they could figure it out together.

I paced around the house like a mad man, while the two spoke… and that's when I had a moment of clarity. I stunned Lizette with the following assertion:

"So, after hanging out for back to back weeks, I haven't seen you in over a month…"

"Okay, let me exp…"

"No, let me finish!" I interrupted. "When I inquire about meeting up, you quickly mention school and work – yet, you blow my phone up – on the hour, every hour! How busy are you?"

Once chiming in, she initially giggled, claiming how she didn't want to travel – due to her concerns of the *subway motion* affecting the "pregnancy".

"You must think I'm a fuckin' fool! Okay… so, I'll come to you", I insisted.

"No. You know I can't have company… plus, my schedule. *Papi*, I'll try to come over in a few days… I swear! I haven't been working, so my money is a little low."

Lizette was certainly skilled at lying, but her story was falling apart quicker than the career of a Disney Channel child star!

- She went through my wallet on the first day we met – which is where I foolishly kept my social security information.
- There weren't any accidents to speak of with the condom.
- I noticed she wore *oversized shirts* on both occasions – unfashionable for a one-hundred and twenty-five pound 20-year-old (who often bragged about having a "designer wardrobe").
- She called from a *Detention Center* on Valentine's Day.
- She claimed to be pregnant about a month after her last visit.
- She didn't try to see me, refusing all my attempts.

Did that sound like someone carrying the child of her *new* boyfriend?

Plot twist: Lizette *was* pregnant! ... by her boyfriend who was locked up. The pregnancy likely occurred right before we met, *possibly* during a prior visit to the correction facility.

The Valentine's Day visit to the facility wasn't caused by a fictitious "neighborhood fight" ... she was paying the *real father* a visit! Likely finding out that he'd be facing extended time. Unwilling to share the pregnancy news and in sheer panic mode, she looked to pin the pregnancy on gullible me!

It further explains why she combed through my personal belongings. Lizette needed enough information in case her worst nightmare came true: Becoming a single parent!

Those oversized shirts worn to the house were none other than maternity shirts, but I didn't know any better. The pregnancy also explained why she wouldn't remove her clothing until the room was entirely dark. The girl was slim with a nice figure. Perhaps she was concerned I'd spot the "bump".

Sure, she could've attempted to puncture a hole in the condom (to validate her story), but her strategy was supposed to instill fear – and it worked! A declaration of, "It's your child" or "I only had sex with you", can startle any man, especially one who's inexperienced and stupefied by love. She could easily detect that I came from a good home. I was supposed to be her safety net.

I was undoubtedly blinded by her "pretty face and cute ass" and had it not been for my analytical mastery, I may have fallen for her trickery. But I was hellbent on not having kids and I was going to find out the truth.

After reading Lizette the riot act, she slammed the phone in my ear – like a telemarketer after informing them to stop calling your phone! Her scheme was genius, but she was messing with the wrong guy. I called the phone company and had her number immediately blocked – but there was still the cell phone which she called for weeks, pleading for forgiveness... even offering to see me again. I felt bad for her and as much as I found her attractive, I wouldn't budge... it was too late. I changed my number and we never spoke again.

* * * * *

The chatline experiment became an addiction, but I managed to stay away for several months after the Lizette debacle. Once returning, I met a few "normal people" for once, but no one who knocked my socks off. Nonetheless, my life was drama-free ... until that *lonely* New Year's Eve evening, when I began to question *why hadn't I found love yet?* I called the line once more and regrettably, made a connection.

Hi – this is Hershey. I just listened to your profile... I think I might be what you're looking for.... Well, there's only one way to find out, I thought, as I made the unwise decision to leave my phone number in her voice mailbox.

Chapter Tidbits:
To those wondering about the bank representative? Well, I avoided her – like Charlie Sheen avoids clean living! I was in a discontented relationship of my own with a newborn on my hands and didn't want to play 'homewrecker' with the newly married bank rep... even after finding out we lived in the same apartment building! Son of a...

Chapter Thirteen: Friends: How Many of Us *Don't* Have Them?

I thought I'd be in contact with Zepan a lot longer than most. He started to act differently upon moving on to Murrow. In what was an abbreviated stint at the school, he became a chronic smoker, alienated himself from most, and came to be barely recognizable. In fact, we seldom spoke by the time he abruptly transferred midway through our freshman year – leaving Slavik, Gerald, Connor and Mike as the remaining Geek Squad members at Murrow. As years passed, I lost all contact until finally reconnecting with Gerald and Connor through Facebook, before eventually deleting my account. Any thought of reviving the group, as adults, was pure fantasy.

* * * * *

Through the years, I've met a lot of interesting people and I only wish I could've maintained a few friendships to cope with the loneliness that I encountered as an adult. It truly saddens me how many of these one-time friendships couldn't stand the test of time, because once I've granted you access to my life, you're usually stuck with me… for good! Like the Chucky doll: *I am your friend 'til the end.*

I am accessible- rain or shine, morning, noon… up until around *9 p.m.,* which is normally when my pillow takes precedence over all. Bottom line? *I'll be there for you* – like the cheesy theme from *Friends.*

You are officially tagged as my *brother* (or *sister*) and together, we'll withstand life's ups and downs. I'll be your listening ear, offer encouragement, tell you when you're wrong and partner-up to fight some of your battles! But of course, it all goes out the window if reciprocity isn't a part of your vocabulary.

My friendship will not be taken for granted. I have no problem 'taking my ball and going home', but I'll usually give you a shitload of opportunities to make up for it before severing ties. Moreover, I value 'sound friendships' – like a stripper values dollar bills. Once we've bonded, you've become an unofficial family member. Family *should* stick together.

* * * * *

A year after settling into his new digs, my father and I paid Kodwo a visit in our old Hamilton Heights stomping grounds. It was the middle of summer and Kodwo needed assistance packing since he was on the verge of moving. Much to our surprise, we found parking in the usually car-busy neighborhood, only having to walk a few houses to lend Kodwo a hand.

After spending several minutes catching up, I thumbed through a few *National Geographic* magazines, taking one last sip of cranberry juice before getting started on the task. Thankfully, there was a moving van parked in front of the house, simplifying matters as we exited his second-floor apartment with boxes.

I was distracted by the gathering of teens leaned against the parked cars a few feet from my father's Honda Civic. It wasn't an unusual site; the weather was warm and kids like to be seen (and heard) when the temperature climbs. But I continued to watch, as two guys were surrounded by a group of girls in cutoff shorts. *Those lucky bastards...*

My royal blue Adidas shirt was drenched with sweat and I was exhausted! I didn't realize how much Kodwo kept inside the studio apartment – or maybe there weren't as many items as I thought, and I was simply annoyed about the process. I've always hated moving and couldn't wait for the whole thing to be over.

Finally, we wrapped up. After taking a few minutes to cool off, we parted from Kodwo and approached the car. The crowd of teens had decreased, but left standing was a guy leaning against a car surrounded by three girls – all who appeared dazed, looking as if they were ready to take turns blowing him.

"Kenny!" He yelled, "bring me two blunts!"

Kenny? As we approached, I was drawn to the seductive movement of one of the girls, as she danced to Adina Howard's "Freak Like Me" which was blasting from the portable radio on the ground. She turned her back to the guy, grabbed his hands and allowed him to feel her up – as she rubbed her body against his. The mysterious teen's N.Y. Yankees baseball cap sat low on his head – almost hiding his eyes, as he bobbed his head to the beat.

Was I on the set of a low-budget rap video? As much as I hated to stare, I couldn't help myself – this guy looked vaguely familiar. My father inserted the key into the driver's side door and that's when it hit me.

"Fran!" I yelled excitedly.

The music wasn't overbearing, but loud enough where I raised my hand in an attempt to get his attention. No response. Puzzled by the snub, I looked at my father – seeking confirmation that I had the right guy. He followed up with a deeper, more imposing voice.

"Fran… How are you?!"

His face appeared a little fragile as Fran looked at my father with uncertainty.

Sidebar: *A few years passed since we last saw one another, but my father bumped into Fran during a recent visit to Hamilton Heights – eventually picking up on his voice. However, there was no excuse for him not to recognize his boyhood best friend.*

"That's Ernest", my father announced, pointing at me as if to lend Fran a hand with recognition.

I walked over to my *best friend,* looked directly into his glassy eyes and extended my hand. Fran struggled to make sense of what was going on... and then it struck him.

"Ooohhh! What's good?!"

We shook hands and I immediately noticed a series of track marks along his forearm. Either he'd been bitten by a gang of mosquitos – and went on a scratching spree, or this dude was entrenched in the perils of the neighborhood. Whatever it was, he didn't recognize me at first site and I was hurt.

We shared a few words and by this point, the girls gathered around him. I walked over to the passenger side, offering a *peace sign* hand gesture – to which he responded with an affirmative head nod. That was all.

My father pulled away as I sat silently trying to keep my emotions in check. Fran was obviously a changed man and it hurt me to my core, but there wasn't much I could do. We were of different minds, far removed from the days of goofing off in the middle of his grandparents living room. It appeared that I lost my friend to the fast life, never to see him again.

* * * * *

I was sprawled out on the living room couch one Friday evening, scrolling through my list of contacts, while the sounds of *screeching sneakers* stemmed from the TV. Paying very little attention to the game, my mind wandered: *Who was worthy of a phone call?*

I'd grown lonely in my one-bedroom apartment and my phone was unusually quiet. The bill collectors clocked out for the day – sparing me some mercy until Monday morning and aside from the chatty basketball announcers, the only other noise was the *pleasant* sound of a steady rain fall against the window pane.

Fully convinced the rain was causing a service issue, I promptly rebooted my cell phone. The phone powered up and minutes later, I was greeted by the same silence. Now concerned, I knew I could rely on Gran's availability. She has always been there when in need, so I called for a quick phone check.

"Hello?"

"Hey Gran – are you alright?"

"Yea? I was asleep, boy! What's the matter?"

"Asleep??? it's 7:40! Anyway, nothing much. The phone was quiet, I thought there was a service issue..."

"Join the club... my phone is always quiet!" she said, giggling.

That summed it up for me. There was a point in my 20s when I received so many calls, I thought about hiring a personal secretary! The list of names was long, ranging from women, childhood friends, friends of friends, friends of ex-girlfriends, co-workers, psychos and more!

And then, there was social media. Keep in mind, I've never won a popularity contest, nor have I ever aspired to become a social media darling. If it matters any (and it doesn't), I was *lucky* enough to have 100 "friends" on Myspace and Facebook many moons ago. That's right! *One hundred!* Sad, right? But it was all a farce.

I've never known 100 people (at one time) in my entire life... not even *Tom* from Myspace! (and why couldn't that bastard be removed)? No longer could I stomach sending *friend requests* to random people or to someone I recognized from school, but hardly spoke to, or accept *friend invites* to give the illusion that I knew a massive amount of people. My family is small, my circle of friends has always been modest and 90 percent of the people on my "friends list" didn't have my phone number! I had absolutely no intentions of speaking to these people on or offline! What was I trying to prove?

It took long enough, but I'd finally accepted it: I'm *really* not that important. In fact, these days, my phone contacts consist of more *take-out restaurants* and *job references* than friends!

When you perform a little "cell phone cleansing", maybe you'll notice the same phenomenon.

* * * * *

Author's Note: *Social media is a great tool if you're looking to network or connect with long-lost friends/family (for special gatherings), but I don't need to communicate with friends and family on that platform with exposure to their everyday lives. For what? when I can simply call them.*

* * * * *

Some friendships are meant to be seasonal, it took a while to understand that. During my 5th grade valedictorian speech, I specifically advised all members of the graduating class to *stay in touch*. I didn't realize how farfetched it sounded, but I meant every bit of it. *Why should we lose contact if solid friendships have been established? Don't take it for granted. The world can be cold and lonely. Find ways to communicate and sustain it!*

Many of us have been fortunate to carry on a childhood friendship or two, but occasionally, life has an ugly way of getting involved – *if* you allow it. That one-time, *unbreakable* partnership can suddenly deteriorate, you'll go from speaking on the phone multiple times a week to receiving (or sending) the dreaded "K" (a.k.a., *okay*), or isolated "Happy Birthday" text. This has become all too normal in the age of cell phones.

Landline phones have become yesterday's news. There are various *dead spots* that will interrupt the flow of a cell phone conversation – why *many* prefer the convenience of a quick text message. But if you're a member of my immediate circle, I wish to hear your voice from time to time, because it is too easy to get lost in technology.

I had childhood friends who I spoke to regularly... until we reached our 30s. Suddenly, the phone calls ceased, yet I was the only idiot still reaching out! It pained me that the calls weren't reciprocated, but it was my own fault: I really didn't have many friends! We need to revisit what a *friend* truly is.

As I alluded to in the opening of the chapter, a friend *should be* to the very end. An *unofficial* member of your family, who you can count on through the good times and bad. Not a 'friend of convenience' – *someone who only reaches out when it is to their benefit.* No thank you.

If there is a misunderstanding – as friends, let's discuss the issue and work it out. If time should pass between calls or emails – pick up the phone and check on them.

In my estimation, that is what a friend does. Friends shouldn't lead each other on with the guessing game of:

I wonder if we're still cool?

Why doesn't he/she call anymore?

I wonder who will call first?

Have I done something wrong?

These are childish games. Again, reciprocity goes a long way. As friends, we spend a lot of time and energy sharing valuable information. Communication should *never* come to a screeching halt – at least not without explanation. That type of behavior is inexcusable. Think about the common denominator that brought you together in the first place. If that glue doesn't hold you together, then sadly, you've found your answer. *The friendship served a purpose for its period and it is time to move on.*

To those who *still* wish to believe they're friends with individuals they haven't spoken to over an extended period – sorry to burst your bubble, but the ship has sailed. Delete the phone number from your contacts at once!

Ask yourself one simple question: *Are you really friends with someone you haven't spoken to in a year?* Think about it. That's 365 days (8,760 total hours) with *zero* communication! Maybe you were on the receiving end of a mind-numbing *YouTube link text* or included in a nauseating *mass text message* – but that's not enough to secure the friendship.

There's a perception that *everyone* is "too busy". Life is going at a speed where a simple phone call or "hello, how are you?" text is virtually impossible. I call bullshit! I am not talking about conducting *daily* 30-minute conversations. That's completely unnecessary and as working adults (some with families), there isn't a need for it. But how harmful would a 'hello' administered every few weeks, *even* once a month be, if you're as tight with the person as you claim?

If anyone feels my suggestion is "overkill", then explain why I need to save your contact information? The best part is when someone calls (or texts) and you've deleted their number.

Who is this?

"It's (*insert name*), have you deleted my number?"

Abso-fuckin'-lutely!

Don't give them the bullshit line of, "I just got a new phone and didn't add my contacts." Just be honest and let it sink in for a bit.

Please note: When removing a number, don't do it out of malice or spite. Take the high road. Hell, remain amicable – just remove yourself from the angst concerning the status of the friendship. Out of sight, out of mind!

We all have *friends* and *acquaintances*. I'm not advising that you completely remove the phone numbers of the latter. Acquaintances can serve a purpose – *if* you've relegated them to that status. But if they were once friends, someone you've spent time with, someone who knows your family, someone you've shared personal information with and they've been demoted to an *acquaintance*, then it's best to delete… delete… delete!

I've moved on from people who probably have no idea their phone numbers have been obliterated! If we've been reduced to an *annual* "what's up?" text … after 20 years of friendship? Let me be the first to say… nice to know ya!

But if you're reading, thank you for purchasing my book!

Call me petty, but I grew tired of being the only person interested in preserving a friendship. It's a two-way street. Have I been the "perfect friend"? No, I'm the pot calling the kettle black. I've *wrongfully* distanced myself from one-time 'brothers' – not because I didn't value their friendships, but due to personal experiences that shamed me. I feared being judged.

Becoming the first in my group to have a child was the fire starter. I watched from a distance, as my one-time friends flourished – evading drama – while I committed inexcusable blunder after blunder. Was having a child the end of the world? No, but it sure felt like it.

My priorities changed. I was dealing with serious adult matters, while the guys traveled, hung out at will, doing what *20-somethings* do. I received plenty of invite offers, but declined them, usually due to my finances not being up to par. Eventually, the invites stopped altogether.

The moment of truth arrived, when I received an invite as a *guest* – not one of the *five* groomsmen – to the wedding of a childhood friend. Someone I spoke to regularly, someone my grandmother fed. Perhaps my new *parental life* and unreliability as a "hang out friend" was to blame, but I was deeply bothered by the snub. Unfortunately, the nucleus of these one-time brother-like friendships have yet to be restored and at this point, I'm afraid they never will.

* * * * *

Author's Note: *I've lost a few friendships through jealousy and misunderstandings – usually with women. To the guys: Do not get chummy with the best friend of your female friend – even if it's the best friend who is actively pursuing you, unless you're Jack Tripper from 'Three's Company', or your friend is in a happy relationship of her own. Rest assure, someone is bound to show a little insecurity and the situation will get messy!*

Finally, do not attempt to build friendships with women who claim to be 'okay' with the 'friends with benefits' label. It's a trap! They will immediately turn on you once you've entered a committed relationship with somebody else (neglecting to understand why they weren't the chosen one).

Chapter Fourteen: *Unlike* Father, *Unlike* Son

As a child, we watched the movie "Like Father Like Son" starring the late Dudley Moore and Kirk Cameron, but my father and I greatly underachieved. I've been determined since day one to avoid a recurrence with my daughter. I cannot stress the importance of open-communication. It is everything!

* * * * *

My father has never openly stated the following, but I'm unafraid to say it: I absolutely failed him as a son! If you are of African descent and haven't excelled as a *surgeon, college professor, lawyer* (or someone in a respected field), then you have shamed the family. Africans are as prideful a group as any; children are prepped for greatness from the upstart. A bookcase of encyclopedias, a room full of science kits and being asked to 'limit my television intake' was a blueprint for success. Parents relish the moment they can tout their children's accomplishments and I dropped the ball... becoming a college dropout – who produced a child out of wedlock.

It's easy to pin the mishaps on my parents' divorce, but that wouldn't be fair. In all honesty, they probably had no business being married in the first place. Even more? I understood this as a child and handled their divorce better than most kids would under the circumstances. My shortcomings fall solely on me. I had a strong desire to 'fit in', while doing things *my* way and I put myself through unfathomable obstacles in the process.

I didn't experience the complications of those growing up in single-parent households and I was fortunate to have my father's guidance from day one. Through him, I've been exposed to extraordinary people, visited many places and experienced a quality of life that many kids would die for. I've truly been blessed, and I can never repay him for those opportunities. But the missing ingredient to what could've been a dynamic relationship? Communication. We had none. *There's a good chance I would be writing this book out of leisure, instead of a last resort, had we only spoken more about life.*

I truly believe my *being born* American (of African descent) kept us at a distance. We are so alike, yet, culturally and contrastingly different. While my father put in twice the effort educationally (through boarding school before arriving to the states), I was handed opportunities on a silver platter, taking education for granted. *Education is viewed as the 'only way' in most countries; it is the key to survival. But America rewards opportunists and I wanted to become one. This is where we butted heads.*

I was drawn to the concept of "thinking outside of the box", gravitating to the success stories of athletes, musicians, overnight sensations and innovative college dropouts. My father preferred the methodical approach and I couldn't fault him for that. *Overnight sensations* are the minority in the world, but it wouldn't stop me from dreaming of becoming *anything* other than a doctor or lawyer.

No offense to those making an honest living in their respective fields, but this is where that 'P word' rears its ugly head: Passion! You must have devotion to enlist in four-years of college, grad school and years of medical (or law school). I simply wasn't that interested.

Our personality traits are comparable, but we had vast differences and it didn't help that he was a disciplinarian – with very little patience – at a time when I was underdeveloped. When my father attempted to teach me how to ride a bike, not only was I scared of falling to the ground but was also terrified of his reaction had I done so! He'd yell my name with his heavy accent, displaying a look of disgust.

Ernest Sr. was a proponent of *first-rate* vocabulary usage, proper walking poster and etiquette, commonly correcting me when I mispronounced words, walked hunched over, or used improper table manners, i.e.; opting to use my fingers for 'finger foods' instead of cutting it with a fork and knife. *Terrific life lessons, if I must say so myself!*

But I was entirely afraid to make a mistake; there wasn't any pleasing him. His gruff voice and intimidating demeanor was peerless, his stern approach ignited a divide, where I favored the softer (yet stricter) methods of Mom and Gran. To have a healthy fear of your parents is one thing, but to walk on egg shells all the time is another!

COMMUNICATION

The accounts I've shared in this book will come as a surprise to many – including my father, because I never felt comfortable sharing personal stories with him. Due to our lack of communication, there lived an uneasiness that continued well into adulthood. I've been transparent throughout this journey, taking accountability for *99 percent* of my actions, but the communication barrier is something I refuse to take the blame for. He set the tone as the adult and I countered by omitting him from my escapades.

Through all the time spent together, seldom did my father open up and I didn't get a chance to know him. It could've paid dividends! Many of our conversations dealt with the present and I became far removed from asking him anything regarding his past. *My daughter knows everything about me, from embarrassing childhood stories – like the time I was savagely pounced on by an alley cat, to my favorite sports teams!*

I grew familiar with my father's occupation in banking and finance, as he regularly took me to his job near the Twin Towers. I was the apple of his colleague's eye and he'd revel in my moment when the women marveled at my cuteness – nodding with approval when a male colleague announced how *well-spoken* and *decorous* I was.

"Man, Ernie! Your son is just like you!"

It was the ultimate compliment and more importantly, it was true. But I was conflicted on who he was as a parent. My father often frowned, spoke very little and had a terrible habit of *giving commands*, leaving very little room for suggestions. Were we *really* alike?

* * * * *

Author's Note: *Parents, please get out of the habit of giving commands to your adult children (who are parents themselves). It is truly uncalled for. Thanks.*

* * * * *

We had our playful moments and there are hundreds of photos of us enthralled in fun activities – but being a goofball didn't suit him. He was *all* business, seemingly imbalanced and our conversations were limited to adult topics:

- The ills of society
- Politics
- Education
- Sports

We never talked about girls, the birds and the bees, his childhood crushes, heartbreaks, or life as a teenager. Outside of his love for soccer, writing and music, I didn't get many childhood stories out of him, nor did I thoroughly know about the relationships he shared with his parents and siblings. I desperately wanted to make the distinction to some of my behavior patterns and the opportunity was there... but he remained shielded... and I wasn't comfortable asking. Again, one can attribute this to a cultural disparity, or maybe this was typical behavior between fathers and sons... but it never sat well with me.

My father loosened up *some*, after the divorce from Mom. We'd share occasional laughs during our limited weekend time. But there remained an uneasiness on my end. Our best times occurred watching sports, as we'd crack up at NFL players and their end zone celebrations or collectively cringe at the inept broadcasting abilities of former NBA players – turned announcer. We'd watch news magazine programs and the public-affairs series, *Like It Is,* where I was educated on prominent black/African political and cultural figures and the important issues facing the black community. Finally, there were plenty of lazy Sunday afternoons, where following church, we'd head over to the park to play basketball or tennis, or lounge around the apartment with an assortment of music playing in the background. He was a music connoisseur and I truly miss those days. A time when life was simple. *My parents claim to have attended several concerts while Mom was pregnant, namely Bruce Springsteen. Maybe that explains my fascination for 80s music.*

Over time, my father found a happy medium to my sports obsession, running alongside as *camera man* – where he'd focus the camcorder on me and fire away with random sports questions. He assisted with my valedictorian speech, offering pointers on how to overcome stage fright, advising on techniques that would allow for speech mastery and confidence. Lastly, during a rare conversation about females, he assured that women would gravitate towards my dark skin as I got older. *He was telling the truth.* My father was (and remains) a prideful man and it was finally rubbing off.

PACK YOUR BAGS...

Mom and Gran fought earnestly with him for months, but I traveled to Milton Keynes, England... *alone*, at the tender age of seven! Yes, I know how unbelievably insane and cruel it sounds – as I'm sure many of you couldn't fathom your children boarding a plane by themselves to travel across the ocean (neither can I for that matter), but my father was persistent about making it happen. *I cried my eyes out on the night of the flight, but I was in good hands on the plane and upon landing where I was immediately greeted by the family of one of his childhood friends.*

I was exposed to culture during my summer breaks – visiting countries (Canada is another) instead of summer camps, but the summer vacation to top them all was my first visit to Ghana. There were prior discussions about visiting Ghana at an earlier age, but through the turmoil of my parents' marriage – coupled with Gran's brainwashing and preconceived notions about the continent – no thanks to America's mainstream media, it struck enough fear into Mom that Africa became an afterthought.

"You're not sending my baby over there!" she'd exclaim.

She was right, as far as I was concerned; I shivered at the thought of visiting the Motherland! Was this man crazy?! *Clearly, ignorance is strength to those with an agenda – as was the case concerning the misconceptions of Africa.*

* * * * *

Following high school graduation, my father rewarded my efforts with a planned visit to Kumasi, Ghana – West Africa. I was eighteen, somewhat immersed in African culture and the timing was just right. We took the nine-hour flight out of New York's Kennedy Airport and I was exhilarated. It was as if I could feel the cultural shift on the plane. Finally, a *country* with plenty of faces that resembled ours!

Hard stares followed as we drove through town, but I was unbothered. I wanted to embrace those looking our way. Based on their gazes, I got the sense that most knew we weren't from the area, but they couldn't help themselves. Our features were similar, our attitudes and style of dress weren't. I sported cornrows – not a favorable look for men in the country at the time, but I honestly felt like a rock star.

In what was a long overdue visit, it was the first time meeting my *other* family. I came across plenty of pictures of my relatives in the past, but I finally had the opportunity to meet my grandmother and cousins. They embraced me from the start, beaming at me and I was treated like a king. The feeling was surreal.

In Kumasi, I welcomed the imperfections of the infrastructure; namely the *dirt roads* and *limited street lighting*. I was captivated by the open sky, where gorgeous sunsets and a collection of stars were viewable at night. There were recurring *blackouts* after dusk – which would've caused mass hysteria back in the States. But I found it calming – as everyone sat on their front porch taking in the evening breeze. It was business as usual. I'd snap pictures at every piece of life surrounding us – even the annoying rooster that unabashedly woke us up each morning. *This* was home!

In addition to Kumasi, we traveled to Accra, the capital of Ghana, where I'd stare in amazement at the luxury cars and *chic* buildings resembling some of the major cities in the States.

There was a visit to Cape Coast, where I was invigorated by the architecture, namely the University of Cape Coast. I was in awe of the Gulf of Guinea which connects to the Atlantic Ocean, yet shaken by the sight of the Cape Coast Castle – where the British once jailed African slaves during the Transatlantic slave trade.

Ghana is amazingly beautiful; the imagery is everlasting! But it saddens me, how Americans will never experience Africa's inner and outer beauty through the likes of television – and just think...I *almost* missed out! *If you're someone who enjoys travel, make certain to add Ghana to your bucket list (cheap plug for Ghanaian tourism – go visit!). There is a ton of history in the multi-cultural country.*

* * * * *

Author's Note: *Africa is considerably greater than the singular images of South Africa, poverty and wildlife.*

* * * * *

Regrettably, I didn't take advantage of the gift of having a parent from another country and it haunts me to this day. I showed negligence towards my family prior to the visit, because I didn't know any better. I was *uninformed, uninspired* and *inundated* with thoughts of a typical child born in the western world – where many of us don't give a rat's ass about anything outside of our personal desires.

My father didn't have the ideal temperament to handle my reasons for being *uncomfortably* African. He took it personally when I shunned the opportunity to learn the language or mingle with children of African descent. The teasing he endured as a school boy didn't compare to what I'd gone through in the American public-school system. Frankly, it was like comparing apples to oranges. But during our three-week stay, we bonded unlike ever before and our relationship was looking up.

REBEL WITH A CAUSE

My father is the quintessential role model for any young man to emulate: *educated, confident, charming, well-traveled* – truly an astute individual. I share many of his traits and being around him has always given me a great sense of pride. He tried diligently to put me on the right track… but along the way, my train derailed.

The goal was to follow in his path to success, while somehow creating a lane of my own. We already shared the same name – I just needed *my own* identity, because the "Big Ernie, Little Ernie" chatter got old. When I worked at his job as a summer intern, I tried envisioning myself as a permanent employee. *Would I be up for the challenge of working in a corporate environment?* I was aware of the opportunities that would arise upon completing school and the thought excited me – some.

The company was reputable, the salaries were excellent, and my father was a recognized name in his division. I even heard through the grapevine that a few 'non-degree' employees made upward of $60,000 annually at the start. Not too shabby for a 20-something year old! But the thought of wearing suits five days a week wasn't appealing and the surrounding personalities were too snobbish for my liking (more on this topic in the next chapter).

My focus was on something greater – I just didn't know what. As I transitioned from school to work, I grew tired of the corporate *monotony*. I couldn't shake off companies imposing *administrative uniformity* and stripping away individuality. I hated how most men were *clean shaven,* sporting the same *unimaginative* haircuts. My father's response to that was simply, "that's the way it goes!" That answer wasn't good enough.

As an adult, I've watched the reaction of women when I arrived at work in a blazer (as opposed to a more casual look). Make no mistake, I've *always* been a fan of dressing up and I understood the power of a suit the moment I put on my very first Easter outfit. A dressed-up man is a man of power! My beef has always been with authority figures dictating what "professionalism" is – usually older white men with infinite zeroes in their bank accounts.

Another beef? Hairstyles! Allow me to wear my hair in a style of my own choice (obviously, nothing excessive – like *pink* hair). This is a major issue for black women in corporate, why should *anyone* be forced to wear somebody else's appearance? Hair has no bearing on whether a job can be performed accordingly. So long as I don't give the appearance of a hobo – leave me alone!

* * * * *

Author's Note: *Why is long hair on men, or braids worn by women, considered 'unprofessional'? If the hairstyle is groomed, what's the problem?*

* * * * *

For my 18th birthday (months before the trip to Ghana), Mom accompanied me to a tattoo shop in the East Village section of the city, where I received my first tattoo – opting for a *skull* with two swords intersecting it and flames emerging from the background. Completely dumb – but thankfully I covered it up years later. The tattoo was meant to signify a "rebel", not my devotion to the Pittsburgh Pirates logo, because I wanted to break free from maintaining the status quo. I respected my father's position on tattoos... but not enough to listen. Moreover, I lived with Mom, so if she was on board – that's all that mattered.

Fitting in with the "popular" crowd was still my main objective and I was the first guy in my group of friends with a tattoo, but you know there's a healthy fear of your parents when you're eighteen – still afraid to reveal your new ink. I spent the entire Ghana trip hiding my left bicep!

Following the ink job, I decided to get my ear pierced – another move I knew he'd frown on. My father commonly targeted male athletes and entertainers with earrings – particularly, hoop earrings, but I was about to enter college and didn't see the harm with getting a diamond stud in my left ear.

The affairs were just the beginning of my off-kilter 20s, where I banished a system that was set in place since taking my first baby steps. I wanted to be free! I wanted to be daring! I wanted attention! I wanted the women of the world to know that I had arrived. I was going to do whatever it took.

I never had an interest in being under the influence of drugs or alcohol because there wasn't a need for it. I didn't care about *that* crowd, nor did any of my friends seek their attention. Our *highs* came through sports, video games and… you guessed it – women! But I was in desperate need of some adventure, which is why I explored *multiple* hairstyles, a single ear piercing became *two*, a skull tattoo turned into an *arm full and* unlike former President Bill Clinton – I admittedly inhaled! None of which was caused by "peer pressure". I wanted this!

The credit card I obtained during freshman year in college (and eventually used on chatlines) was swiped throughout clothing stores citywide, as I added the latest fashions to my dated wardrobe. Once women took notice, I was as good as dead! There would be plenty of date nights, *booty-calls* and high interest on a growing credit card balance! But for the love of God, it was happening… my name was growing and I loved every moment! But deep down, I knew it wasn't the right way. It wasn't the *African* way. My act was pure westernization rubbish at its best – but I didn't know how to let go.

Did I expect the awful decisions of my early 20s to bury me for almost two decades? Of course not. Body markings are innocuous – considered a form of expression if anything, plus I had a job which could easily resolve my impending credit card debt. But I didn't expect my "bad boy" experiment to back fire, attracting women from *different* walks of life: *The types who grew up fatherless – with abandonment issues, those who oozed promiscuity, the ones with little ambition and drive.*

* * * * *

Author's Note: *Of course, when a father inexplicably chooses not to be involved in their child's life (particularly a daughter), a mother is left to play both roles. Those who succeed should be commended for their efforts. However, when that child grows up, their behavioral patterns will eventually reveal the 'male deficiency'. I think we can all agree: a woman **cannot** fill in that void.*

* * * * *

Women growing up under these conditions, tend to have an increased dependency on the men they're dating. As someone who *claims* to have great 'people evaluator skills', well... I clearly missed the signs. Before long, I was dealing with drama, pregnancies and a bevy of real-life matters.

When I finally introduced my father to a couple of the young ladies I elected to date, he privately shared how much he disapproved.

"She doesn't compliment you well."

I'd get extremely annoyed when he'd play matchmaker, attempting to connect me with the daughters of his *Ghanaian* friends instead:

"She's intelligent, pretty and currently studying for her Masters!"

Why does he have to throw the whole master's thing in there? Who cares! I'd say to myself. What was this guy's deal and why was he assuming *my* women choices weren't fit?

Because they weren't, you DUMB ASS!

I didn't socialize with Africans namely because I didn't find them relatable. It was all work – no play and the guys were commonly missing that "cool factor" that I preferred. In addition, I became heavily influenced by hip-hop culture. My appearance from head to toe exemplified that of a typical American black male. I walked with a certain swagger and conducted myself like someone from the city – because after all... I was.

Africans couldn't quite make the distinction. *Is he one of us, or is he trying to separate himself?* African men tend to adopt the hip-hop fashion trends upon arriving to New York (looking for a way to fit in), but there's still an underlying thought of "we're better" than non-accomplished black American males. I received many hard stares in passing – almost like they were collectively thumbing their noses at me. *Let's face it, what's the initial thought when face to face with an individual sporting cornrows, a do-rag, 4XL white t-shirt and baggy jeans?*

- Is he going to mug me?
- He probably sells drugs
- *Who is his stylist and why hasn't that person been fired?!*

On many accounts, the hip-hop uniform signified "thug" – but I was far from one. I was simply a byproduct of my environment and it was my preferred style of dress.

I rebuffed African girls, as I found them boisterous and quite arrogant (no different than 99 percent of the women in New York City). In addition, the city didn't offer many *young* American women of African descent, or *westernized* Africans. The types I came across didn't attract me at the same rate as those from other ethnic groups seen around the city. *Of course, that narrative has completely changed, so we can debunk the non-attraction crap.*

I didn't want my father playing matchmaker nor did I care as much about his opinion on their academic achievements. I'll be the first to admit it, his observations on the young ladies I introduced him to were spot on – but I knew the type of women I yearned and that's all that mattered. Was she:

- A quality human being?
- Attractive?
- Well versed on various subject matters?
- Ambitious?
- Someone I'd consider marrying?

I was sure I'd find her on my own – except I tripped up, finding myself expecting a child with an unpopular choice. So, there I was, out of school, in and out of jobs, trying to figure out life... with *another life* on the way. What had I done?!

How would I break the news to my father, after he *just* found out about his mom's passing? How would I dodge the shame and embarrassment of becoming another statistic? Why did I have to take things so damn far?! *Perhaps if I moved to New Jersey after the Summer of '95 (as he suggested), I'd be in a better position.*

I was still under his tutelage despite the divorce and I had betrayed the man who quietly showed faith in me. The man who instilled a sense of book smarts, confidence and pride. I was "Little Ernie" ... I wasn't supposed to fail... *I wasn't supposed to fail.*

I didn't grow up under the best of circumstances, but I never exhibited the signs of a child who needed the watchful eye of their parents. I was "too smart" to fall victim to life's deceptions. But I chose to play with fire and got burned by two notable subjects he clearly tried to steer me away from... just without explanation: *Poisonous women and television!* It all made sense – but it was too late.

* * * * *

I'd been on the straight and narrow for years and when children show good faith, you reward them with trust. My parents did that – but turning into a *malcontent* was simply my way of breaking free of life's chains. I was tired of society dictating what *I could and could not do* and I was sick and tired of my father's close-minded, sheeple ways.

I wanted to be accepted, I wanted to take risks... and it bit me in the ass. Sorry, *Dad...*

Chapter Fifteen: The Lifetime *Underachievement* Award Goes To...

Overtaken by anxiety, I placed my left hand on my face and proceeded to massage between my eyebrows – right above the bridge of my nose. The pressure in that area was insurmountable – but the motion of my fingers was pacifying. I closed my eyes for a couple of minutes and thought, 'what am I doing here and how did I get to this point?'

The sound of my co-worker openly passing gas at his cubicle (for the fifth time) unquestionably lit my fire. Why was I the only one in the office disturbed by these unforgivable sounds? I needed to remove myself from this environment at once! Too many personality types, too many egos and not enough hours in the day to continue putting up with the bullshit. The time was now. I was sick and tired of being sick and tired!

* * * * *

If you fail to plan, you plan to fail...

You can all put your hands down, the *Lifetime Underachievement award* goes to *me!* I am a proven loser and will claim my prize! Thank you. Am I being a bit too hard on myself? No. These are the cold facts and I realized the sooner I accepted how *little* I've accomplished, the easier I could make the declaration (though it's still a tough pill to swallow).

It may not seem like the "end of the world" to some, but my life has been one big red *incomplete* stamp... and it was time I did something about it. As you've learned, I've given half efforts on almost everything I've been associated with – from school, sports, hobbies (which could have potentially turned into careers) and my reasons varied. Sometimes, it was through laziness, other times, out of fear and insecurities. But the culprit? My *intuitive conviction*.

In other words, I've always been in tune with my subconscious. If something didn't feel right, I didn't do it – no matter the instant reward, no matter how greatly I'd benefit down the road. But the spirit moved me to get started on a book – *twice!* That was all the conviction I needed. *Nothing hits me twice.* I've deemed this period as the third quarter in life and it was imperative that I finish my assignment come hell or high water – in fear of the *fourth quarter blues*.

Fourth Quarter Blues: *If you're in the referenced fourth quarter age group – having already explored various career choices, continue to find yourself unhappy (whether professionally or financially) with essentially no escape plan? Then maybe it's time to hang it up and accept your reality.*

That thought alone, was about as disturbing as my former co-worker playing what sounded like the "Star-Spangled Banner" with his ass. But my pride wouldn't allow me to go out that way. The fourth quarter was near, I needed to get a move on.

Leaving this planet without accomplishing *anything*, became my greatest fear (next to going bald), leading to many nights where I'd shiver and grind my teeth as I attempted to sleep. But once I stopped concerning myself with nonessential matters, that's when life *finally* started to make sense.

I've chased "success" through the pitfalls, trying to figure out exactly what it was: *Was it based on an individual's opulence, or was it a mind state?* The *younger* version of me would've selected the former (like many of you have), but the older, wiser *Ernest*, opts for the latter.

* * * * *

I'll shoulder the blame for not obtaining success the *conventional way*. In what was a case of the blind leading the blind, I thought playing a game of Russian Roulette with my life was more titillating than being conservative. Such illogical thinking led me to a place called *No Man's Land*. But it was *there* where I found the creative space to put the pieces of Life's puzzle together.

While everyone frantically scrambled through school and the *systematic exploitation of humanity* (a.k.a. employment), trying to find their place on the financial scoreboard, I had time to reflect and meticulously pick apart my flaws (most importantly, learn from them).

- I restored my credit score (to the point where no one can deny me)

- I learned the importance of saving, investing and living modestly
- I developed an interest in controlling my destiny – rather than participating in the *psychological entrapment* of the matrix

And the icing on the cake:

- I would no longer be a contributor to the *overpopulation* of the planet... a.k.a., no more kids!

God said: *Be fruitful and increase in number; fill the earth and subdue it.* I did. And *one* time was enough! To put it mildly, no more careless decision making!

* * * * *

Life can be simple, but we tend to make it harder by answering temptation's call – instead of sending that son of a bitch to voicemail! Our time is limited, I refuse to spend my remaining years going through any more pain and suffering. Some of us are governed by thoughts of invincibility.

"Oh, that will never happen to me!"

And that type of mindset put me in a *near* lifelong rut where I was exposed to things I'd never seen:

- Debt
- Drama
- Jail
- *Plenty of women with the names of exes tatted across their private areas!*

I knew I was in a heap of trouble when I continued attracting those types. I don't care what anyone says, no man wants to find the name, 'Tyrone', scribbled across the erogenous zones of their new partner!

* * * * *

Author's Note: *Ladies, why do you do this?!*

* * * * *

Experience is the greatest teacher. As you've learned, one of my biggest regrets was bringing a child into the world out of wedlock. It goes against everything I stand for. Children should not be conceived through *trial runs* – because essentially, that's what relationships are:

- Is there an attraction?
- Is this person worthy of my time?
- Are we compatible?
- Is he/she emotional/mentally sound?
- Do we share the same moral compass?
- Does he/she strengthen my weak areas?
- Are the conversations inspiring and invigorating?
- Are the families formidable and dependable?

And not:

- Does he have a degree?
- Does he make a lot of money?
- Does he have a big penis?
- Is her ass fat?

* * * * *

Author's Note: *My sorry behind knew the answers to the top portion of questions long before any pregnancy, yet, I intentionally ignored them because I was bitten by the attention bug! What a shame.*

* * * * *

By no means should children be conceived during *sexual encounters* either. I can't begin to tell you how many times I've been told of how a hot fling turned into, "my baby-daddy ain't shit!" ... followed by court battles and thousands of dollars per year spent towards child support! *Don't set yourselves up for the okie doke! Allow birth control to be your friend.*

When women (without children who partake in reckless sexual activities) receive the immediate news about an impending pregnancy, the tables will immediately turn and you, my friend, don't want to be involved in the following:

"I know we were only messing around, but I may *never* get this chance again."

Say what now???

Disclaimer: *Guys, don't try to see how effective your pull-out game is. Keep a condom on!*

* * * * *

Author's Note: *Ladies, do not fall for the 'I want to get you pregnant' line either! It sounds obscene at first, but some of you are gullible enough to fall for it – especially after he tells you "he loves you" and wants to do right by you. Any man who makes an open request to impregnate you – and doesn't really know you? – is a fuckin' idiot! Don't be one too.*

* * * * *

Yes! We are being 'judgmental' by creating checklists during the *trial period*, but that isn't a crime. This is your life, be as selective as you want! The purpose isn't to make someone feel bad about themselves – this isn't a game of, 'I think I'm better than you'. The goal is to find someone who meets your requirements, where perhaps you'll consider tying the knot (if marriage is your thing). Contrary to popular belief (especially in this era, where many feel empowered to live and do things on their own), I can confidently say that *most* people would rather have some form of a companionship, than to grow old alone.

In my case, I was young and really had no business thinking that far ahead – considering I've always been independent, self-centered and goal-driven. The relationship which sent me to jail was initially meant as a 'personal exercise' – get in – gain some experience – get out! I lacked relationship experience and was *only* looking to make up for the missed opportunities of my past. It's the only logical explanation I can think of. I grew tired of putting women through the rigors of a checklist... especially when my requirements were long enough to be read on a scroll! So, I caved in. *Do not cave in – ever!*

My negligence resulted in a *18-21-year sentence* and it led to becoming a statistic, where I became *another* name in the system, followed by a multitude of financial hurdles. Furthermore, I missed out on valuable time spent with my daughter (not being the first to teach her how to tie her shoe laces or ride a bike *really* stung), constant bickering and badgering with the other parent, a lifetime of resentment and roughly *$80,000* in child support payments when it's all said and done! You wanted to know what my dumbest act of all-time was? There you have it! *I sure know how to pick them, don't I?*

THE OFFICE...

I've accepted my *mediocrity* label with pride – particularly in the workplace, where my desire to be "great" was negligible. As someone who lives for setting and executing goals, I knew I could shift the focus to finding a lifestyle suitable to me, removing myself from poisonous people and nagging financial debts. Achieving a personal goal – such as becoming an author, brought a feeling of happiness that only playing sports did. No longer did I want to be at the mercy of my employer.

My new way of thinking (after receiving countless rejections) was to set low expectations in the workplace (to soften the blow of disappointment) and make *my life* rich. I grew disinterested in *name recognition and promotions,* usually sought after by most employees – and I refused to have a "make top dollar or die" attitude (you can keep that type of stress). But of course, it didn't always start out this way.

I was once an eager twenty-something, looking to make my mark in corporate – fully aware of how my *non-degreed-ass* would have a sure fight on my hands... until I realized that didn't even matter much! I came across plenty of educationally advanced black males, *marginally* recognized for their academic success – let alone, their hard-working efforts on the job and it completely took the steam out of me. If companies were overlooking those types, then what sense would it make to bust my ass for acknowledgment?

Soon, I adopted the 'work smart' mantra, where the objective was to gain as much experience in as many fields as possible – to become a *super* employee and compensate for the lack of degree. I'd command a feasible salary to maintain what I deemed a "comfortable lifestyle", instead of attempting to climb the *never-ending ladder* as a black male in corporate ... because as I found out... that was about as pointless as a Hollywood marriage.

* * * * *

Author's Note: *Of course, with every rule, there is an exception. Yes, there are many "successful" black men in corporate – my* *father was one – but black men remain at the bottom of the totem pole. It isn't even debatable.*

* * * * *

By no means would I suggest anyone forsake challenging themselves at work. Continue to set goals and aim high! You lose absolutely nothing by trying (except, *maybe* a bruised ego). I am simply admitting that method of thinking wasn't conducive for ME.

I grew tired of workplace snubbing:

- Being informed on interviews how *over-qualified* I was (after making it abundantly clear that I was satisfied with both the pay rate and day-to-day responsibilities).
- Being overlooked for positions that I was qualified for, while my white counterparts (especially those who I would befriend), with less experience, were granted interview opportunities and awarded the position.

Yet, the final straw occurred, when a company refused me on *three* separate occasions for three different positions (in as many months) – although I was repeatedly recommended by the company's recruiter. I met the job requirements for each position, leaving *two* of the three interviews feeling like a million bucks! (I admittedly bombed on one interview). The managers appeared equally elated, almost revealing their poker hand too soon. I just *knew* I'd gotten the job when I received a call from the recruiter only 10 minutes after one of the interviews.

After following protocol (writing a nauseating kiss ass 'thank you for the opportunity' e-mail), it was a matter of time before I'd be on the receiving end of good news. The company had other plans.

"It was a pleasure meeting you today, Ernest! We have a few more people to interview, but you'll *absolutely* hear back from us in about two weeks."

Fair enough. Two weeks turned into three, then four and before long, I was second guessing myself. *Am I a bad interviewer? Did I do enough to convince them? Should I have asked more questions?* Aaah, fuck it!

So, I did what I do best – I wrote a letter to the Department of Labor! *What was I to do?* When you're interviewed by a company on three separate occasions and denied each time... you become a tad suspicious of their hiring practices, not to mention there weren't any black males in the office as I headed to the conference room to interview. I am big on paying attention to my surroundings.

Was I really that bad of an interviewer, or were these bastards playing hot potato with my resume to meet some stupid quota? As one can imagine, the experience left a nasty taste in my mouth – but it led to this: My first book!

* * * * *

Author's Note: *To Human Resources – If the rule of thumb for potential employees is to respond accordingly (post-interview), how hard is it to follow up with a rejection e-mail if the company elects to move on with other candidates? Staying mum is truly the ultimate slap in the face!*

* * * * *

THE LISTS!

After nine long months composing a book, I'd become mentally and emotionally spent. There were many agonizing days and sleepless nights, where I'd open my laptop at 3 a.m., *type, revise, edit, repeat,* until my eyes bled! Was it worth it? You betcha! Why? Because I've procrastinated far too long and there wasn't a moment left to spare.

Third quarter: *Type or die!*

Aside from growing tired of the unsuitable behavior of a gassy co-worker, there were a list of motivating factors to drive me to completing this book. I desperately wanted to become the voice for those fitting under the following categories:

- *American-born* Africans
- Dark-skinned
- Underachievers
- Introverts
- Weirdos and assholes
- Black baseball lovers
- 80s fanatics
- Deep Thinkers
- Non-Conformists
- And those who were sick and tired of being sick and tired!

On my pursuit to happiness, I wanted to use the book as a platform to list some of the *many* topics that ruffle my feathers.

UNSPOKEN SOCIAL ISSUES

- The psychological damage of social media
- Mainstream media's obsession with asses!
- *The unfairness of the terribly flawed child-support system*

* * * * *

Author's Note: *To the chagrin of my ancestors, I made the executive decision to forego my voting rights, until a Commander in Chief has the gall to amend child support laws. Whether it's a Federal or state matter, why couldn't there be healthy dialogue on the topic? Just as dead-beat fathers permeate the land, so do unfit mothers who reap the benefits of the system! Hard-working fathers have no voice and instead, have lost hope. Although many hard-working, single-parent women reading are likely to become emotionally invested on this issue, try looking at my thoughts/opinions objectively. Not every father deserves to have his pay check decimated because a judge woke up on the wrong side of the bed!*

* * * * *

The *unspoken social issues* set the car in motion, but when I thought about additional talking points, that's when I *really* put my foot on the gas!

OFFICE FOLLIES

- Being the only black male in my department
- Being overlooked for *non-black* counterparts
- Taking useless mandatory training activities
- Spray tanned, six-figure earning executives who prefer being called 'Dick' (instead of Richard)
- Self-entitled men hogging up executive positions
- Nepotism
- "Big shot" executives who walk around the office whistling

- That co-worker who wants to engage in a full-fledged conversation *the moment* you walk through the door, because a simple 'Good Morning' pleasantry won't do
- Women who refuse to initiate pleasantries in passing
- Tight-lipped smiles
- That annoying co-worker who says, "Happy (*fill in the day of the week*)" each and every day!
- Open-mouth coughers (you all suck!)
- Employees with work-from-home privileges, who come into the office when sick, contaminating us all
- The black guy who stares like a deer caught in headlights upon spotting another black male in the office
- The black guy who doesn't like the idea of *another* black guy in the office
- The black guy who strategically positions himself around the office to get the phone numbers of multiple women
- The black guy who gossips about the *other* black guy to ensure he has those hot women to himself!
- The "token black guy" who laughs at unfunny jokes to fit in
- People who perform double-takes when a black male (of little workplace significance) wears a suit jacket (what are you looking at and why are you stunned?)
- The loud laughter that follows once a staff meeting completes
- The "Good Morning game" and who says it first upon crossing paths
- The annoying "Good Morning, how are you?" – "I'm doing great!" banter (can we at least *lie* sometimes?)
- The obnoxiously loud, balding delivery guy who enters the office and doesn't care that he's being disruptive
- Meetings around the clock
- *30-minute* lunch breaks
- Eating lunch… at the desk
- Being terror-stricken to eat fried chicken at work…

- People and their salad obsessions!
- Management rewarding employees with *pizza*, like they're seven-year-olds
- Employees *behaving* like seven-year old's once the pizza arrives!
- The bored employee who takes two-toilet breaks per hour
- The guy who stands at the sink (way too long), as you patiently wait to unleash all types of noises (on the toilet)
- Taking a dump at work and dreading the embarrassment of seeing a familiar face as you're leaving the toilet area
- The lack of courtesy flushes when someone is using the toilet
- Standing at the urinal – holding your breath, hoping not to take in the odor
- When the culprit of the 'restroom bombing' washes his hands, scurries off and someone new enters ... as *you* approach the sink
- The moment you realize: 'Oh no! they're going to think I'm responsible for this smell!'
- The person who *doesn't* wash their hands after using the restroom
- That awkward silence when standing next to someone at the urinal
- That awkward moment when the very same person (standing at the urinal) takes a glance at you
- That awkward conversation at the urinal about the big football game
- The *married* female co-worker who dresses for work like she's going out to the club
- When you stare at her outfit in disbelief, yet elated to have her body on full display for eight-hours!
- The *single* woman, who "can't find a man", but walks around the office man-shaming all day long (perhaps *you're* the problem?)
- The *married* guy who has a "work wife"

- The "happily married" woman with the obnoxiously big wedding ring – who openly flirts with you
- The "I got married too soon" woman who flirts *and* gives you her number
- The "I married the wrong guy" woman who flirts, gives you her number *and* fucks you during lunch breaks

I can't be the only one bothered by this? *By the way, if I struck a nerve? Good!*

Suddenly, I was speeding, the car was spiraling out of control, but I needed answers! Why were these talking points taboo?

- The *fair skin, dirty-blonde, blue eye* depiction of Jesus Christ (sooo, no one has an issue with this?)
- Calling a U.S. customer support number and connecting with foreign call center representatives!
- Black people constantly inventing new dances
- People pronouncing the word *aunt*, as 'ant' (don't tell me the 'u' is silent – bullshit!)
- The "N-word" obsession; has there been *any* other word in the history of vocabulary that society has been so eager to use – or refuses to let go?
- The obsession for wearing 'black face' and 'afro wigs' (when does that get old?)
- Those who respond to questions answering, '*what?*' instead of, "excuse me?" or, "I'm sorry?" (have you no manners?)
- Men wearing jeans tighter than their girlfriends
- Women who have more leggings in their wardrobe than pants!
- The fake eyelash obsession
- The *idiocy* of butt injections
- The *stupidity* of face tattoos
- Black men dyeing their dreadlocks *blonde*
- Black women wearing bright colored wigs (am I supposed to believe your hair is *naturally* green?)
- Women who take initiative with everything *except* for approaching men!
- Women who wear open-toe shoes... *with bad feet!*

- America's obsession with celebrities
- Mainstream media's obsession with 24-hour news coverage
- Mainstream media's obsession with "breaking news"
- America's obsession with pharmaceutical drugs
- Americans and their obsession with *using* recreational drugs
- Radio programmers who play songs promoting sex and drugs – during the *morning* drive to work and school!
- Why the F.C.C. continues to sit back with their feet up?
- *PEOPLE® Magazine* dictating the "sexiest man/woman alive" (did they conduct a worldwide poll or something?)
- The South *still* declaring how they'll "rise again!" (you couldn't possibly *still* be upset about the Civil War?!)
- The flawed judicial system
- Daylight savings being *worthless* (get rid of this rule, please!)
- Groundhog Day being *stupid* and *worthless*
- Valentine's Day being *stupid, worthless* and *comical!* (seriously, what are we celebrating? Stop it!)
- Watching the *ball drop* (at Times Square) to kick off the New Year (I can think of a million other things I'd rather do)
- The sense of urgency to wish everyone a Happy New Year! at midnight... because God forbid you wait a few hours later! (the New Year doesn't magically disappear at 9 a.m., you know?)
- Wishing others, a 'Happy New Year' ... in February! (a little late?)
- The lack of diversity on television commercials
- Why *neutral* skin tones are never used in books/TV illustrations
- The token black lady featured in the *Popeye's* chicken commercial (I don't care *how much* Popeye's offered you contractually)

- White celebrities adopting African babies (there is *something* to this, I swear there is)
- Reality TV becoming the death of television
- People who wear rock-band t-shirts, but *never* listened to the group in their life
- Women who publicly spit onto the ground (classy! ... said no one ever!)
- Men who publicly blow snot out of their nose, one nostril at a time (seriously?! you feel good about yourself doing that in front of everyone?)
- The obsession with six-pack abs
- The obsession with jogging in all types of weather conditions
- Why some of the most aggressive drivers on the road are those with *handicap* license plates!
- Cops who aren't around to ticket bad drivers, but willing to pull you over for having an air freshener in your rearview mirror!
- The never-ending *Fast and Furious* movies (enough already!)
- *Sharknado*...
- The lunacy of a *Sharknado* sequel!
- Vince McMahon monopolizing wrestling
- Black comedians who *constantly* make white jokes
- Athletes who openly 'thank God' during triumphant times, but not during slumps and adversity
- Fans who *still* feel it's cool to taunt black players with racial slurs
- Beyoncé refusing to take a break from the spotlight (go away! How can anyone miss you if you won't leave?)
- Michael Jordan re-releasing sneakers at astronomical prices!
- "Sneakerheads" who continue to fall for it!
- People who wear crucifix chains, but live Un-Godly lives
- Sports fans who tuck-in their team jerseys (I understand if you have a beer gut, but cut it out!)

- Rappers and their strange obsession for jewelry
- White men and their obsession for *Oakley* sunglasses
- *Right-handed* people who wear watches... on their *right* wrist!
- Those stupid trainer shoes that look like feet!
- Bumper stickers on *luxury* vehicles (don't do it...)
- Excessive bumper stickers on cars (you're *so* not cool)
- The "My child is an exceptional student..." bumper sticker (nobody cares about your child!)
- Driving around with rims bigger than your car
- Guys who try to look tough (sitting at a red light) because they've *just* souped-up their Toyota Prius (am I missing something? is the Prius the new *Porsche?*)
- Blasting music in your car... with distorted speakers (don't be an idiot!)
- People who drive around with loud mufflers (get that fixed or get off of the road!)
- Grainy UFO footage... in the *High-definition* age
- Why the Government continues to downplay UFO's in the *Information age?*
- Pepperidge Farm discontinuing Lemon Nut Homestyle cookies! (I haven't been the same since)
- Caribbean/Hispanics and their obsession with showcasing their country flags
- Country flags placed in the review mirror *and* on the head rests of their cars (okay, okay, we get it!)
- People who pick their noses at red lights in sight of other drivers
- People who say, "conversate" (sorry! not a word)
- *Homographs* – words that are spelled the same, but have different meanings – like, *tear, bass, etc.* (couldn't we find other words?)
- Last names featuring all consonants and no vowels (how do you pronounce *'SKRVJ?'*)
- Two first names acting as one (Jim-Bob)
- People using the letter 'Z' in place of an 'S' (I'm guessing 'Z' is cooler?)

- Celebrities who name their kids after fruits!
- Names like, 'David Davidson', 'Robert Robertson', 'John Johnson', 'Edward Edwards' (that's just dumb!)
- Bigen dyed beards
- Bigen dyed hairlines
- Bozo the clown hairstyles (it's over, dude, just cut it off)
- The old, out of shape man at the gym – with the Bozo the clown hairstyle – who tends to draw all the pretty women his way!
- People who pronounce *Target*, "Tar-zhay" (you're not cool)
- The horrific *Madea* films
- How most of the *big* lottery winners are old and… (you figure out the rest)
- Opinions being classified as "hate"
- Paying for necessities, such as electricity and water! (why are we paying bills for items we can't live without? Are there alternatives for water???)

AND THE GRAND-DADDY OF THEM ALL:

- Alexis Texas refusing to act out interracial scenes in her films!

* * * * *

That was fun! Now, let's recap my list of *all-time dumb acts*:

5) **Using the bathroom on *myself* instead of heading home** – Self-explanatory
4) **Turning down the opportunity to play varsity baseball** – Life changer!
3) **Electing not to go to an out of state college** – I should have gone for the experience alone (or not gone to school at all)
2) **Chasing love** – This *should* be number one, except…
1) **Having a child out of wedlock** – Takes the crown!

*It has become less of a big deal in the 'what is wrong is RIGHT and what is right is WRONG era', but **number one** can single-handedly take you out of commission (especially if the parents-to-be aren't compatible).*

Additionally, in a split home, you lose the ability to raise your child under the set of rules/values that you were once accustomed to. Everything tends to be one-sided and you can only influence your child so much from afar. Whatever you do, find a way to separate the bitterness and love your child unconditionally! They didn't choose their bonehead parents.

FINISH LINE

I've indisputably flopped.
Production budget: *One-million dollars*
Box Office Gross: *$325.42!*

Gigli flopped... LeBron James taking a charge, flop... Robin Thicke's *Paula* album, flop...

I've let myself down in more ways than you can imagine, rehashing my truth has been nothing short of bittersweet. As you've learned by now, the parental guidance was there, but the confidence to be "great" wasn't. Settling for societal mediocrity has never been a concern – settling for mediocrity, *without a clear site of direction,* was. Until I woke up and got a whiff of the Folgers.

America couldn't sell me on her dream. I am a person who rebels when restricted and have sought *independency,* long before the *white picket fence and accumulated debts* of said "dream".

I am an advocate of teaching, but I never envisioned being a parent. I wanted to travel the world, meet interesting people, eat different foods, mingle and seduce multiple women and teach through coaching, counseling, or my personal writings.

My thoughts can be aberrant, yet, I am attracted to *intelligence, simplicity and ambition.* I had every opportunity to go through life unscathed... but I haven't sunken into the quicksand yet.

Through the grace of God, I found my purpose and despite the parental *downs and downs* (when I can think of an 'up', I'll be glad to share it), I have a connection with my daughter that is indestructible – until I start to reject *every* future boyfriend of hers. If dealing with adversity was a prerequisite to becoming a best-selling author – I wouldn't change a thing...*well, on second thought...*

As an underachiever, and more importantly, someone who has learned not to chase money, writing a book had very little to do with hopes of receiving a "lavish payday" and *everything* to do with proving (to myself) that I wasn't a failure. It was imperative that I achieve something – maintaining the status quo was senseless and quite depressing. I needed to break away from the ordinary and act fast! I couldn't afford to be in the *fourth quarter,* counting down to death, without a form of personal gratification.

For any thoughts of prosperity, you must obtain a mental and emotional shrewdness. I greatly lacked this in the previous quarters of my life, but the faster you grow tired of your woeful ways, the quicker you'll acquire the rudiments of basic survival. I swear by this!

Forecasting my paycheck from week to week with the constant reminder of where I stood financially in a country obsessed with monetary classification left a bitter taste in my mouth. After spending forty hours a week (sometimes more) achieving nothing but *ill will and nagging migraines*, I couldn't continue to pad the pockets of a CEO – allowing valuable years to go by the wayside. As a result, I took a long – hard look in the mirror and made a declaration: I will do my part!

My Part – *Put forth the effort in any endeavor and through prayer and obedience, allow for synchronicity. Basically, if you follow this formula, one door will open, then another and soon, there will be an abundance of opportunities staring back at you!*

Enlighten your mind, ride that energy wave and pay attention! Opportunities await us all regardless of your education or financial state. Do *your* part, develop healthy practices and most importantly: Do not get blindsided!

I've never feared death, but there hasn't been *one* area of my life that turned out how I'd imagined: *professionally, relationally, parentally.* If you ask me, that was the closest thing to death. But through it all, I found my *purpose* – find yours!

As long as you have breath left in your body – it is *never* too late. I'm just being Earnest...

* * * * *

Folks, we've reached the finish line and it puts a *tear in my eye...* which I'll gladly allow to fall down my cheek... if that's alright with you? Writing my first book, has allowed for sitting comfortably inside of my 'happy bubble', reminiscing on merrier times. As I often tell my daughter, no matter how problematic your childhood, try to enjoy it – because adulthood sucks! But, as we've learned, it doesn't have to (*if* you pay attention). *Paying attention comes at no cost!*

As I move forward, it is important that I step outside of my comfort zone and present my little 'bundle of joy' to the world. Mixing with humans is on the horizon and it won't be easy – I've come to dislike humans, but I promise to do my best. *I can't afford to allow "junior" to miss out on some of the opportunities I passed up.*

Pardon my impertinent behavior, it just so happens I've become comfortable being a lone wolf. I've always been someone who appreciated *quiet time* even more so since the start of the 2000s – where every day feels like a *Twilight Zone* episode. I run towards quietness when human beings become ruthless and overwhelming. It is a peaceful addiction.

The older I get, the less relatable I find people – with their bizarre and unusual behaviors. It is undeniably attributed to an increase in meds, recreational drugs and stress. But the main culprit? Hint: *Rhymes with 'Tocial Pedia'!*

For the sake of humanity, I am crossing my fingers (and toes), *praying* for a director to yell, "Cut! That's a wrap!"

intercom sound "Hi Ernest, I have Jesus, on line one?"

Yes! Please – send Him through!

We desperately need to snap the population back into shape, awakening from this nightmare called the 21st century. Until then, I'll continue my bromance with my laptop – meaning, more compelling stories, more books, more laughter!

I was once shielded from the perils of the outside, but life's plights prepared me for this *very* moment. Now, I can bear the weight of similar personalities, lead *us* to the promised land and cement *our* flag to the pavement!

There is a lane for us – the perceived "weirdos" of the world *and* I am living proof! Do not be ashamed of who you are and do not succumb to the pressures of humanity. Love yourself... be a standout. Everything else is trivial. Until next time...

* * * * *

Final Author's Note: *I believe everyone should make a lasting impression while they're still breathing... well... this was mine.*

About the Author

Ernest K. Aning's debut publication, *Can I Be Earnest?* was inspired by many personal events. The public travesty that got the ball rolling was the discovery of a Texas man who was ordered to pay $65,000 in child support – for a child that wasn't his! Let's just say, Ernest was fed up!

Not only would he pursue a platform to shed light on his own life, but he wanted to notify the uninformed about the blatant degradation of good fathers and men who are wrongfully accused of being one! In addition, Ernest has a passion for an array of topics, including the downfall of our systematic design, which includes: college, the judicial court system, nine-to-five work structure and the worst…daylight savings! He commonly questions why those in power are complacent about a conspicuously flawed system.

One of Ernest's many interests is traveling. Apart from childhood visits to London, Toronto, and Ghana, he lists *Rio de Janeiro and Tokyo* as future destinations.

He is a lifelong sports fan and plans to coach a group of kids with a passion for baseball. In his spare time, Ernest enjoys working out, visiting local beaches, and attending concerts. He is a documentary buff, a frequent YouTube viewer, and an avid fan of 80s and 90s music. *Married with Children* and *The Office* are his favorite TV shows.

Born in New York City, Ernest currently resides with his family in the Delaware Valley where he has become a proponent of peace, quiet… and *obedient* neighbors! You can connect with him through his website at www.canibeernest.com.